Scholars have often drawn attention to William Blake's unusual sensitivity to his social context. In this book Nicholas Williams situates Blake's thought historically by showing how through the decades of a long and productive career Blake consistently responded to the ideas, writing and art of contemporaries. Williams presents detailed readings of several of Blake's major poems alongside Rousseau's *Emile*, Wollstonecraft's *Vindication of the Rights of Woman*, Paine's *Rights of Man*, Burke's *Reflections on the Revolution in France* and Robert Owen's utopian experiments. In so doing, he offers revealing new insights into key Blake texts and draws attention to their inclusion of nations of social determinism, theories of ideology-critique and utopian traditions. Williams argues that if we are truly to understand ideology as it relates to Blake, we must understand the practical situation in which the ideological Blake found himself. Williams' study is a revealing commentary on the work of one of our most challenging poets.

CAMBRIDGE STUDIES IN ROMANTICISM 28

IDEOLOGY AND UTOPIA IN THE POETRY OF WILLIAM BLAKE

This series aims to foster the best new work in one of the most challenging fields within English literary studies. From the early 1780s to the early 1830s a formidable array of talented men and women took to literary composition, not just in poetry, which some of them famously transformed, but in many modes of writing. The expansion of publishing created new opportunities for writers, and the political stakes of what they wrote were raised again by what Wordsworth called those "great national events" that were "almost daily taking place": the French Revolution, the Napoleonic and American wars, urbanization, industrialization, religious revival, an expanded empire abroad and the reform movement at home. This was an enormous ambition, even when it pretended otherwise. The relations between science, philosophy, religion, and literature were reworked in texts such as *Frankenstein* and *Biographia Literaria*; gender relation in *A Vindication of the Rights of Woman* and *Don Juan*; journalism by Cobbett and Hazlitt; poetic form, content and style by the Lake School and the Cockney School. Outside Shakespeare studies, probably no body of writing has produced such a wealth of response or done so much to shape the responses of modern criticism. This indeed is the period that saw the emergence of those notions of "literature" and of literary history, especially national literary history, on which modern scholarship in English has been founded.

The categories produced by Romanticism have also been challenged by recent historicist arguments. The task of the series is to engage both with a challenging corpus of Romantic writings and with the changing field of criticism they have helped to shape. As with other literary series published by Cambridge, this one will represent the work of both younger and more established scholars, on either side of the Atlantic and elsewhere.

For a complete list of titles published see end of book.

IDEOLOGY AND UTOPIA
IN THE POETRY OF
WILLIAM BLAKE

NICHOLAS M. WILLIAMS

Indiana University

 CAMBRIDGE
UNIVERSITY PRESS

PUBLISHED BY THE PRESS SYNDICATE OF THE UNIVERSITY OF CAMBRIDGE
The Pitt Building, Trumpington Street, Cambridge CB2 1RP, United Kingdom

CAMBRIDGE UNIVERSITY PRESS
The Edinburgh Building, Cambridge CB2 2RU, United Kingdom
40 West 20th Street, New York, NY 10011–4211, USA
10 Stamford Road, Oakleigh, Melbourne 3166, Australia

First published 1998

Printed in the United Kingdom at the University Press, Cambridge

Typeset in Baskerville 11/12.5pt [CE]

A catalogue record for this book is available from the British Library

Library of Congress cataloging in publication data

Williams, Nicholas M.
Ideology and Utopia in the poetry of William Blake / Nicholas M. Williams.
p.   cm. – (Cambridge Studies in Romanticism, 28)
Includes index.
ISBN 0 521 62050 3 (hardback)
1. Blake, William, 1757–1827 – Political and social views.
2. Utopias in literature.
3. Literature and society – England – History – 19th century.
4. Literature and society – England – History – 18th century.
5. Romanticism – England.   I. Title.   II. Series.
PR4148.U76W55   1998
821'.7 – dc21   97–25204   CIP

ISBN 0 521 62050 3 hardback

For my parents

Contents

Figures

Preface

Like so many critical books on Blake, the present study stands very much in the shadow of two masterpieces of Blake scholarship: Northrop Frye's *Fearful Symmetry* (1947) and David Erdman's *Blake: Prophet Against Empire* (1954). In a way perhaps unprecedented in the study of any other single author, these two books have served as a standard and as a resource for almost all the critical projects which follow them. They provide the language and, in many cases, the tools for much of the scholarship of the last thirty years. One can depart from their conclusions and from their techniques, but only with an intimate and assured knowledge of what it is that one is departing from.

But if many Blake critics have felt the double burden of these two critical monoliths and the necessity of coming to terms with them, surely many have also experienced a sense of the strange incongruity of the two. This incongruity can be most simply expressed by juxtaposing Frye's statement on the importance of Blake studies – "What makes the poet worth studying at all is his ability to communicate beyond his context in time and space"[1] – with Erdman's general statement of intent – "With the growth of interest in Blake as a poet of social vision the need has grown for a methodical study of his thought and art in relation to the history of his own times."[2] Of course, Frye does not deny the need to relate Blake to patterns of thought dominant in the eighteenth century (a thing which he does brilliantly), nor does Erdman's book cast itself as the definitive and conclusive interpretation of Blake's poetry. But the fact remains that these two major productions of the so-called Blake industry approach their subject from almost diametrically opposed directions and so reach almost diametrically opposed conclusions. Indeed, the process of reading Frye's and Erdman's books consecutively is rather like that of ingesting two medicines which stand in relation to each other as mutual antidotes: Erdman's hard-headed methodical identifications are the perfect antidote to Frye's wide-ranging anagogic speculations, while Frye's expansiveness serves as the ideal antidote to Erdman's sometimes narrow readings. We find ourselves in an odd situation: our twofold panacea appears split down the middle, each part claiming to be the cure for the other part's disease.

It should come as no surprise, however, to find ourselves so quickly at an intersection in Blake criticism, for surely Blake stands at one of the busiest intersections in English literature. Even a partial list of the traditional boundaries which Blake's poetry seems openly to defy would have to include: pictorial art versus textual art, literature versus philosophy, literature versus theology, allegory versus symbol, psychology versus politics, mind versus body, sociology versus phenomenology, science versus art. Blake parades a constant disrespect for the internal coherence and distinctiveness of most traditional Western discourses and even those which have developed since his death. The reader of Blake must constantly be prepared to change the frame of reference for any single poem, from psychology, to politics, to literature, to theology. This is only one element of the "Mental Fight"[3] waged between the reader of Blake's text and the text itself, a fight which has been lost by more than one audacious reader.

But if it is impossible to eliminate the element of struggle in the confrontation with Blake's work ("Without Contraries is no progression," *The Marriage of Heaven and Hell*, 20, E42), the purpose of the following study is at least to describe the field of battle, to identify the common ground upon which antagonistic discourses wage their "intellectual War" (*The Four Zoas*, 139:9, E407). My presupposition is that the barriers which have been placed between the various schools of Blake criticism are neither necessary nor desirable. For too long critical studies have self-consciously adopted their political Blake, their Christian Blake, their Gnostic Blake, without acknowledging that these critical constructs are merely parts of one and the same man. One is tempted to place these critics in the lists of those fallen workmen who "view a small portion & think that All, / And call it Demonstration" (*Jerusalem*, 65:27–8, E216). Clearly, for there to be a war of discourse (even if only an intellectual war) in the poetry and in the interpretation of that poetry, we must be able to imagine a point of contact between the antagonists. Unfortunately, the practice in the criticism has been all too often to place the combatants in separate cork-lined rooms. What is attempted in the following is an articulation of antagonistic forces in Blake studies or, in directly Blakean terms, a transformation of Negations into Contraries. The concept of Contraries in no way lessens the force of opposition between elements in Blake's work, but it does offer a context against which to consider oppositions in meaningful ways.

In pursuing this study, I have abandoned several critical fictions which have been useful in previous decades of Blake criticism, but which have been questioned more and more convincingly by recent interpreters. The most important of these is the idea that Blake's career presents one integral whole, the entirety of which is expressed in each of the parts. This fiction made possible the more synoptic readings such as (most prominently) Frye's, which read early works such as the *Songs of Innocence and of Experience* and *Poetical Sketches* in terms of the fully developed mythology of *The Four Zoas* and *Jerusalem*. My own study, on the contrary, attempts to pursue a single theme through its progression over the course of Blake's life. Although my idea of the progression in Blake's career is different than his, Morton D. Paley, along with E. D. Hirsch in *Innocence and Experience* (1964), must be cited as an early proponent of the progressive (in all senses of the word) school of Blake criticism for his *Energy and the Imagination* (1970).[4]

A fiction related to that which sees Blake's career as a temporal unity is that which sees his thought as a conceptual unity. The critics who have subscribed to this point of view are those who paint him as a self-assured philosopher, in complete control of the wholeness of his thought, who has only to communicate its meditative fullness in a series of poetic visions. The leading debunker of this critical myth is Leopold Damrosch. In his *Symbol and Truth in Blake's Myth* (1980), Damrosch identified a number of central inconsistencies in Blake's thought which plagued him throughout his life.[5] One might say that Damrosch opens the door to synchronic heterogeneity in his work on Blake, while Paley opens the door to diachronic heterogeneity in his. The result is a more complex, more various and, hopefully, more historical Blake, the inhabitant of a changing historical landscape. This is the Blake that I have tried to describe in the following pages.

In abandoning these two fictions of unity, I have also abandoned the conceptual ordering devices which many critical books employ. These devices organize an interpretation of Blake around a series of conceptual categories such as "Blake's Theology," "Blake's Mythology," "Blake and Mysticism," and so on. Clearly, this ordering scheme implies both the synchronic and diachronic unity of Blake's work, in that it ignores the diachronic dimension almost completely and stresses a unity of thought which holds for the entire Blakean corpus. My own study, after an initial survey of Blake's ideology, will consist of a series of readings of Blake's texts arranged in a roughly chronological order and embedded in considerations of various contexts I consider useful for the study of Blake. I say "roughly chronological" because it has been my concern here to outline Blake's progression through a series of historical strategies, and this concern has necessitated my considering *Europe* in the same chapter with *Visions of the Daughters of Albion* in a wider consideration of the place of the female in Blake's poetry, even though *Visions* precedes *Europe* in order of composition. The chronological axis, however, is very important to my thesis, for the purpose of this study is to portray a Blake whose program for social change was always situated in an historical context which conditioned his strategical decisions and finally contained them.

On the question of context, certain readers might accuse me of lying entirely within the camp of David Erdman and tending to "explain" Blake's genius by referring it to patterns of thought prevalent in his time. They may rest assured that such is certainly not my intent, as may be attested to by my lack of attention to strict datings of analogue texts and to considerations of whether Blake had read any given document. My concern is much more with providing analogues to Blake's manner of thought than with providing literal sources for that thought. In Walter Benjamin's term, I am concerned with certain "correspondences" between Blake's solution of the problem of change and the solutions of others – poets, philosophers, scientists, political thinkers.[6] The analogues serve both as a way of defining the problem as it was historically articulated and as a comparative pole for discussing the peculiarity or the conformity of Blake's solutions. In terms of the "mutual antidotes" discussed above, I intend my conceptual background to be the expansive part of a study which will remain intensive in its readings of Blake's texts. Perhaps the most surprising conclusion of this investigation will be that where Blake appears to be at his most transcendent, and least subject to historical precedent and limitation, is precisely where he is reacting most closely to historical pressures and social conditions. In particular, I hope to suggest that those personages who go by the name of the "religious Blake" and the "political Blake" – who, in some accounts would seem never to have met, or rather, to be sworn enemies – are actually more closely aligned than usually thought. One aspect of the "utopianism" of Blake's text which I have highlighted throughout is the notion that, at least in this historical period, religion can be a powerful form of political radicalism.

As for other analogues quoted throughout my text, references which have no pretension to contemporaneity with Blake's poetry, such as those to Ernst Bloch, Karl Mannheim, the Frankfurt School, Marxists and others, these are intended to express Blake's powerful presence within a tradition of writing which is usually called ideology-critique. Although my intent, once again, is never to propose Blake's identity with the beliefs and vocabulary of the ideology critics, I do intend to suggest a continuity of thought between Blake and the work of those writers whose dominant concern was to describe the limitations of their society and to effect a change of that society. The vocabulary might not be that of "fall" and "redemption," but the anguish in the face of what exists and the passion for its complete eradication remain much the same. In short, I understand and sympathize with E. P. Thompson's side-by-side placement of Blake and Marx in his pantheon of heroes, although I spend much of my time in the following pages illustrating their differences as well as their similarities.

Acknowledgements

Although I could not hope, in the manner of Blake's Los, to remember every "Word, work, & wish" that contributed to this project, the most prominent acts of generosity and fellow-feeling are truly unforgettable. For the earliest encouragements in the practices of thoughtful reading, I must thank Larry Thibodeau, Roger Sprague and, especially, Tony Brinkley, whose classes still serve me as a model of non-oppressive inquiry. Lore Metzger, Walter Reed, and John Sitter each offered invaluable advice, much of which has found its way into the final text. Since that earliest hobbled stage, the arguments have been nursed to health and put on their feet by many helpers, to whom much thanks is owed: Judith Anderson, Patrick Brantlinger, Mary Favret, Brian Goldberg, Ken Johnston, Gene Kintgen, Joan Linton, Laura Lovasz, Andrew Miller, Janet Sorensen, and the Indiana University Romantics Reading Group. Special thanks go to Jon Mee, who always had "manuscript-assumed authority" for me, in his exemplary readings of the radical documents of the 1790s, but whose careful and intelligent comments in the later stages of writing left me more directly indebted to him. Josie Dixon and others at Cambridge University Press, particularly Marilyn Butler and James Chandler, have made this first adventure into book-length print much easier than it had any right to be.

Robbie, David and Brynn McCurry, if they look carefully, will also find their influence here. And finally, as a gesture of defiance to those acknowledgements she so hates to read, thanks to Julia McElhattan Williams, who did not type the manuscript for this book nor minister to flagging intellect, but whose effects appear on every page.

Note on the text and abbreviations

The texts of Blake's works referred to are those in David Erdman's *The Complete Poetry and Prose of William Blake* (newly revised edition), Garden City, New York: Doubleday Press, 1982 (with commentary by Harold Bloom). The question of stability in Blake's texts is an endlessly vexed one, but I have accepted a "limit of contraction" in using Erdman's stable texts in order to perform the task at hand. I have also accepted Erdman's unnormalized versions of Blake's poetry, in the belief that the occasional grammatic and syntactic undecidability of the poetry is significant and intentional.

The following abbreviations will be used throughout the volume to refer to Blake's works.

ARO	*All Religions are One*
A	*America a Prophecy*
BA	*The Book of Ahania*
BU	*The Book of Urizen*
E	*Europe a Prophecy*
FR	*The French Revolution*
FZ	*The Four Zoas*
J	*Jerusalem: The Emanation of the Giant Albion*
M	*Milton a Poem in 2 Books*
MHH	*The Marriage of Heaven and Hell*
NRR	*There is No Natural Religion*
PS	*Poetical Sketches*
Songs E	*Songs of Experience*
Songs I	*Songs of Innocence*
Song L	*The Song of Los*
VDA	*Visions of the Daughters of Albion*
VLJ	*A Vision of the Last Judgment*

In multiplate or multipage works, the note will first list the plate or (Blake's) page number, next the line number (for verse works), then the page number in Erdman's revised edition, designated with the letter *E* – e.g., *FZ*78: 9–14, E353.

CHAPTER I

Blake, ideology and utopia: strategies for change

Rouze up O Young Men of the New Age! set your foreheads
against the ignorant Hirelings! For we have Hirelings in the
Camp, the Court, & the University: who would if they could,
for ever depress Mental & prolong Corporeal War.

(*Milton* 1, E95)

I

The present state of Blake criticism can be said to resemble, as it
has for several decades past, a state of war. What distinguishes this
war in purely Blakean terms, however, is the fact that it cannot be
classified easily as either a mental or a corporeal war, but is rather
a war between the mental and the corporeal themselves. This is
the war between Blake's socially oriented critics and those who
would interpret his poetry as an internally coherent, largely mental
and necessarily ahistorical triumph. This war is sometimes waged
through selectivity: Blake's social critics sometimes neglect *Jerusalem*
in particular and the more explicitly religious content of Blake's
vision in general; the aesthetic (as I will call them) critics overlook
America and *The French Revolution*, as well as Blake's detailed
descriptions of contemporary working conditions. Sometimes a
more frontal assault is waged: I need only recall a rather ugly
confrontation in some recent issues of *Blake: An Illustrated Quarterly*
which began over the question of how thoroughly Blake's poetry
could be put in a social and intellectual context, but quickly
degenerated into charges of "First World arrogance" (against the
aesthetic critic) and "projection and denial" (against the sociological critic).[1]

What the present book attempts is a consideration of Blake
which suggests that he partly anticipates this debate, that, to put it

another way, Blake himself proposes that thought and culture are historically conditioned. Such an explanation goes a long way towards accounting for an odd feature of Blake's poetry, a simultaneous sense of the exhilarating newness of his conceptions – a newness which seems hardly to have faded since the poems' composition – and of a crushing, almost debilitating pessimism. As a way of registering this doubleness, and of introducing the concepts which will control the following analysis, we might first turn to a poem from the Pickering Manuscript, an unilluminated, unpublished collection of ten lyrics usually dated to the first years of the nineteenth century, during Blake's Felpham period. "The Mental Traveller" is an odd production not only for its appearing in this context of manuscript verse, but for the way it rehearses some of the major themes of his poetry without recourse to the mythological apparatus for which he is best (and most fearsomely) known. Even without this apparatus, the startling newness of Blake's vision is apparent in the double story of a "Babe" given to a "Woman Old," who gets progressively older as she becomes young, only to end once again as an infant, a "frowning form" whose fate recapitulates the poem's opening:

> And none can touch that frowning form
> Except it be a Woman Old
> She nails him down upon the Rock
> And all is done as I have told.   (101–5, E486)

The elements of this text which mark it as "Blakean," and which have encouraged some to see Blake as a creator distinct from his historical setting, are the seeming freedom from traditional frames of reference and the unusual vividness of the stark imagery. If this is an allegory, and as much is suggested by Blake's tone of normative explanation ("And if the Babe is born a Boy / He's given to a Woman Old" [9–10]), then it is an allegory like no other, whose ties to established cultural codes (the Christian story, classical myth, etc.) are at best oblique. Despite attempts to translate it by reference to these codes or to Blake's own "mythology," the poem retains the characteristics of an interpretive scandal, and seems always fresh in its capacity to resist easy codification.

But if the poem carries with it a shock of newness, a sensation that here is a poetic voice like no other, such a feeling rests uneasily beside the subject matter of the poem itself. That tone of normative certainty which gives to Blake's poems their sense of urgency and importance, also lends to them a claustrophobic sense of limitation, of already determined futures and of indefinite repetition. That tale told by the Mental Traveller is one of mental bondage and violence, the Old Woman's crucifixion of the Babe mirrored by his later revenge:

> Till he becomes a bleeding youth
> And she becomes a Virgin bright
> Then he rends up his Manacles
> And binds her down for his delight.   (21–4, E484)

Indeed, the persistent mirroring in the poem – the boy "Babe" of the opening and the "Female Babe" of the middle, the Old Woman and the man "blind & age-bent" (55), as well as the parallel bindings at the poem's core – all suggest that this world's inhabitants are forced to repeat the same limited repertoire of actions again and again. The feature of the text that has received the most attention, which influenced W. B. Yeats's theory of history, that inverse structure whereby the Woman gets younger as the Man ages and vice versa, itself suggests that the poem depicts a self-contained universe, one in which no amount of recapitulation could create anything new. Although the Man and Woman seem to bear to each other something of the relationship of "Contraries," they resist the logic of Blake's earlier formulation that "Without Contraries is no progression" (*MHH*3, E34): here we would seem to have contraries with no progression, but a sterile round of repeated torture. The complacent cruelty of the last line – "And all is done as I have told" – bids its reader to continue the cycle *da capo*, as if this were a hellish circle which could never end. The manacles of the text are thus extended to the reading process itself.

What are we to make of such an anomaly, such a discontinuity between a seeming originality of insight and the apparent denial of any originality whatsoever? One option, of course, is to attempt to translate the allegory, to figure out what Blake "means" by this strange narrative, most often by interpreting his characters as the equivalents of general concepts, of externalized Nature (the Woman) or Humanity (the Man). But in addition to not respecting the non-specific terms of Blake's poem, such an approach risks overlooking a central element of its powerful effect. It attempts, in a sense, to overstep the boundaries that Blake evocatively establishes in the poem's opening stanza:

> I travld thro' a Land of Men
> A Land of Men & Women too
> And heard & saw such dreadful things
> As cold Earth wanderers never knew.   (1–4, E483)

We might take the speaker here to mean that he is reporting on a non-Earthly scene in the lines that follow, that he is a kind of proto-spaceman recording extra-terrestrial happenings for the home planet (such science-fictional frameworks are not inappropriate for the author of "An Island in the Moon"). But what is more likely is a logical opposition of the "Mental Traveller" of the title and the "Earth wanderers" of line 4, distinguishing between two modes of travel rather than two destinations. What the lines suggest, in other words, is an even more striking anomaly at work in the poem, a contradiction between the uniformity of event described ("all is done as I have told") and the complete lack of knowledge of those events on the part of those who are forced to suffer through them. One might, of course, simply take this as an assertion of poetic vision, in the transhistorical sense, making a claim for the poet's ability to see beyond the time-bound, mundane conceptions of the "Earth wanderers" to the effulgent realities of transcendent truth. By such an interpretation, the poem's opening stanza represents a strong instance of what might be called the "aesthetic ideology" or, even more specifically, the "Romantic ideology," in its privileging of the ideal over the real, the mental over the physical, the intellectual over the corporeal.[2] But what complicates this picture is the fact that what the Mental Traveller sees is a vision of extreme corporeality, or, to put it another way, what the poem develops is itself a theory of ideology. If the opening stanza proposes an opposition between what the Mental Traveller can hear and see and what the Earthly wanderers can know, we have yet to consider the later description of the perceptual abilities of the "Guests" who invade the old man's cottage:

> The Guests are scatterd thro' the land
> For the Eye altering alters all
> The Senses roll themselves in fear
> And the flat Earth becomes a Ball.   (61–4, E485)

Juxtaposed with the magisterial eye of the Mental Traveller, whose vision seems to be raised above the physical, we have this very material, sense-bound "Eye" whose power, or lack of power, effectively creates the world around it. Beside the transcendent recording of reality, the objective "knowing" glance of an authoritative viewer, we have something much closer to what has come to be known as the social construction of reality, the sense that the viewer him/herself plays a large role in creating the observable world, or, in Blake's extremely condensed formulation, that "the Eye altering alters all."

It is as an attempt to trace the convolutions of this double perspective in Blake's work that the following book is designed. In particular, it suggests that the excellent work already done in ascertaining Blake's ideology, placing him in his social, historical, and political contexts, needs to be supplemented by a consideration of the role played by Blake's own deployment of a proto-concept of ideology.[3] And as this brief initial analysis of "The Mental Traveller" suggests, it looks particularly at the way an extreme formulation of ideology as the total determination of consciousness – what Blake might have called "fallenness" – interacts with other perspectives which posit a limit to, an escape from, ideology. The Mental Traveller tells stories of limited sensual abilities, paralyzed consciousness, but the very ability to tell these stories presumes a point beyond their purview, a point from which they can be "known" and, in some cases, changed. I take as a founding presupposition of what follows that Blake's goal in most of his work is a kind of traveling, a kind of change, but that rather than be satisfied with mere "mental traveling," the path of this career is a search for the route to that total engagement of human capacities, in both individual and social forms, which he called "Eden." The path to Eden will not be found by an evasion of ideology, by a mentalized ideal vision of easeful love (what Blake called *Beulah*), but instead by a harsh imagining and reimagining of the ideological world. It is in this sense of a hard-won and reimagined vision of the ideological world that I will call Blake's Edenic visions "utopian," distinguishing this use of the word from its other, less politically viable meanings.

The reader will find in what follows numerous comparisons to writers contemporary with Blake, as well as to twentieth-century theorists of ideology and its critique. This partly expresses my notion that the end of the eighteenth century sees a shift in thought which can broadly be related to the development of the modern concept of ideology (a shift indicated by more than the simple fact that the word was coined during this period). It is also intended to suggest that Blake's works might reasonably be illuminated by comparison to thinkers who struggled to square their notion of the social determination of reality with a desire for meaningful liberational change. In addition, my choice of analogues for the various periods of Blake's career (Rousseau, Wollstonecraft, Burke, Paine, and Owen) is meant to counter the belief, largely dispelled but still occasionally encountered, that Blake is a thinker outside of time, not subject himself to ideological constraint. It is my belief that if we are truly to understand ideology as it relates to Blake, to understand "Blake's ideology," then we must understand the practical situation in which the ideological Blake (both the Blake submitted to ideology and the Blake who used ideology) found himself and the task he had at hand. As such, the following sequence of chapters attempts something half way between a chronological tour through Blake's development of his concept of ideology and a thematic treatment of issues pertinent to the topic. The current chapter, after a brief typology of concepts of ideology and their range of meaning, turns to a general consideration of the place of both ideology and utopia in Blake's work by means of a few examples. Chapter 2 then considers a sector of vital importance for the study of ideology, the educational system, comparing Rousseau's plan for humane schooling in *Emile* with Blake's experiment in transformational children's literature, *Songs of Innocence and of Experience*. Chapter 3 turns to a problem which continues to be of central importance to any discussion of Blake's ideology, his attitude towards and representation of women. Two Blake poems which feature central female characters, *Visions of the Daughters of Albion* and *Europe: A Prophecy*, are read in the light of Mary Wollstonecraft's *Vindication of the Rights of Woman*, a work with which Blake would no doubt have been familiar due to his and Wollstonecraft's participation in the Joseph Johnson circle. The remaining chapters trace a more determinate arc of progression, modeled in part on Karl Mannheim's identification of the "utopian mentalities" he labeled the "liberal-progressive," the "chiliastic" and the "socialist–communist."[4] My argument, broadly stated, is that rather than interpreting Blake's move from the historical poems of the 1790s (*America, Europe*) to the prophetic books of *Milton* and *Jerusalem*, as a rejection of politics or a retreat into religion,[5] as they are still sometimes characterized today, they should instead be seen as separate attempts to solve a central sociopolitical problem: how (to use Marx's terms) does a realm of freedom emerge from a realm of necessity? Chapter 4, comparing Blake's vision of history to Burkean historiography, suggests that the answer in these poems might relate to a liberal–progressivist belief in the salutary effects of time. Chapter 5, which compares the apocalyptic *Milton* to Thomas Paine's *Rights of Man*, sees Blake's solution in this period lying closer to an individualistic, chiliastic break with the past. Finally, in a consideration of a work which has too often been marked with an imaginary warning, "For Blake enthusiasts only," *Jerusalem* is compared with Robert Owen's turn-of-the-century experiments in communal societies, as a way of thinking about Blake's broadening focus in the last work of his life.

II

Although the (French) word *idéologie* was coined by the philosopher of education Destutt de Tracy during Blake's lifetime, in the period of the French Directory, the modern analytic concept of ideology properly begins in the works of Karl Marx and Friedrich Engels.[6] Indeed, many of the complications which I intend to explore in this thumbnail sketch of the concept can most easily be derived from Marx's famous statement of 1859, dating some thirteen years after his first use of the term in *The German Ideology*: "It is not the consciousness of men that determines their being, but, on the contrary, their social being that determines their consciousness."[7] The debate within Marxism and within non-Marxist theories of ideology revolves around the precise sense in which social being can be said to determine consciousness, as well as around conflicting definitions of all three of these central terms, "social being," "determination," and "consciousness." It is through examination of the shifting meanings of these terms that we can construct a typology of ideology and ideological strategies with which to compare Blake's own strategy of ideology-critique.

The strategic dimension of Marx's concept of ideology is foregrounded in his early works, the *Critique of Hegel's "Philosophy of Right"* (1843) and *The Economic and Philosophic Manuscripts of 1844*, for his intent in these works is a selective critique of specific targets rather than a universalization of the concept. The *Critique of Hegel*, although not using the word itself, develops a model of ideology as inversion which, as we shall see in chapter 6, is of particular interest in assessing Blake's strategies in *Jerusalem*. Here, Marx criticizes Hegel for his abstract philosophy of right which assigns agency to the state considered as a theoretical entity rather than to the lived experience of "actual men" (*sic*): "The German thought-version [*Gedankenbild*] of the modern state . . . which abstracts from the actual man, was only possible because and in so far as the modern state abstracts itself from actual man, or satisfies the whole man only in an imaginary way."[8] Ideology, as expressed here, is Hegel's inversion of the real agency of government, his tendency to make "actual man" the predicate of an action for which he is really (in Marx's view) the subject. The process of ideology-critique then becomes, as Paul Ricoeur insightfully names it, "the reversal of a reversal" (*Ideology and Utopia*, 27); the righting of an upside-down perspective on the world. As the later Marx famously puts it, the dialectic in Hegel "is standing on its head. It must be inverted in order to discover the rational kernel within the mystical shell."[9]

What is important for our purposes in this concept of ideology as inversion is the strategic nature of Marx's formulation at this early stage of his career. At this period Marx is not attempting, as he and his followers would later do, to posit the universality of ideology or to propose a universal methodology of ideology-critique. The process of inversion is very practical and very localized. It involves an active procedure of reinversion which one might imagine is different for each case: one cannot reinvert Feuerbach in precisely the same way one reinverts Hegel. Neither is the concept of inversion an indictment of consciousness or of ideas as a whole: the process of reinverting Hegel results in a consciousness grounded in material practices, not in the elimination of consciousness *per se*. The *Critique of Hegel* still works very much within the mainstream of Western philosophy, merely tinkering with some of its formulations as expressed in *The Philosophy of Right* and attempting to ground them in practical human experience.

The universalization of ideology only begins with Marx's explicit use of the term in *The German Ideology*. He still retains his concept of inversion, giving it perhaps its best-known formulation: "If in all ideology men and their circumstances appear upside-down, as in a *camera obscura*, this phenomenon arises just as much from their historical life-process as the inversion of objects on the retina does from their physical life-process."[10] But the concept of ideological inversion intended here is much more sweeping, as all-encompassing, in fact, as the universal process of an object's inversion by the lens of the eye.[11] Although Marx's explicit target here is the Young Hegelians, the scope of his metaphor has expanded the scope of ideology's application. The stated intent of the analysis is to ground thought in reality, but at times Marx retreats into a universal condemnation of thought itself, as when he issues his challenge in the preface: "Let us revolt against the rule of thought" (*German Ideology*; 37). The assignment of ideology to consciousness *per se* no longer serves a purely strategic purpose – that of debunking Hegelianism – but also serves a universal purpose – the calling into doubt of consciousness itself. Marx's general dissatisfaction with philosophy, with consciousness, as a whole can be detected in his titanic declaration in the "Theses on Feuerbach," composed the year before the publication of *The German Ideology*: "The philosophers have only interpreted the world in various ways; the point is to change it."[12] The break with philosophy is complete here and the concept of ideology is used as a springboard to propel Marx beyond philosophy into a properly material dialectic.

The universalization of the concept of ideology continues to occupy Marxist and non-Marxist theorists into the twentieth century, particularly in the works of Karl Mannheim and Louis Althusser. Mannheim's contribution to the concept of ideology was his realization that ideology expanded to incorporate his own position as philosopher and observer of history. The curious position of the ideology critic, whose own critique is itself subject to the charge of ideology, has become known as "Mannheim's paradox." While Mannheim's subsequent attempts to regain the Archimedean point from which to critique ideology have met with general contempt in both Marxist and non-Marxist circles, the potency of his initial discovery and its widespread implications cannot be ignored in a discussion of ideology. One thinker who has not ignored Mannheim, and whose theoretical formulations are more widely appreciated, is Louis Althusser. Althusser incorporates a universal theory of ideology within his larger structural system by defining ideology as a "lived" relationship to the world, which, as all living people have a "lived" relationship to the world, is necessarily universal.[13] Althusser's formulation is definitively posed in his book *For Marx*:

In ideology men do indeed express, not the relation between them and their conditions of existence, but *the way* they live the relation between them and their conditions of existence: this presupposes both a real relation and an *"imaginary," "lived"* relation. Ideology, then, is the expression of the relation between men and their "world," that is, the (overdetermined) unity of the real relation and the imaginary relation between them and their real conditions of existence. In ideology the real relation is inevitably invested in the imaginary relation, a relation that *expresses a will* (conservative, conformist, reformist or reactionary), a hope or a nostalgia, rather than describing a reality. (*For Marx*, 233–4)

It is worthwhile quoting this rather difficult and lengthy section of Althusser's argument because through it we can begin to appreciate the complications introduced into the Marxist theory of ideology by a particularly narrow reading of Marx's idea of social being determining social consciousness. For Althusser's complex machinery of overdetermination, real versus imaginary relations between men and their world, is largely the result of his lifelong struggle with the late Marxist model of base and superstructure. Within this model, which is fleshed out from some passing comments Marx made in *A Contribution to the Critique of Political Economy* and later canonized by more doctrinaire forms of Marxism, the cultural output of a society is reduced to a mere reflection of its economic base. The appeal is to an architectural metaphor, where the economic system – the means of production and the relations of production – serves as the base to support the secondary and derivative productions of culture – the superstructure – whether they be art, law, religion, or philosophy. Althusser's concept of overdetermination is an attempt to come to terms with the obvious inadequacies of this model, its failure to account for the diversity and seeming independence of cultural productions. But as Paul Ricoeur has noted, Althusser finally remains dogmatically faithful to the base/superstructure model and is led to oppose culture to the "real" conditions of existence, thus relegating ideology to the dubious sphere of "imaginary relations" (*Ideology and Utopia*, 331). The correction of ideology's illusions, as one might expect, is left to the "scientific" system of (Althusserian) Marxism, itself immune to ideological traps by virtue of its suprapersonal objectivity.

One of the most cogent critics of the base/superstructure model, Raymond Williams, has offered a convincing diagnosis of the problems which led to such a narrow formulation and has himself

made suggestions for a new theory of ideology and cultural production. According to Williams, the promulgation and tenacity of
the base/superstructure model can partly be attributed to a particularly limited reading of determination as it appears in Marx's
text. This narrow idea of determination, which Williams calls
"abstract determinism," employs a quasi-religious notion of absolute
control, "in which some power (God or Nature or History) controls
or decides the outcome of an action or process, beyond or irrespec-
tive of the wills or desires of its agents".[14] Thus cultural production
is absolutely predetermined (the echo of Calvinism is significant) by
the general mode of production prevalent in a particular society,
whether it be primitive communism, capitalism, or socialism. Williams, with his characteristically keen etymological sense, would
choose to rely on a concept of determination which bears a closer
relation to its root meaning: "setting bounds" or "setting limits"
(from the Latin *de* plus *terminus*, an end or limit) (*Marxism and
Literature*, 84). Within this sense of determinism, ideology would be
the product of real laborers who proceed freely in their production
until they, so to speak, "bump up" against the limits of their material
and social conditions. This idea begins to allow for some of the
diversity and some of the subversiveness which any thoughtful critic
of cultural production (and Williams is certainly an astute critic of
particular artistic works) cannot help but feel is an integral part of
art and culture.[15] Williams completes his concept of determination,
perhaps to the satisfaction of those who would see the "limiting"
idea of determination as too optimistic, by allowing for a degree of
purposefulness, of willfulness, in his full formulation of the term, as
in being "determined" to do something (*Marxism and Literature*, 87).
Williams thus accounts for a type of determination which conforms
more closely to our experience of compulsion, of domination by one
stronger than ourselves, a necessary complement to the more
autonomous notion of self-creativity within the limits only of
material conditions.

We have considered the use of ideology as a strategic concept and
as a universal concept, as a mere reflection of a more fundamental
base and as a material practice operating within the limits of
material conditions; the only thing that remains, for our purposes, is
to assess the intersection of the notion of class with the concept of
ideology. Like so many ideas at the center of twentieth-century
political and intellectual debate, the idea of class as it designates a

particular segment of a socioeconomic structure derives from the
period of industrial revolution and the political revolutions in the
USA and France.[16] As I shall hope to show in my consideration of
Milton, this idea's contemporaneity with the composition of Blake's
poetry is of no casual significance. The conjunction of this idea with
the concept of ideology, however, properly begins, as we might
expect, in *The German Ideology*. Although previous writers had spoken
of art forms or forms of consciousness peculiar to a certain section of
society – one thinks of Wordsworth's analysis of melodrama and its
relation to the working class of Britain in the 1802 preface to *Lyrical
Ballads* – a full analysis of ideology and its connection to class had to
wait until the publication of Marx and Engels's book in 1846. Here
ideology is specifically identified as the product of the division of
labor: one class is able to produce ideology, while the other is
relegated to material production in support of the thinking class.
The notion of class thus takes its place in Marx's general condemnation of consciousness in *The German Ideology*: ideological production
is the collective illusion of a class which has shifted the burden of
material necessity to an oppressed underclass. The idea of a
working-class ideology is largely ignored here in the service of a
universal indictment of ideology as superfluous and frivolous.

The potent combination of a revolutionary proletariat with a
corresponding revolutionary ideology appears in the later Marx and
perhaps most powerfully in the work of Georg Lukács, especially in
his *History and Class Consciousness* (1923). Marx theorized that a
proletariat continually thrown together in the position of oppression
would naturally and necessarily identify itself as a class whose
interests and problems are held in common. Although Marx had
previously denied the validity of all consciousness under the rubric of
ideology, he allows that the consciousness of a collective proletariat
would have universal validity because it would represent the right of
all people to the fruits of their labor. Lukács extends this analysis by
describing the process by which the proletariat would be freed of the
illusions inherent to commodity capitalism and would realize a
liberating consciousness of its own. For Lukács, commodity capitalism is characterized by its propensity to fixate on individual objects
as whole unto themselves, independent of any history of production
or use. This epistemological (and ideological) stance Lukács labels
reification. It is largely the product of a class which has never been
compelled to learn the details of an object's production, but has

instead always experienced objects as commodities, without history and occurring naturally for the purposes of consumption. The proletariat's unique position within modern society, paradoxically enough, consists in its exclusion from this system of commodity capitalism: condemned to comparative poverty and the role of production rather than consumption, the working class realizes the illusory nature of reification and restores process and history to its perception of the object. In what Lukács describes as a "moment of crisis,"[17] the laws of commodity capitalism fall apart for the proletariat, revealing the chaos of history and process that lies beneath. The knowledge gained through this shattering realization of reification's falsity is then the necessary prerequisite for its elimination, history beginning in earnest at the critical moment of reification's unveiling. No longer are objects perceived as naturally occurring, ahistorical commodities, but instead as the products of a dialectical historical process.

But there remains a serious challenge to the class theory of ideology. Regardless of Marx's claims that capitalism's contradictions would bring it to destruction and despite Lukács's claims for the priority of a proletarian consciousness, capitalism and its reifying vision have shown a remarkable tenacity in their grip upon the world's economies. In large part Marx's and Lukács's miscalculations can be assigned to the inadequacies of their class theories of ideology. For the lesson of capitalism, as theorists such as Herbert Marcuse continually remind us, is that capitalist ideology has a strange ability to insinuate itself into the minds of the very workers it oppresses. Whether this fact be illustrated by the anti-union sympathies of poor urban laborers or by the tendency of Southern slaves in the nineteenth century to adopt the religion of the slaveholders, the fact remains the same: capitalist ideology, whatever its origins, is peculiar to neither the ruling classes nor the proletariat. Marcuse describes this dynamic in terms of a "repressive tolerance" by which he means capitalism's ability to maintain control by satisfying the needs of a majority of the population.[18] Industrial capitalism, as it has developed in the twentieth century, has become a machine for inventing new needs and then satisfying those needs, so as to defuse any dissent that might otherwise emerge. According to Marcuse, however, all the while these invented needs are being satisfied, real human needs are going unmet. Whatever one thinks of Marcuse's humanistic vocabulary, the challenge to a class theory of ideology is significant: consumer capitalism and the ideology which is its product is the property of no single class, nor is any class exempt from its illusions. The escape hatch of a working-class consciousness free from reification and the limitations of industrial capitalism is thus effectively closed.

But if escape through class consciousness is precluded does any other escape remain? Or is the lesson of ideology that one has no choice but to repeat the same round of oppression, trapped within an ineluctable false consciousness? Blake expresses his early concern for this problem and also hints at his solution in the pamphlet "There is No Natural Religion": "If it were not for the Poetic or Prophetic character. the Philosophical & Experimental would soon be at the ratio of all things & stand still, unable to do other than repeat the same dull round over again" (E3). However, with the idea of the "prophetic character" and the nature of Blake's escape from the "dull round" of ideology, his strategy of change, we are already invading our other area of concern in this study of Blake's poetry: the subject of utopianism and its relevance to a theory of change and ideology. The tendency within Marxist theory has been to collapse the boundaries between utopia and ideology and thus reduce utopianism to a species of false consciousness characterized, as they might say, by wishful thinking. Given the central position which a utopian vision holds in Blake's work – the apocalypse to which his poetry always points and occasionally reaches – part of my purpose will be to interrogate this position and see whether there is a utopia which is not mere wishful thinking. At least we can assess the function of Blake's utopia before dismissing it out-of-hand as naive optimism or solipsistic daydreaming. But, as we have seen, the utopian lies at the outskirts of a concept of ideology, so it will first be necessary to outline a basic description of Blake's ideology and his premonitory use of the concept, before turning to his particularly utopian vision.

III

William Blake, as one might expect, never used the word *ideology.* The word, although coined during his lifetime, was largely unavailable to him: it was part of a language foreign (although comprehensible) to him and limited in its application to a rationalistic school of social engineers who no doubt would have been abhorrent to him.

Why, then, do we speak of Blake's ideology? Even more significantly, why do we speak of Blake's conscious use of the concept of ideology when it is almost always used (in its modern sense) in a negative way, as an accusation or denunciation? Paul Ricoeur has analyzed this strange property of the word *ideology* by contrasting it to the word *utopia*. Utopias are the products of authors who consciously choose the utopian genre: it is in this sense that we can speak of Thomas More having written the first utopia conceived as such and thus having created the genre. Ideology, on the other hand, is always assigned to another against his will, as an act of discovery, and is never owned by its "author." As Ricoeur puts it, "no proper name is affixed to an ideology as its author. Any name joined to an ideology is anonymous; its subject is simply *das Man*, the amorphous 'they'" (*Ideology and Utopia*, 15). The question then becomes one of the function of the word *ideology* in the discourses in which it is used and whether a similar function is served by any word or group of words in Blake's text. While it would be too facile to effect a one-to-one translation of Blake's text into the text of ideology-critique, I believe that such a group of words and concepts can be found in Blake's text as demonstrates his contemplation and conscious deployment of the series of strategies that we have seen at work in the texts of the ideology critics.

First of all, a universalized concept of ideology is operative in at least three distinct aspects of Blake's text: the equation of the Fall with Creation; the theory of fallen perception; and the systematic description of society. (1) The equation of the Fall of Man with the moment of earthly Creation is repeated in one way or another in each of Blake's major prophecies, but its first appearance is in Blake's parody of the biblical Genesis myth, *The Book of Urizen*. The poem opens with Urizen, "a shadow of horror," rising within undifferentiated Eternity, "[u]nknown, unprolific! / Self-closd, all-repelling" (3:1–3, E70). The scene occurs at a time before the creation of Earth (3:36, E71), so the parallel to the biblical God of Creation seems evident. But this God is portrayed in singularly unsympathetic terms. He yearns for "a solid without fluctuations" (4:10, E71) and in his anguish for such stability engages in a fit of monomaniacal creation, establishing "One command, one joy, one desire, / One curse, one weight, one measure / One King, one God, one Law" (4:38–40, E72). In a typical Blakean dialectic, the creation of the One Law quickly results in the emergence of the "seven

deadly sins of the soul" (4:49, E72), which exist to transgress it. The
consequent gap opened in Eternity sends Urizen fleeing for shelter.
It is only at this point in Blake's version of the Genesis myth that the
creation of Earth occurs:

> And a roof, vast petrific around,
> On all sides He fram'd: like a womb;
> Where thousands of rivers in veins
> Of blood pour down the mountains to cool
> The eternal fires beating without
> From Eternals; & like a black globe
> View'd by sons of Eternity, standing
> On the shore of the infinite ocean
> Like a human heart strugling & beating
> The vast world of Urizen appear'd.   (5:28–37, E73)

For the most part, Blake's account of Creation as it appears here
and elsewhere in his work is merely cited by critics as evidence of his
debt to Gnostic systems of thought. Certainly the notion of a
demiurge creating Earth as an act of rebellion owes much to Gnostic
thought, but we must look more closely at the section to understand
its function in *The Book of Urizen* and in Blake's work as a whole. First
of all, we must recognize the motive of Urizen's creation: the
Creator does not, as in the biblical account, create Earth as an act of
love, eventually creating man in his own image, finding the whole
"good"; instead Creation is an act of subterfuge for Urizen, shelter
from the "eternal fires beating without / From Eternals." Secondly,
while Blake's account of Creation does not explicitly mention the
creation of man (that will be invoked in the seven ages during which
Los creates a body for Urizen (10:35–13:18, E75–6)), still the idea of
human ontogeny is involved even in the creation of Earth. Urizen
frames the world around him "like a womb," with "thousands of
rivers in veins / Of blood"; from an Eternal perspective, the newly
created world looks like "a black globe," but also like "a human
heart strugling & beating." All this suggests that Blake is collapsing
two events that appear separately in the biblical account, the work of
the second day and the work of the sixth day, the creation of Earth
and the creation of man. In Blake, the creation of Earth *is* the
creation of man, the two occurring simultaneously, this idea being
expressed most forcefully in the violent combination of the human
and the natural in the image of "thousands of rivers in veins / Of
blood."

What does it mean to say that there is nothing which is not always already human and that the human itself was created in an act of dissimulation, to hide one's head from the wrath of the (humanly conceived) Eternal? It partly means that one has no recourse to an object or an idea that is not already contaminated with the condition of fallenness. It is as if Blake had pushed the idea of Original Sin back beyond the frontier of God's Creation so that even the saving idea of a primal garden is disallowed. Wherever one looks in Blake's Created world, the only reflection which is returned is that of fallen humanity. Blake's distrust of the idea of Creation is also expressed through the ambiguous figure of Los. In *The Book of Urizen*, Los is the figure who creates a body for the perplexed Urizen and also for himself, thus establishing what Blake will call in the later prophecies a "limit of contraction." But the very act of self-incarnation shuts the avenue of right thinking: after Los has reproduced himself by fathering Orc on Enitharmon, the poet announces that "[n]o more Los beheld Eternity" (20:2, E80). The burden of Blake's version of the Creation myth is just this universal denial of the Eternal perspective, a perspective which can only be imagined from a human position of loss. To an Eternal, Earth will still seem "a black globe"; but to an inhabitant of the Earth, the vision of Eternity will be blocked, as by a covering cherub, by the "human heart strugling & beating." The contamination of the Creation itself testifies to the universality of the Fall; there is no escape from this ideology.

(2) Blake's theory of fallen perception is already involved in his idea of Creation, for the ambiguous status of Los as Creator is, as we have seen, the result of his inability to perceive Eternity after having engaged in an act of creation. The *locus classicus* of Blake's theory of perception, however, is the second chapter of *Jerusalem*, where he describes the process by which the senses of men were degraded by the Fall. In one of those pithy aphorisms which are sprinkled throughout the otherwise tangled text of the poem, Blake summarizes in two lines the entire phenomenological dimension of his thought: "If Perceptive Organs vary: Objects of Perception seem to vary: / If the Perceptive Organs close: their Objects seem to close also" (30:55–6, E177). Certainly this is one of those doctrines that commentators have praised for its uncanny anticipation of later philosophical and scientific developments, and one is tempted to recall Marx's own metaphor for the action of ideology in *The German Ideology* – the inversion of the object by the lens of the eye. And the

comparison is well taken: as we remember, Marx's use of a physical metaphor served to universalize the concept of ideology by making it an inescapable element of experience. I would suggest that Blake's perception theory has the same result. Although it is presented as an if – then proposition and therefore seems to leave some room for alternatives, the lesson of Blake's text supports a different, more universalized reading. The progress of the next two plates depicts a process of sensual degradation by which the eyes, nose, tongue, and ears of a continually expanding cast of characters – Reuben, the "Seven Nations," Hand, Hyle, and Coban – are reduced to fallen proportions and, in that resonant Blakean phrase, "they became what they beheld" (32:14–15, E178). The lesson of *Jerusalem* is not that perceptive organs *may* vary, but that they *do* vary, and when they do their objects vary also and eventually close. Blake's indictment of fallen perception is entirely as damning as Marx's indictment of ideological consciousness, for it once again extends the dimensions of perceptual contamination until they engulf the whole of earthly existence, even the act of seeing.

(3) Finally, in establishing a universalized concept of ideology for Blake's text, we must acknowledge one of the most striking aspects of his poetic insight – his ability to describe society as a unified, coherent structure. Where else is the power of the poem "London," returned to by commentators again and again, but in Blake's prescient insight into the systematic complicity of an entire society in the perpetuation of its own evils? What other previous poet had the perspicacity to link together in one sustained lyrical moment the powers of labor, church, army, and state?

> How the Chimney-sweepers cry
> Every blackning Church appalls,
> And the hapless Soldiers sigh
> Runs in blood down palace walls. (E27)

Blake was also able to suggest the underground sympathies between prostitution, marriage, and death:

> But most thro' midnight streets I hear
> How the youthful Harlots curse
> Blasts the new-born Infants tear
> And blights with plagues the Marriage hearse.

Blake takes *discordia concors* – "the Marriage hearse" – beyond the realm of intellectual amusement which it had inhabited for the

Cavalier poets and the Metaphysicals, and forces it to express a bitter new recognition of the dialectic of master and slave, priest and pauper, soldier and victim, husband and harlot. The fact that the manacles which bind society are "mind-forg'd" is not an acknowledgement of their ephemerality or flimsiness, but rather their very insurmountableness, for the mind cannot effect an escape from a situation which it itself has created. Blake's identification of the "mind-forg'd manacles" is the equivalent of Mannheim's paradox, for it extends ideology even to the position of the poem's speaker, who can "mark" weakness and woe in the faces which he meets but cannot perceive the mark of woe branded into his own consciousness. The power of "London" is just this tendency for ideology to assume universal proportions, to subsume first the position of the harlots and chimney-sweeps, then the position of respectable citizens (even seemingly innocent infants), and finally the position of the poem's speaker and even its reader. "London" is the concrete representation of a universal complicity between the victims and the unconscious perpetrators of social oppression; it is a vision of the chain which links all segments of society in a fallen whole and which ultimately binds consciousness itself.[19] Blake will return to images of chains, nets, and webs over and over again, but perhaps never so potently as here.

Without downplaying this universal concept of ideology, however, we must also acknowledge a more particularized concept of ideology in Blake's text. It is to this end that we note Blake's attacks on specific targets – Locke, Rousseau, Voltaire, Newtonian physics and, most powerfully, the dominant school of British painting as represented by Joshua Reynolds. It is fitting that the strategic concept of ideology should be illustrated by a series of interlineations in Reynolds's text (the *Discourses*), for this dimension of ideology concerns the inversions, denials, and denunciations proper to the confrontation of one mind with another. In the annotations to Reynolds, Blake shows himself a master of the art of reply and counterpoint, working his way between Reynolds's arguments to reveal the interests which they unknowingly serve. Although Blake's harsh responses often speak to the content of Reynolds's theory of art – his praise of mere technical ability, his injunction to paint nature as it is seen, his positing of a general nature which subsumes particulars – Blake also displays the ability to trace a position to its material and political interests, a strategy more characteristic of ideology-critique. In a note written in the introduction to *The Works of Sir Joshua Reynolds*, where Reynolds's editor is justifying the writing of the *Discourses*, Blake summarily declares, "This Whole Book was Written to Serve Political Purposes" (E641). Blake similarly sees through Reynolds's praise of various artists and overturns his arguments by reinverting what only seems praise to restore the malevolence which Reynolds truly intends:

I consider Reynolds's Discourses to the Royal Academy as the Simulation of the Hypocrite who Smiles particularly where he means to Betray. His Praise of Rafael is like the Hysteric Smile of Revenge His Softness & Candour. the hidden trap & the poisoned feast. He praises Michael Angelo for Qualities which Michael Angelo Abhorred; & He blames Rafael for the only Qualities which Rafael Valued, Whether Reynolds knew what he was doing. is nothing to me; the Mischief is just the same, whether a Man does it Ignorantly or Knowingly. (E642)

Blake's purpose is the "reversal of a reversal" characteristic of ideology-critique: the feast is reinverted as poison, the candor as a trap, the smile as betrayal, praise as blame, and blame as praise. Part of Blake's savvy in the technique of reinversion can be attributed to his experiences with that other gentle hypocrite, William Hayley, experiences which led him to warn of the dangers of inversion: "Mark well my words! Corporeal Friends are Spiritual Enemies" (*M*4:25, E98). It is tempting to see all of these preliminary reinversions as preparation for that most significant of all strategic reinversions which will occur near the end of *Jerusalem*: the reinversion of Antichrist into Christ. Whatever the case, Blake's grapplings with particular foes, from Joshua Reynolds all the way to the Antichrist himself, show him in full control of the techniques specific to a strategic concept of ideology.

We may approach the question of the base/superstructure model in Blake's text by understanding to what degree he assigns the deceptions of ideology to the system of industrial production. We will not be surprised to find Blake a pioneer in this species of analysis also. One of the most fiendishly effective moments of *The Four Zoas* occurs in Night the Seventh when Urizen (now the industrialist workmaster) rehearses a speech designed to grease the wheels of production:

Listen O Daughters to my Voice Listen to the Words of Wisdom
. . .
Compell the poor to live upon a Crust of bread by soft mild arts

Smile when they frown frown when they smile & when a man looks pale
With labor & abstinence say he looks healthy & happy
And when his children sicken let them die there are enough
Born even too many & our Earth will be overrun
Without these arts If you would make the poor live with temper
With pomp give every crust of bread you give with gracious cunning
Magnify small gifts reduce the man to want a gift & then give with pomp
Say he smiles if you hear him sigh If pale say he is ruddy
Preach temperance say he is overgorgd & drowns his wit
In strong drink tho you know that bread & water are all
He can afford Flatter his wife pity his children till we can
Reduce all to our will as spaniels are taught with art.   (80:2, 9–21, E355)

The "art" which Urizen speaks of is drawn largely from the list of ideological ruses which industrialists used at the time: pointing to their own charity as a way of avoiding deeper injustices, accusing the poor of drunkenness, limiting reproduction, denying the deplorable physical condition of the workers. Ideology as expressed here occupies the position of a superstructure because it is simply the expression of a more fundamental base: the mode of capitalist production and the exigencies of its continuing operation. Blake's analysis also conforms to Marx's class theory of ideology, for clearly one's position with regard to the machinery of production would determine one's position within this ideological framework, whether as ruling-class ideologist or as the working-class object of ideological portrayal.

But do we find a clear distinction between the consciousness of the ruling class and the working class in Blake's text? I believe that the lesson of Blake's text, as well as the lesson of history, is otherwise. Urizen's dominance within the sphere of industrial production can be attributed to his ability to freeze the consciousnesses of the workers who labor beneath him, thus reducing them to a state of ideological confusion equal to his own. Urizen achieves this partly through the alienation of the worker from his product, a result of the division of labor which Adam Smith had celebrated some twenty-five years before Blake wrote *The Four Zoas*. Still in Night the Seventh, Blake describes the process by which the Sons of Urizen condemn the peaceful arts of the hourglass and the waterwheel in order to gain complete control of the workers' consciousnesses:

To perplex youth in their outgoings & to bind to labours
Of day & night the myriads of Eternity. that they might file

And polish brass hour after hour labourious workmanship
Kept ignorant of the use that they might spend the days of wisdom
In sorrowful drudgery to obtain a scanty pittance of bread
In ignorance to view a small portion & think that All
And call it Demonstration blind to all the simple rules of life.

(92:27–33, E364)

The confusion and deception of the workers is merely the first step in a process that will result in the total cooptation of the workers' consciousness by the system of capitalist production. Blake describes this process several times throughout his work, in terms of the rigidification and, to borrow a Blakeanism, the "stonifying" of individual bodies and minds:

> Then the Inhabitants of those Cities:
> Felt their Nerves change into Marrow
> And hardening Bones began
> In swift diseases and torments,
> In throbbings & shootings & grindings
> Thro' all the coasts; till weaken'd
> The Senses inward rush'd shrinking,
> Beneath the dark net of infection.   (*BU*25:23–30, E82)

The temptation to compare this process to the process Georg Lukács describes as "reification" is too strong to resist, for both processes describe a degradation of the senses by which objects (and, in Blake, people themselves) come to seem static and lifeless. But whereas Lukács theorized that the worker's alienation from his product was the prerequisite for a class consciousness which breaks through the rigidities of reification, Blake offers little hope of a revolutionary consciousness which will escape the limitations of ruling-class ideology. Both thinkers are contemplating the dynamics of industrial production, but Lukács is allowing an exemption from reification for the working class with which Blake cannot agree. A class theory of ideology is here collapsing beneath the weight of a universalization of ideology which allows no escape.

But Blake's portrayal of labor and the consciousness proper to it is not always so gloomy, for work is the method of escape as well as the source of enslavement. For the purposes of establishing a redemptive class consciousness in Blake's text, we must turn to those images of positive labor, mostly in *Jerusalem*, involving Los's construction of Golgonooza. Golgonooza is the city of art which will spell the end of mankind's subjection to the tyranny of time and the workmasters, but Golgonooza, like every city, requires labor for its existence. Borrowing partly from the description of the temple in the Book of Ezekiel, Blake portrays Golgonooza in one of the most famously intractable sections of *Jerusalem* (12:45–13:55, E156–7). But unlike Ezekiel's temple, Golgonooza is portrayed as the result of active and continuous constructive labor:

> [T]he thundering Bellows
> Heaves in the hand of Palamabron who in London's darkness
> Before the Anvil, watches the bellowing flames; thundering
> The Hammer loud rages in Rintrahs strong grasp swinging loud
> Round from heaven to earth down falling with heavy blow
> Dead on the Anvil, where the red hot wedge groans in pain
> . . .
> Scotland pours out his Sons to labour at the Furnaces
> Wales gives his Daughters to the Looms; England: nursing Mothers
> Gives to the Children of Albion & to the Children of Jerusalem.
>
> (16:8–13, 22–4, E159–60)

Blake is involved in the redemption of labor as a constructive practice and also necessarily the redemption of the class consciousness peculiar to the working class. Within a seemingly esoteric and solipsistic text, he is reaffirming the integrity and efficaciousness of collective labor and the consciousness of a working class which remains true to itself despite the deceptions of industrial capitalism. A class theory of ideology has here seemingly found the fissure which will allow its escape from "stonified" capitalism.

But we seem to have happened upon a contradiction between a reified proletariat and an activated class-conscious proletariat. And since the evidence of Blake's time and our own suggests that the working class adopts the ideology of its oppressors, we are perfectly within our rights to ask whether the redemptive class consciousness as Blake here proposes it is feasible or mere wishful thinking. The strengths of Blake's descriptions of universal ideology, universal fallen perception, have lain in their inescapability, the conviction that Blake's picture of the fallen world represents a tragically accurate portrayal of existence as it cannot be avoided. The questioning of Blake's contradictory theories of ideology, of universal and nonuniversal ideologies, will necessarily lead us to an appraisal of his posited utopias of redeemed labor, redeemed perception, redeemed communication, and redeemed artistic production. Are these utopias reasonable exceptions to the otherwise universal ideology or are they merely the projections of a naive ideological consciousness? Ultimately our inquiry will bear on the validity of the central dynamic of ideology-critique: the negation of what is. The value of Blake's strategies for change finally rests on the fundamental negation of the "here" of ideology for the "nowhere" of utopia.

IV

That which is cannot be true. Ernst Bloch[20]

The subject of utopianism has always enjoyed an ambiguous status within Marxism.[21] Although at the heart of many proto-Marxist social theories, such as those of Robert Owen and Charles Fourier, utopianism has largely been denied any validity within the system of orthodox Marxist thought. For the most part, the origin of utopia's exclusion from serious discussion can be traced to the publication of Friedrich Engels's *Socialism: Utopian and Scientific* (1880) and the subsequent redirection of Marxist theoretical efforts into scientific channels. In that book, originally issued as part of a critique of the social reorganization scheme of Eugen Dühring, Engels voices the main criticisms which will continue to be leveled against utopianism for the next century. It is worth quoting Engels at length to understand the content and the vigor of scientific Socialism's distrust of the utopian:

The Utopians' mode of thought has for a long time governed the socialist ideas of the nineteenth century, and still governs some of them. Until very recently all French and English Socialists did homage to it. The earlier German Communism, including that of Weitling, was of the same school. To all these Socialism is the expression of absolute truth, reason, and justice, and has only to be discovered to conquer all the world by virtue of its own power. And as absolute truth is independent of time, space, and of the historical development of man, it is a mere accident when and where it is discovered. With all this, absolute truth, reason, and justice are different with the founder of each different school. And as each one's special kind of absolute truth, reason, and justice is again conditioned by his subjective understanding, his conditions of existence, the measure of his knowledge and his intellectual training, there is no other ending possible in this conflict of absolute truths than that they shall be mutually exclusive one of the other. Hence, from this nothing could come but a kind of eclectic, average Socialism, which, as a matter of fact, has up to the present time dominated the minds of most of the socialist workers in France and England. Hence, a mish-mash allowing of the most manifold shades of opinion; a mish-mash of such critical statements, economic theories, pictures of future society by the founders of different sects, as excite a minimum of opposition; a mish-mash which is the more easily brewed the more the definite sharp edges of the individual constituents are rubbed down in the stream of debate, like rounded pebbles in a brook.[22]

The criticisms Engels brings to bear against utopianism are the same as those used against ideology: it is ahistorical ("independent of time, space, and of the historical development of man"); merely super-structural, determined by a material base ("conditioned by . . . conditions of existence"); and divisive, as if along class lines ("no other ending possible in this conflict of absolute truths than that they shall be mutually exclusive one of the other"). Utopianism's effects on the mind, as Engels portrays them here, are also reminiscent of the effects of a dominant ideology: the "mish-mash" of muddled utopian thinking has "dominated the minds" of French and English socialists and has "rubbed down" the sharp edges of otherwise clear-headed thinkers. The anti-utopian move, in this originating gesture of scientific Marxism and in its later development, is the elision of the line between utopia and ideology, or what's more, the identification of utopia as a particularly virulent form of ideology.

The first step in recovering the concept of utopia then lies in establishing a fruitful opposition between the two. Once again, Ricoeur has offered useful suggestions. In his regressive analysis[23] of ideology and utopia, Ricoeur isolates a specific function of uto-pianism precisely in its claim to exist "nowhere":

May we not say then that imagination itself – through its utopian function – has a *constitutive* role in helping us *rethink* the nature of our social life? Is not utopia – this leap outside – the way in which we radically rethink what is family, what is consumption, what is authority, what is religion, and so on? Does not the fantasy of an alternative society and its exteriorization "nowhere" work as one of the most formidable contestations of what is? (*Ideology and Utopia*, 16; Ricoeur's emphasis)

The radical contradiction between utopia and ideology thus begins to generate a progressive dynamic, much the same as Blake referred to when he declared that "Without Contraries is no progression" (*MHH*3, E34). As Ricoeur characterizes the relationship between ideology and utopia, "It is always from the depth of a utopia that we may speak of an ideology" (*Ideology and Utopia*, 251). We can thus begin to understand, though not resolve, the incompatibility of contradictory notions of ideology, as universal or particularized, as determined by class or not. The significance of a universal concept of ideology, as we have seen, is the realization that there is no escape from ideology, no place from which to critique ideology. A strategic concept of ideology, on the other hand, is that used within the context of ideology-critique itself, which always finds a point from which to bring judgment. What else is the import of utopianism but the realization that, if there really is no place from which to critique ideology, the ideology critic must position him/herself in the "nowhere" of utopia? Utopianism is the only concept which simultaneously allows the breadth of a universal concept of ideology and the possibility of ideology-critique.

But the skeptic will accuse me of sophistry or, worse still, a brand of philosophical punning. "Surely," one may say, "we have seen utopias come and go, and they always express the interests of a certain class and are as subject to the charge of ideology as the most repressive law or the most conservative novel." The beginnings of an answer to this objection can be found in a consideration of the role of utopia in Marx's text itself. Ricoeur claims that "accomplished communism" plays the role of utopia in Marx's early manuscripts (*Ideology and Utopia*, 55). It is only against the utopian background of an accomplished communism – when modes of production will have been fully humanized – that the critique of alienated forms of production makes sense. Similarly, we might add that the critiques of commodity fetishization, the false totalization of bourgeois ideology, and many other elements of Marx's critique of capitalism, only become coherent within the framework of a utopian reconciliation at the end of time. Even the central Marxian formulation of the disjunction between the realm of nature and the realm of freedom only becomes significant as it prefigures a world in which the two are united. Scientific as the Marxist analysis claims to be, it finally cannot exclude the utopian dimension which gives form to its critique of alienation. The contradictions of ideology only make sense against the unity of utopia.

Utopia plays a similar role in the Blakean text. As we have seen in our consideration of his concept of ideology, Blake portrays a world in which the mind and the senses are completely ensnared by fallenness. Political and economic life is characterized by the tyranny of kings and workmasters over alienated subjects and workers whose consciousnesses are eventually reduced to a condition of universal degradation. Man is in a state of self-alienation, or, as Blake would state it, Albion has fallen into disunity, into the confusion of irreconcilable forces at war with each other, the four fallen Zoas. But if Blake offers a diagnosis of alienation, decay, and degradation, he also offers a prognosis of reintegration and redemption. The song which the Daughters of Beulah sing at the beginning of *The Four Zoas* tells both sides of Albion's story, "His fall into Division and his Resurrection to Unity / His fall into the Generation of Decay & Death & his Regeneration by the Resurrection from the dead" (4:4–5, E301). Indeed, one might say that the utopian dimension of Blake's thought is present even in the fiercest attacks on ideological fallenness. How else are we to understand the anguished imagery of chains, nets, and cages, but against the unrealized utopia of freedom? The alienation of the workers under the tyranny of Urizen – "In sorrowful drudgery to obtain a scanty pittance of bread" (*FZ*92:31, E364) – only carries its full weight of despair when compared with the realized utopia of humanized labor, the Great Harvest of Night the Ninth and the endless recreation of Golgonooza in *Jerusalem*. Ultimately, one reads Blake's symbols correctly only when one extends them into their utopian dimension, realizing Albion's fall as a proleptic form of his resurrection, his disunity as a proleptic form of his unity. Blake suggests just such a utopian hermeneutic in *A Vision of The Last Judgment*:

If the Spectator could Enter into these Images in his Imagination approaching them on the Fiery Chariot of his Contemplative Thought if he could Enter into Noahs Rainbow or into his bosom or could make a Friend & Companion of one of these Images of wonder which always intreats him to leave mortal things as he must know then would he arise from his Grave then would he meet the Lord in the Air and then would he be happy. (82, E560)

We will return to the consideration of a proleptic hermeneutic and its importance in a portrayal of utopia in the chapter on *Milton*.

But we have not considered all of the objections to utopianism. If it is true that any critique of ideology necessarily involves a posited utopia, there remains the fact that utopias can sometimes be naive, idealistic, and unrealizable. Engels is expressing dissatisfaction with just such utopias when he criticizes utopian Socialism for being "independent of time, space and of the historical development of man." Utopianism has been criticized by the scientific Marxists as the equivalent of religion, an "opiate of the masses," naive wish-fulfillment and ideological daydreaming. In its attention to "absolute truth" it fails to acknowledge mundane reality and glosses over the real pain and anguish suffered by the victims of an economic system highly resistant to change. What utopianism needs, these opponents say, is a bracing dose of reality. The "epoch of rest" (William Morris) and the country without money (Thomas More) are all very well for the leisure class, but the rest of us have to make do with things as they are.[24] The cause of revolution and of substantive change would seem to be served very ill by these idle dreamers who merely dispense tranquilizers to a population in need of a violent cure.

Telling as these criticisms are, the interest of Blake's utopia lies precisely in its capacity to account for the facts of fallen existence, the pains and deceptions of the everyday world. It is on the fine line between universal ideology and universal utopia that Blake situates his reflections on the life of Eternal Man. He eludes the criticism of "wishful thinking" by confronting the recalcitrant material of fallen history, the "Minute Particulars" of earthly existence. One can begin to get a sense of the breadth of his utopian vision by measuring it against the criterion of that other "theologian of revolution," Ernst Bloch. In his massive study of utopian phenomena and mentation, *The Principle of Hope* (1959), Bloch distinguishes between what he calls "abstract" and "concrete" utopias. Abstract utopias, although useful for their effort to resist the hypostasization of the merely existent, are nevertheless limited to individualistic, largely compensatory dreams, psychic distractions from the horrors of the ideological world. But Bloch is not willing to surrender the realm of reality entirely to ideology, recognizing also a dimension of the current situation which constantly thrusts itself towards a realizable utopian future. These tendencies, both mental (the "Not-Yet-Conscious") and material (the "Not-Yet-Become"), are "concrete" in two senses: in their grounding in actual elements of the present world, in hopes, stories, objects, organizations; and in their actual realizability in future social formations. The "concrete utopia" thus represents a "*docta spes*," an "educated hope," which exists as a surplus to the ideological determination of the existing world: "Only thus does utopia fetch what is its own from the ideologies and explain the progressive element which continues to be historically effective in the great works of ideology itself."[25] Utopia here is neither a rejection of the ideological thesis nor a collapsing of utopia into ideology, but instead a recognition of the inter-implication of the two. And as I hope to

show in what follows, the strength of Blake's utopia and its relevance
to a revolutionary program for change lie in Blake's careful balan-
cing of the ideological and the utopian, the fallen and the redeemed.
Blake cannot endorse the endless cycle of universal ideology –
"unable to do other than repeat the same dull round over again"
(*NNR*, E3) – but at the same time his utopia is not the negation of all
that has come before, but rather its culmination.

Although it is the purpose of this study to show the tension
between ideology and utopia throughout Blake's work, we can turn
specifically to two moments from the major prophecies as preliminary illustration. As Blake describes it in the second book of
Milton, there are two ways open to the imaginative person desiring
entry into Eden. The first is the Wild Thyme, which "appears only a
small Root creeping in grass" (35:56, E136). The second is the Lark,
"Los's Messenger thro the Twenty-Seven Churches" (35:63), that is,
Los's messenger through history, the twenty-seven ages of the world
thus far. Blake describes the passage of the Lark backwards through
history, from the gate of Golgonooza and eventually back to the
central location of his Felpham garden:

> When on the highest lift of his light pinions he arrives
> At that bright Gate, another Lark meets him back to back
> They touch their pinions tip tip: and each descend
> To their respective Earths & there all night consult with Angels
> Of Providence & with the Eyes of God all night in slumbers
> Inspired: & at the dawn of day send out another Lark
> Into another Heaven to carry news upon his wings
> Thus are the Messengers dispatchd till they reach the Earth again
> In the East Gate of Golgonooza, & the Twenty-eighth bright
> Lark met the Female Ololon descending into my Garden.
>
> (36:1–10, E136)

Besides the sheer beauty of this passage, in its recollection of the
mercy seat at the top of the Ark of the Covenant, its value lies in
Blake's stubborn refusal to relinquish a single moment of the fallen
earth's history. The Wild Thyme is the timeless (a Blakean pun?)
path to Eden, but the Lark is Blake's acknowledgement that history
itself must not be forgotten in the utopian realm. The "Twenty-
eighth bright Lark" will usher in the apocalypse held in abeyance at
the end of *Milton*, but it will not be an apocalypse which explodes the
world, but one which fulfills it. The twenty-eighth lark is the
companion, not the rival, of his twenty-seven forbears. The particu-

larity of this vision of utopia is also implicit in the lark's descent into Blake's very real garden at Felpham, here identified with, and thus conferring a new reality upon, the biblical Eden.

Blake's refusal to abandon history in utopia is even more forcefully expressed in the first chapter of *Jerusalem*. Los is described surveying the city of Golgonooza in ways that reveal its significance and composition:

> He views the City of Golgonooza, & its smaller Cities:
> The Looms & Mills & Prisons & Work-houses of Og & Anak
> The Amalekite: the Canaanite: the Moabite: the Egyptian
> And all that has existed in the space of six thousand years:
> Permanent, & not lost not lost nor vanishd, & every little act,
> Word, work, & wish, that has existed, all remaining still.
>
> (13:56–61, E158–9)

In the repetition of "not lost not lost" Blake reveals the passion for wholeness and for recollected particularity which characterize his utopian vision. Los's hall, as Blake describes it a few plates later, is similarly a museum of remembrance and actuality, whether good or evil:

> All things acted on Earth are seen in the bright Sculptures of
> Los's Halls & every Age renews its powers from these Works
> With every pathetic story possible to happen from Hate or
> Wayward Love & every sorrow & distress is carved here
> Every affinity of Parents Marriage & Friendships are here
> In all their various combinations wrought with wondrous Art
> All that can happen to Man in his pilgrimage of seventy years.
>
> (16:61–7, E161)

Were it not for his well-known distrust of memory, one might be tempted to compare Blake's hall of historical sculptures from which "every Age renews its powers," to Wordsworth's "spots of time" with their "renovating virtue."[26] But where Wordsworth's memories are personal and compensatory for the losses associated with maturity, Blake's are social ("Every affinity of Parents Marriage & Friendships") and transformative of reality as it exists. To put the distinction perhaps too bluntly, Wordsworth's evocative memories represent the "abstract utopianism" opposed to Blake's "concrete" invocations of actual historical tendencies. Blake's utopian city, Golgonooza, is to be built from the good and bad, the happy and sad, experiences of real men and women in real social conditions, "All that can happen to Man in his pilgrimage of seventy years."

The problem of a utopia, then, as it is expressed in Blake, is not that of an escape from history, but instead the strategic problem of history's culmination, how to retain the particulars of history while bringing them to utopian perfection. This is the problem of a revolutionary consciousness faced with seemingly intractable fallenness, the utopian problematic of change.

As such, it is also the battleground for that war of the intellectual and the corporeal, the aesthetic and the social, with which we began this chapter. If the intellectual and the corporeal are ever to find the common ground on which to fight their Blakean war, the war which has not been properly waged up to this time, it will be on the field of a material, a concrete, utopia. Utopianism, as conceived by Blake and theorized by Bloch, is the element of art and literature which incorporates both the material conditions of artistic production and the utopian longing for perfection. The utopian hermeneutic restores the full meaning of an image in its material context but also carries it to the utopian fulfillment which is its artistic destiny. Only a hermeneutic of such breadth can do justice to both elements of the Blakean text, the corporeal and the intellectual, the social and the apocalyptic, the ideological and the utopian. But as is proper to a study which purports to maintain contact with an historical and material reality, we must abandon bold generalizations from the entire corpus of Blake's work and descend to a work-by-work analysis of Blakean strategies for change. We must descend through the twenty-seven churches of Blakean particularity to map the tensions of ideology and utopia, so that we might ascend with the twenty-eighth Lark to experience the final apocalypse. And the fittest place to begin that journey is with an examination of Blake's most widely read, and seemingly most simple, works, the *Songs of Innocence and of Experience.*

CHAPTER 2

The ideology of instruction in Emile *and* Songs of Innocence and of Experience

> If it were not for the Poetic or Prophetic character. the Philosophic & Experimental would soon be at the ratio of all things & stand still, unable to do other than repeat the same dull round over again.
>
> *There is No Natural Religion* [b], E3

> By doing away with giving explicitly to everyone what it implicitly demands of everyone, the educational system demands of everyone alike that they have what it does not give.
>
> Pierre Bourdieu, "Cultural Reproduction and Social Reproduction"[1]

I

By positioning himself within the instructional genre of the child's reading book with the 1789 publication of *Songs of Innocence*,[2] William Blake indissolubly links his poetry with a theme of interest to both the ideologists of his own time and the ideology critics of ours: the theme of education and literacy. We do well to remember that the word *ideology* itself, which, as we have seen, was coined in a positive formulation by Destutt de Tracy in 1796, emerged in an explicitly educational context: de Tracy imagined his science of ideas, *idéologie*, as the basis for a new educational system, freeing the French citizenry, young and old alike, from the prejudices of the past.[3] Modern students of ideology, although reversing the significance of the term, also see the school and education in general as a locus of key significance in the maintenance of social order and repression. Louis Althusser, for example, in his crucial "Ideology and Ideological State Apparatuses (Notes towards an Investigation)," identifies the school as the substitute for the church in modern (post-Enlightenment) society's transmission of the civic "virtues" which maintain social order:

[C]hildren at school also learn the "rules" of good behavior, i.e. the attitude that should be observed by every agent in the division of labour, according to the job he is "destined" for: rules of morality, civic and professional conscience, which actually means rules of respect for the socio-technical division of labour and ultimately the rules of the order established by class domination. They also learn to "speak proper French," to "handle" the workers correctly.[4]

This last point, the speaking of "proper French" and its role in business "management" (to adopt an American parallel for Althusser's euphemistic "handle"), indicates the way in which the seemingly neutral skill of linguistic competence is implicated in larger social structures. In particular, education is of vital importance for Althusser's desire to move beyond a mere thinking of the conditions of production to the more crucial question of the *reproduction* of the conditions of production. The school (in alliance with the family) is the place where the social structure negotiates the precarious transition from one generation to the next or, in the most extreme formulation, from one moment to the next. The school is an incubator, the place where society reproduces itself, transmits its structures as completely as possible.

The metaphor of education as a quasi-biological reproduction seems to open up some room for variation, however, since we all know of children who show little or no resemblance to their parents. Althusser seems to leave such a space for the incomplete functioning of the school in his later encomium of "those teachers who, in dreadful conditions, attempt to turn the few weapons they can find in the history and learning they 'teach' against the ideology, the system and the practices in which they are trapped" ("Ideology," 157). But we should be wary of accepting too quickly, within Althusser's prophecy of doom, a saving heroic remnant that might allow us to ameliorate the force of his critique. If Althusser is a half-hearted doomsayer in this context (although in few others), we might turn to the proper Jeremiad of Pierre Bourdieu, who, picking up on Althusser's notion of reproduction in education, leaves us in a state much closer to Blake's Ulro of unvarying fallenness. In a work of central importance to the sociology of education, *Reproduction in Education, Society and Culture*, Bourdieu unites the structures of the family and the school in a formulation which seems infallible in its reproduction of social structures of domination. Bourdieu concludes from the nearly ubiquitous failure of pedagogic communication (as judged by tests of students' command of educational content) that the primary function of the school is not the communication of a body of knowledge, but rather the inculcation of a *manner of relating* to that knowledge, whether conceived of as a humanistic "culture" or a scientific or technical "know-how." However, students who succeed in achieving this "manner of relating" – a "style" of behavior, what Bourdieu calls a "*habitus*," reflected in gestures, manners of speech, clothes, "personality" – are preselected, since the manner of relating to culture which the school teaches is the manner of the dominant class in society, and therefore requires the background of a preschool immersion in a family environment only to be found in those dominant classes. The message of the schools is thus already coded in its earliest manifestations, and the only key to this code is provided by the upper-class family: "the academic market value of each individual's linguistic capital is a function of the distance between the type of symbolic mastery demanded by the School and the practical mastery he owes to his initial class upbringing."[5] While we might imagine, along the lines of Althusser's heroic teachers, exceptions to this iron-clad rule of class dominance, Bourdieu, in another but related context, claims that these exceptions (whom he calls, in a Blakean manner, the "elect") are really "the best testimony of [a spurious] academic democracy" ("Cultural Reproduction," 497). The structure is not changed by the various personnel who occupy its slots, and the seeming "freedom" of the educational structure must finally be read, according to Bourdieu, in terms of the legitimation function of the school, the necessity to make the current social structure appear just. Bourdieu's analysis of the system of education, with its capacity for near total self-reproduction and reproduction of society, tightens the noose in much the same manner as Blake's "same dull round," a similarity of which Bourdieu reminds us in lamenting that "it is difficult to break the circle in which cultural capital is added to cultural capital" ("Cultural Reproduction", 493).

Cultural reproduction and the accumulation of cultural capital were particularly salient processes in the decades leading up to the publication of Blake's *Songs*, as a growing entrepreneurial middle class staked its claims for legitimacy not on the unavailable prerogative of birth, but on the attainment of culture and its mastery in the schools. Numerous Dissenting Academies, the creation of necessity rather than innovation, arose in response to the 1662 Act of

Uniformity barring non-Anglicans from established teaching posts, and these schools gradually developed over the course of the next 100 years into the breeding ground for the new entrepreneurial class.[6] As scholars of the period have realized, however, the eighteenth century stands as the focal point of a crisis in social reproduction, a crisis that can usefully be summarized as the necessity to fulfill two logically opposed functions: (1) to provide for the ascendancy of the new entrepreneurial class while (2) not destabilizing the current social order. The eighteenth-century school is thus the site of an odd game of societal musical chairs, orchestrating the effective transfer of power while resolutely avoiding upsetting the furniture of polite society. According to John Guillory, one of the best observers of this delicate balance and its effects on literary production and reception, the eighteenth-century bourgeoisie found two ways of achieving this contradictory goal: emulation and exclusion.[7] The bourgeois educational system encouraged its students to emulate the values of the previously dominant class, to behave like "little gentlemen" (a skill inculcated in the Dissenting Academy) or like "little ladies" (a by-product of the bourgeois home). Exclusion, however, characterizes the bourgeoisie's attitude towards the working classes and their education, best expressed in Soame Jenyns's harsh appraisal of 1757, that ignorance is "the appointed lot of all born to poverty and the drudgeries of life . . . a cordial, administered by the gracious hand of providence, of which they ought never to be deprived by an ill-judged and improper education" (quoted in Altick, *English Common Reader*, 31–2). By means of this careful negotiation of competing goals, each staking its claim in the eighteenth-century school, a rising class insured its own reproduction in its containment of the spread of popular education and social improvement.

If such a strategy were completely effective in its goal of consolidating power in the hands of a new class, then Bourdieu would indeed seem justified in his analysis of the school as a perfectly efficient mechanism for the reproduction of social domination, weathering, as it here seems to do, the storm of social change while still maintaining an unequal distribution of power. But such an account of the educational system is incomplete, and ignores, in particular, the extent to which the school is the site of more radically competing claims whose energy cannot be contained as easily as the middle-class will-to-power. The mere fact that eighteenth-century schools were privately-organized institutions rather than the product of state-sponsored public "consensus," as in our own times, might alert us to the contestation of educational ideology in the period. In particular, this submerged dimension of the educational system implicitly structures a debate throughout the century and into the period of Blake's *Songs*, about whether the school should be seen primarily as a means for social advancement or for social containment and whether, along parallel lines, education should be denied to the working class (as Soame Jenyns and others suggested) or whether it played an indispensable role in their indoctrination into a class hierarchy in which they occupy the lowest position. Already, in the first half of the eighteenth century, the Society for Promoting Christian Knowledge had established a system of charity schools to train poor children in the reading of Scripture and, quite explicitly, in obedience to their "betters." But resistance to popular education continued throughout the century,[8] indicating, rather than a simple disagreement about ideological strategies, an instability in the workings of education itself. It is at this point, the point of an anxiety about the efficiency of education's reproductive function, that we can perhaps begin to work out an alternative use and purpose for the school and can begin to place William Blake's intervention in the apparatus of education.

For, as we shall see, Blake enters the discourse of education as a *space of conflict*, a site for contesting voices and opinions about the value of education and its main technique of literacy. The role of children's reading books and collections of nursery rhymes in this conflict has been well documented, serving as they do the function of extending the reach of the educational system into the private home. In order to get a notion of the full dimensions of this contest for the power of instruction, we have only to turn to the example of Hannah More, whose *Cheap Repository Tracts*, first distributed the year following Blake's initial issuance of the combined *Songs of Innocence and of Experience* (1794), specifically oppose themselves to the raucous chapbooks then available: "Vulgar and indecent penny books were always common, but speculative infidelity, brought down to the pockets and capacities of the poor, forms a new aera in our history" (quoted in Altick, *English Common Reader*, 74). Little case can be made for Blake's volume as either "common" (only 24 copies of the combined volume now exist) or "brought down to the pockets and capacities of the poor" (*Songs of Innocence* sold for 5 shillings at a time when the average weekly wage for a worker was 10 to 12 shillings),[9] but we can see him as participating through these lyrics in a war of words which was also a war over education's function. The weapons of education's middle-class guardians were standardization of the language (as witnessed to by the increasing number of grammars written during the period)[10] and standardization of instruction for the poor to include only the indoctrination of polite, socially-stable virtues, all in the service of a reproduction of dominant class values. The weapons of Blake's resistance are an occupation of the dominant mode in order to destabilize it from within and an openness to many of those voices that challenge the polite monopoly on literacy and its values. The outcome of this skirmish – merely one in a long line of struggles between those who wish to realize education's full democratic potential and those who wish to preserve its function as a conveyor of a distinguishing cultural capital[11] – will rest on the ability of this volume which so often takes reproduction as its theme, its own reproduction and its society's reproduction, to suggest ways of breaking the "dull round" of reproduction "in which cultural capital is added to cultural capital." And a major ally and predecessor for Blake in this struggle, an educational theorist who had his own dual legacy in the debate of the period, was Jean-Jacques Rousseau.

II

It would truly be difficult to overstate the importance of Rousseau in the educational debates of the late eighteenth and nineteenth centuries, not only in France but throughout Europe and the United States. He is, as Zachary Leader puts it, "the single most important and controversial educational theorist in Blake's age" (*Reading Blake's Songs*, 22). Leader's dual emphasis – "important and controversial" – is an accurate one, for soon after the appearance of *Emile, or On Education* in 1762 (and its almost immediate translation into English), Rousseau became the focal point for much of the conflict over the proper function of education. On the one hand Rousseau emerges as the Dr. Spock of his age, cited by the large number of mothers who decide to breast-feed their own babies "a la Jean-Jacques"; on the other, the children's author Sarah Trimmer could argue in *The Guardian of Education* (1802) that Rousseau and his followers constituted a *"conspiracy against* CHRISTIANITY *and all* SOCIAL ORDER . . . endeavouring to infect the minds of the rising generation, through the medium of *Books of Education* and *Children's Books*."[12] The most crucial point to recognize in asserting Rousseau's influence and its incendiary effect, as well as its role in providing the backdrop for Blake's composition of the *Songs*, is the manner in which issues of education are inherently and inescapably political in *Emile*. It is no coincidence, as James Chandler has noted,[13] that *Emile* was issued in the same year as the *Social Contract*, and Rousseau's own precipitous flight from arrest in Paris soon after publication would itself seem evidence of the political force of pedagogical theory.

But if Rousseau's immense influence on general educational debates has been unavoidably acknowledged, his influence on Blake has not yet been fully registered. The problem lies in Blake's incorporation of Rousseau as a character in his developed vision of cosmic history, most powerfully stated in the third chapter of *Jerusalem*, addressed "To the Deists": "Voltaire Rousseau Gibbon Hume. charge the Spiritually Religious with Hypocrisy! but how a Monk or a Methodist either, can be a Hypocrite: I cannot conceive . . . Rousseau thought Men Good by Nature; he found them Evil & found no friend" (*J*52, E201). Rousseau, in this late formulation, is the Man of Nature aligned against the Man of Religion, and Blake's version of this complex thinker is here so little nuanced as to "uncover" him as one of Vala's Covering Cherubs: "Her Two Covering Cherubs afterwards named Voltaire & Rousseau: / Two frowning Rocks: on each side of the Cove & Stone of Torture" (*J*66:12–13, E218). But attempts to deduce a consistently negative opinion of Rousseau from this admittedly extreme portrait pay too little heed to generic constraint – to the prophetic condensation which meets Blake's needs in *Jerusalem* but does not necessarily do justice to personal particularity – nor do they take account of the historical context of composition. References to French thinkers, especially those such as Rousseau and Voltaire who were credited with planting the seeds of the Revolution, carry a far different weight in the first two decades of the nineteenth century (when Blake was working hardest on *Jerusalem*) than they might have in the last decade of the eighteenth century. So, in the unpublished poem *The French Revolution*, written in 1791, the pair, although no more carefully delineated, assume a completely different valuation in their guidance of the heroic Lafayette: "Over his head the soul of Voltaire shone fiery, and over the army Rousseau his white cloud / Unfolded" (15:282–3, E298–9). Looking backwards from the perspective of

Blake's death in a monarchic Europe, we thus see Rousseau and Voltaire transform from Covering Cherubs to the philosophical equivalents of the pillar of fire and pillar of cloud which lead the children of Israel to the Promised Land. Interesting in themselves as an example of Blake's visionary transformation of historical detail, these explicit textual references neither help us to distinguish Rousseau from Voltaire (a pairing whose compatibility is anyway open to question) nor do they help us to assess Blake's connections with the details of Rousseau's educational theory. These connections are much more likely to be found in the intricate weave of similar concerns and formulations which suggest *Emile* as a cognate text for the *Songs*.

The most formidable obstacle to establishing such a connection and the most formidable obstacle to any case for Rousseau's early understanding of an ideological critique of education, lies in the formulation most often associated with him, that of the Natural Man. If Rousseau really "thought Men Good by Nature," as Blake puts it in *Jerusalem*, and also thought that the solution to social evils was simply a restoration of the natural state, then he certainly could not be said to have realized the central element of the ideological thesis, the social construction of humanity. But the case in *Emile* is not so simply stated. After the magisterial opening sentence – "God makes all things good; man meddles with them and they become evil" – Rousseau offers a much modified, if not contradictory, assessment of human "meddling": "Yet things would be worse without this education, and mankind cannot be made by halves. Under existing conditions a man left to himself from birth would be more of a monster than the rest."[14] "Made," along with "all things," in the first sentence, mankind is half "unmade" by the start of the next paragraph, and education is granted a power of making to rival God's. Rousseau here betrays some of the ambivalence about education's function that I have suggested characterizes contemporary discourse in general, an uncertainty about education's role as "maker" or "unmaker" of society and citizen. The ground we can surely feel beneath our feet, however, is the "existing conditions" – the world of social reality – which has here been substituted for the abstract realm of natural good. A Covering Cherub, no less daunting than Blake's, blocks Rousseau's access to the Nature he identifies as the ultimate source of good, and he has no choice but to toil in the world of current social conditions, with education as his best available tool.

But the pathos of an ideological understanding of education is the notion that this "making" is itself an "unmaking," the production of educated minds merely a reproduction, in Bourdieu's term, of the same half-made monsters of the past. Rousseau registers this logical bind by addressing the difficulty of finding a teacher who could teach anything but the corrupt values of established society:

> The more you think of it the harder you will find it. The tutor must have been trained for his pupil, his servants must have been trained for their master, so that all who come near him may have received the impression which is to be transmitted to him. We must pass from education to education, I know not how far. How can a child be well educated by one who has not been well educated himself?   (*Emile*, 19)

Education, for Rousseau, is understood in its context of still earlier education, as a reproduction in the present student of an "impression [*impressions*]" received in the past. Hope for any transformative potential in education would seem to depend upon searching the past for an elusive Archimedean point, the "well educated teacher" who would not simply indoctrinate his pupil in the errors of his own training. The price of losing contact with the state of Nature, where God has made all things good, is being confined to a realm where to "meddle" seems logically to imply "evil." The momentum of Rousseau's educational theory would thus seem to compel him to admit that, education or no, existing conditions can only "make" monsters.

Such a conclusion, seemingly damning for any education not conceived of in narrowly reproductive terms, finds its parallel in some of the most pessimistic of Blake's *Songs of Experience*, in, for instance, the concluding stanza of "The Human Abstract" and its location of the obscuring Tree of Mystery:

> The Gods of the earth and sea,
> Sought thro' Nature to find this Tree
> But their search was all in vain:
> There grows one in the Human Brain.   (21–4, E27)

In much the same manner as Rousseau, although with considerably less nostalgia for inaccessible Nature, the experienced speaker locates the (literal) roots of obscurity and ignorance in their human sufferers. If human thought is obscured by "mystery," it is a mystery itself composed of human thought, the recirculated notions which "pass from education to education." The organic metaphor, rather than simply referring to the biblical Tree of Knowledge, suggests the quasi-natural development and reproducibility of Mystery's domain:

> Soon spreads the dismal shade
> Of Mystery. . .
> And the Catterpillar and Fly,
> Feed on the Mystery.
> And it bears the fruit of Deceit,
> Ruddy and sweet to eat;
> And the Raven his nest has made
> In its thickest shade. (13–20)

The placement of this growth in "the Human Brain" comes as a kind of comic deflation after the natural imagery of these two stanzas, much like Rousseau's turn away from the infallible state of Nature in the opening of *Emile*. But the use of natural imagery in "The Human Abstract" suggests a durability in Mystery's power to reproduce itself, to produce attractive and consumable fruit, a durability which seems to exceed human capacities to change it even though it is rooted in the human brain. Like Rousseau's description of a continuous miseducation, the Tree of Mystery embodies a process of transmission in which human action is always already implicated, as if trapped in the branches of "its thickest shade." Rousseau suggests a similar process in the education of an individual child, discussing the way in which, once indulged in his desire for sway over others, he can never be freed of his love of tyranny, even when he possesses the ability to meet his own needs: "the love of power does not die with the need that roused it; power arouses and flatters self-love, and habit strengthens it; thus caprice follows upon need, and the first seeds of prejudice and obstinacy are sown" (*Emile*, 40). Although Rousseau assures us that this unsavory result "does not spring from a natural love of power, but one which has been taught them" (*Emile*, 40), his use of the organic figure of "seeds" suggests the worst combination of human agency with quasi-natural durability.

The power of ideology and its self-reproductive ability are invisible, growing "in the Human Brain," although externalized in the image of the tree. Given this invisibility, the role of Blake's decidably visible illuminated art becomes that much more important. The illuminated plate for "The Human Abstract" shows two blighted trees, to the right and left of the text, sending strangely unnatural feelers into the body of the text (figure 1). At the bottom, an old man

Figure 1 "The Human Abstract" from *Songs of Innocence and of Experience.*

struggles with two ropes that seem to pinion him to the ground.[15] The Gods' search in Nature for the Tree of Mystery, a search "in vain" given the invisibility of its object, here seems at least partially satisfied: if they have not found the Tree and its "thickest shade," then at least we, the readers/viewers of Blake's text, have found this visible scene of bondage at the bottom of the page. This uneven relation between text and illustration (if we can even conceptualize Blake's work in those terms) suggests something about his relation to the tradition of children's book publishing and also something about his relation to the technique of literacy which those books were designed to develop. More than a simple illustration of the text, more than a reproduction of the text's narrative, the scene at the bottom of the page seems to have the power that Louis Althusser grants to all art, not simply to serve ideology, but to render it visible.[16] If tutelage in the literacy of the text is an invisible process by which the skill of the parent is transmitted to the child, then the picture at the bottom of the page would seem to disrupt this process, to make visible what the text claims is sought "in vain." The illustration's making visible of the text, while not directly reproducing it, begins to suggest some means of escaping the dull round of ideological reproduction which Bourdieu presents as the only face of education. Indeed, a viewer, rather than confirming the text's description of Mystery's "thickest shade," might note an odd looseness in the ropes with which the old man is bound and the beginnings of an effort to free himself.

Rousseau, similarly, begins to find some revolutionary potential for education not in its ability to establish continuity, to "pass from education to education," but precisely in the failure of that continuity, in the breakdown of education's transmissibility. In observing the results of a traditional authoritarian education, Rousseau pays most attention to the *lack* of transmission from teacher to student:

> Listen to a little fellow who has just been under instruction; let him chatter freely, ask questions, and talk at his ease, and you will be surprised to find the strange forms your arguments have assumed in his mind; he confuses everything, and turns everything topsy-turvy; you are vexed and grieved by his unforeseen objections; he reduces you to be silent yourself or to silence him. (*Emile*, 71)

As Bourdieu observed of the French educational system some 200 years after this assessment, its fundamental characteristic (and that of perhaps all education systems) is a startling inability to communicate its content effectively,[17] but unlike Bourdieu, Rousseau does not conclude that it therefore must communicate something else, the class *habitus* which for Bourdieu is the true invisible content of education. The problem with Bourdieu's analysis is that it remains within the domain of communication, of transmission: the only alternatives it poses are a straightforward transmission of knowledge or, if that fails (as it does), a transmission of class-specific behaviors, the *habitus*. The peculiar and important innovation of Rousseau's educational theory, and the element most influential for Blake in the composition of his volume, is the acknowledgement of a gap between adult and child, a space which forbids simple transmission: "Childhood has its own ways of seeing, thinking, and feeling; nothing is more foolish than to try and substitute our ways" (*Emile*, 64). The problem with most literacy training, as Rousseau conceives it, is that it attempts forcibly to close this gap. As a prelude to a discussion of that staple of eighteenth-century French children's literature, La Fontaine's *Fables*, Rousseau rejects premature literacy training along lines that might remind us of his earlier discussion of indelible "impressions":

> What is the use of inscribing on their brains a list of symbols which mean nothing to them? . . . No, if nature has given the child this plasticity of brain which fits him to receive every kind of impression, it was not that you should imprint on it the names and dates of kings, the jargon of heraldry, the globe and geography, all those words without present meaning or future use for the child, which flood of words overwhelms his sad and barren childhood.[18] (*Emile*, 90)

We will have to access Blake's connection to this explicit rejection of early literacy at greater length in the last section of this chapter, but for now it suffices to say that both authors reject the invisible transmission of knowledge which early literacy training often implies.

The hallmark of a Rousseauian education, *Emile*'s central contribution to educational theory and the point to which the book continually returns, is the need for freedom in the child's development, a willingness to let happen what will in the early experience of the child. In this, Rousseau firmly rejects the closely regimented instruction which characterized the educational establishment as he found it and which would reemerge in the monitorial system of Joseph Lancaster and Andrew Bell in nineteenth-century England.

Those moments in *Emile* most likely to give a modern parent pause and to go against the grain of an eighteenth-century authoritarian conception of child-rearing, are the points where Rousseau recommends allowing the child to indulge even those whims which may lead to pain, sickness, or death:

[T]he liberty I give my pupil makes up for the slight hardships to which he is exposed. I see little fellows playing in the snow, scarcely able to stir a finger. They could go and warm themselves if they chose, but they do not choose; if you forced them to come in they would feel the harshness of constraint a hundredfold more than the sharpness of the cold. (*Emile*, 60)

The voice of the indulgent parent might remind us of Blake's innocent Nurse, who also indulges children in their refusal to obey her not very hard-pressed curfew:

> No no let us play, for it is yet day
> And we cannot go to sleep
>
> . . .
> Well well go & play till the light fades away
> And then go home to bed.   (9–10, 13–14, E15)

The point in this and others of the *Songs*, particularly in *Innocence*, seems to be to break the round by which one generation's values are impressed on another, and the best means to this end are to allow for the play of the child's willful desires. The authoritarian voice of Experience, on the other hand, will insist on the wisdom of its own advice, cautioning against the potential dangers of the external world: "Then come home my children, the sun is gone down / And the dews of night arise" (5–6, E23). Both Rousseau and Blake seem concerned with the almost imperceptible way in which seemingly caring and nurturative voices come to serve the function of a more explicitly repressive social system, to reproduce, in disguised forms, the mandates of institutional power.

It is around the issue of nursing, however, and nursing conceived of in both its lenient and strict forms, that we can seek out the ideological limits of Rousseau's theory of education and begin to suggest Blake's differences from it. For it is in his opinion of nursing that Rousseau reasserts his ideology of nature and reinserts education in a reproductive framework. In some ways the nurse would seem a figure parallel to that hero of *Emile*, the tutor, to whom Rousseau gives his own name, Jean-Jacques: both of them represent a deviation from the purely "natural" course of the child's being raised by its mother and father. Rousseau suggests such a parallel in his claim that "[t]he real nurse is the mother and the real teacher is the father" (*Emile*, 18), the corollary to which would seem to be that the hired nurse and the teacher are supplemental substitutes. But while he is able to grant a waiver from the course of nature for the tutor, conceived of as someone "more than man" (*Emile*, 19), as Jean-Jacques himself, Rousseau seems to imagine no such exception to the role of the mother as "real nurse." While willing to weigh the claim that a "healthy nurse" is better than a "petted mother," he still concludes that "there is no substitute for a mother's love" (*Emile*, 4). As has already been noted, Rousseau's insistence on mothers breast-feeding their own babies registered in the public consciousness more fully than any other elements of his theory, but such a result is no surprise given the extremity of his posing of the issue:

> Would you restore all men to their primal duties, begin with the mothers; the results will surprise you. Every evil follows in the train of this first sin [i.e., sending children out to nurse]; the whole moral order is disturbed, nature is quenched in every breast, the home becomes gloomy, the spectacle of a young family no longer stirs the husband's love and the stranger's reverence . . . But when mothers deign to nurse their own children, then will be a reform in morals, natural feeling will revive in every heart; there will be no lack of citizens for the state. (*Emile*, 14–15)

In this formulation, Rousseau seems to have abandoned his earlier conception that some additional labor, the work of education, needs to be exerted for the making of citizens. Here education is renaturalized, as a simple and passive transmission of nurturance from mother to child. The mother is figured as Nature, irreplaceable in her salutary effect on the child, a Nature no longer inaccessible in a social world but, rather, the foundation of that social world, the first link in the chain that binds citizen to citizen. And, as Carol Blum points out in her discussion of *Emile*, given the fact that sexual intercourse with a nursing woman was considered taboo at the time, Rousseau's insistence on the maternal "duty" seems part of a rechanneling of women's sexual desire into the naturalized and legitimated sphere of motherhood.[19] Sexual reproduction is here enlisted in the service of social reproduction, as Rousseau the anti-institutionalist puts his entire faith in that most durable of institutions, the bourgeois family.[20]

Although Rousseau makes allowances for an "unnatural" tutor to substitute for the natural father, we might see a complimentary reintroduction of the theme of reproduction in the procedures of the male educator as well. As we have already seen, Rousseau's method for instruction is a calm passivity on the part of the teacher, a leaving of the child to his/her liberty, or, in what he calls "the most useful rule of education," not to "save time, but lose it" (*Emile*, 67). One of the most striking features of Rousseau's pedagogical anecdotes, however, is the extent to which the child's "liberty" is repeatedly manipulated by an omniscient tutor. Rousseau recounts, for instance, his technique for curing the son of an acquaintance of his love of caprice and tyranny over his elders. The child insists on being accompanied in his walks at whatever time he chooses, and Rousseau characteristically takes the negative route of simply refusing to join him, responding to his petulant statement that he'll therefore go on his own with a hearty wish that he enjoy his liberty. Liberty it hardly seems, however, for Rousseau has prearranged the scene that meets the boy as he walks through the streets:

He had scarcely gone a few steps, when he heard, first on this side then on that, all sorts of remarks about himself. "What a pretty little gentleman, neighbour? Where is he going all alone? He will get lost! I will ask him into our house." "Take care you don't. Don't you see he is a naughty little boy who has been turned out of his own house because he is good for nothing? You must not stop naughty boys; let him go where he likes." (*Emile*, 104)

Although claiming to evade the corruptions of social institutions by allowing his student to be educated by his own free experience, Rousseau here invokes the repressive apparatus of social opinion, made only more effective for the invisibility of the machinations which have gone towards the arranging of the scene. Rather than a social contract between non-equivalent equals, tutor and pupil, adult and child, the political system which Rousseau's pedagogy suggests is the subtlest of tyrannies, in which the subject mistakes his subjection for liberty: "There is no subjection so complete as that which preserves the forms of freedom; it is thus that the will itself is taken captive" (*Emile*, 100). The paradox of Rousseau's liberative education, and its reinsertion in the dull round of reproduction, can be stated in the irony that in order to cure the child of tyrannical caprice Rousseau must himself become a tyrant.

This last use of the term *subjection* [*assujettissement*] might remind us of the initial context for this discussion, the ideological critique of education and, in particular, it might evoke Althusser's own double definition of the "subject" as both "a free subjectivity" and "a subjected being, who submits to a higher authority" ("Ideology," 182). For the final product of Rousseau's education, a product which distinguishes his procedures from the educative action of Blake's volume, is precisely this self-regulating bourgeois subject, the subject who, in his very "freedom," chooses his subjection. Rousseau's idea of the "well-educated" citizen, despite his rejection of the explicitly repressive educational regimens of the past, is finally nothing more than a Blakean ratio, a limiting matching of means to ends: "True happiness consists in decreasing the difference between our desires and our powers, in establishing a perfect equilibrium between the power and the will" (*Emile*, 53). Against this careful measuring of desires and powers, Blake asserts a formula which exceeds narrow definitions of human potential: "The desire of Man being Infinite the possession is Infinite & himself Infinite" (*NRR*[b], E3). The textbook in this school of Infinity, the book that pushes against the momentum by which repetition becomes reproduction, is the *Songs of Innocence and of Experience.*

III

[T]hough not all utopia-writers are Platonists, nearly all of them make their utopias depend on education for their permanent establishment. It seems clear that the literary convention of an ideal state is really a by-product of a systematic view of education. (Northrop Frye, "Varieties of Literary Utopias"[21])

Another element that *Emile* and *Songs of Innocence and of Experience* have in common, and one that would initially seem to preclude their participation in the genre of educational literature, is the fact that both are, in a manner of speaking, books written in opposition to bookishness. Indeed, good evidence exists for Blake's participation in the widespread distrust of education and literacy characteristic of much radical and antinomian thought of the time. Jon Mee, in his excellent *Dangerous Enthusiasm*, points to Thomas Paine's influential rejection of "manuscript-assumed authority" in *Rights of Man* (1791) and its echoes in the opinions of popular enthusiasts such as Garnet Terry, who believed that the uneducated understood prophecy more readily than the educated.[22] In Blake's annotations to Robert Thornton's translation of the Lord's Prayer, made in the last year of his life (1827), he claimed, in opposition to Thornton, that "[t]he

Beauty of the Bible is that the most Ignorant & Simple Minds Understand it Best" (E667). And lest we make the mistake of simply assuming an ahistorical continuity in this attitude across the length of Blake's career, we might point to the many uneasy references to books and their power in Blake's works of the 1790s, to the pervasiveness of this theme in, for instance, *The Book of Urizen* or the printing-house allegory of plate 15 in *The Marriage of Heaven and Hell*.[23] This background, drawn from both Blake's texts and the works of the radical political and religious thinkers with whom he is most commonly associated, suggests that Blake's views on books and schools might not be very far removed from those of the School Boy whose song sometimes occupies the penultimate position in the combined volume:

> But to go to school in a summer morn,
> O! it drives all joy away;
> Under a cruel eye outworn,
> The little ones spend the day,
> In sighing and dismay.
>
> Ah! then at times I drooping sit,
> And spend many an anxious hour.
> Nor in my book can I take delight,
> Nor sit in learnings bower,
> Worn thro' with the dreary shower.　　(6–15, E31)

The boy's rationale for this strong dislike of school and the basis of his appeal for relief from his parents echoes the organic metaphor of Rousseau's address to the "[t]ender, anxious mother," to "remove this young tree from the highway and shield it from the crushing force of social conventions. Tend and water it ere it dies. One day its fruits will reward your care" (*Emile*, 5–6):

> O! father and mother, if buds are nip'd
> And blossoms blown away,
> And if the tender plants are strip'd
> Of their joy in the springing day,
> By sorrow and cares dismay,
>
> How shall the summer arise in joy.
> Or the summer fruits appear. (21–7)

But if Blake's schoolboy echoes Rousseau in these many regards – in his combination of metaphors of organicism with those of a necessary human cultivation, in his critique of a "cruel" regimented educational system – then he would not seem to agree in rejecting what Rousseau called "the chief cause of [children's] sorrows, namely their books" (*Emile*, 5). The boy's grievance is not the book itself, but the fact that the context of the school forbids him from "tak[ing] delight" in his book. Indeed, the poem seems to project a situation by virtue of the mere negativity of the schoolroom, where reading can be a delight, not the joyless task it becomes in the context of the school. A similar projection perhaps haunts the boy's second grievance, cited immediately after his inability to enjoy reading, that he cannot "sit in learnings bower, / Worn thro' with the dreary shower." These are difficult lines: do they express his petulant refusal to put up with classroom tedium ("I just *won't* sit there any longer")? Or do they propose an alternative site of education, "learnings bower," access to which is prevented by his attendance at school? The latter reading creates further difficulties with the "dreary shower" which follows, necessitating either a logical supplement provided by the reader – "I can't sit in learnings bower *because* I am worn thro' with the dreary shower of classroom instruction" – or a seemingly paradoxical description of this alternate site of education – "I'm not allowed to sit in learnings bower *where I would be* worn thro' with the dreary shower." The reference to nature, however, to "learnings *bower*," a reference which echoes the child's plea in the last two stanzas, seems to posit this extracurricular alternative to the confined classroom, a possibility also suggested by the vernal outdoor imagery of the illumination (figure ·2). Once again, we cannot say that Blake's visual designs merely reproduce the content of the text, but rather, as here, that they tease out and make visible a possible reading of the text. The vines to the right of the text are not a tree whose "thickest shade" implicates all humanity in its reproduction, but an open growth whose natural latticework allows the children to play upon it or not as they choose (the three at the bottom of the plate prefer marbles), and to use it as the support for their improvised activities, including, in the person of the child in the upper right-hand corner, the activity of reading. By drawing the eye across the plate, from text to design, Blake's illumination takes us from a scene of formal education, where attention to the text is compulsory and therefore joyless (if not impossible), to the site of "learnings bower," where delight in the text seems restored in the child's rapt attention to the book. The

2 "The School Boy" from *Songs of Innocence and of Experience*.

plate, therefore, makes visible the education of its own reader, from the tedious tutelage of a "bookish" reading of the poem's lament to the awakening delight in the reading of both text and design in their many interimplications.

Even in this seemingly most anti-educational of the Songs, then, it is not a wholesale rejection of learning but a careful examination of learning and its mechanism of literacy that is at work. Indeed, the whole volume can be seen to thematize or implicitly invoke the specific situation of reading, especially the situation of reading peculiar to children's literature. The title page to *Songs of Innocence*, a plate that was included in the combined volume as well, depicts one form of the reading triad common in the reception of children's literature: adult reader, text, and child audience (figure 3). The broad outlines of this scene represent the major point of transfer in the cycle of society's ideological reproduction of itself: the adult reproduces her own value system in her childish audience via the technique of literacy, the text operating as a kind of pleasing trap (or a "Cobweb to Catch Flies," as one of the titles to a popular children's book of the time put it), alluring its audience while invisibly inculcating dominant values. The specifics of the scene as Blake depicts it are also worth considering, however: at the knees of the adult (who here appears to be a nurse rather than a mother), the children, a boy and a girl in this case, look at a book significantly turned towards them rather than the adult reader. Of course, one of the main techniques of the children's reading books in their actual use by adults and children in the eighteenth century, as still today, was a monitored repetition by the child of the adult's intonation of the text. By this means, literacy is the result of a literal reproduction of the adult's intonation by the child, a passage from voice to print which serves to regulate and correct the voice by justification with the written word, the adult issuing corrections or reinforcements in accord with the child's performance. The scene as Blake depicts it, however, suggests a much less unidirectional transfer: the children stand entranced, the boy slack-jawed, the girl intent, all three participants responding primarily to the visual appearance of the text, as if Blake's colorful designs furnished an independent source of delight in no need of textual supplement from the nurse. As if to support this transformation of the typical reading situation, the letters of Blake's title seem similarly torn between literal and pictorial representation, as if Blake were suggesting a different source for

3 Title page for Songs of Innocence from *Songs of Innocence and of Experience*.

writing itself, an origin not in the invisible realm of ideological reason, the "Human Brain" of "The Human Abstract," but in the practical realm of pictorial design, in squiggles and doodles, in those first attempts at creativity represented by a child's scrawls.[24] The title page to *Innocence* thus offers a different route to literacy, one not simply administered by an authoritative adult. As if to call attention to the importance of these aspects of pictorial representation, Blake boldly refers to himself as both "Author & Printer" at the bottom of the page, not merely the invisible purveyor of authoritative texts but also the workmanlike presenter of material print and design.

Continuing down this alternative route to literacy, as the little girl seems to be doing by reaching to turn the page, a reader or viewer of Blake's volume would next come upon a plate which seems to posit many of these same questions about authority – the relationship of adult and child, their mutual relationship to the book – but now situates these questions in the realm of textuality. The Introduction to the Innocence volume has, of course, often been taken as a commentary on writing itself, an introduction not just to this particular volume of poetry, but, in a sense, to Blake's entire medium of illuminated printing, a process he had begun experimenting with at around the time of the composition of the Songs. The last two stanzas, in particular, representing a child's demand for reading material, have been discussed in terms of their attitude to the technology of writing and its relation to the pre-textual technologies thematized earlier in the poem:

> Piper sit thee down and write
> In a book that all may read –
> So he vanished from my sight.
> And I pluck'd a hollow reed.
>
> And I made a rural pen,
> And I stain'd the water clear,
> And I wrote my happy songs
> Every child may joy to hear.   (13–20, E7)

Some of Blake's best critics, Heather Glen and W. J. T. Mitchell for instance,[25] have pointed to the ambiguity in these stanzas, to elements which seem both to stigmatize and to celebrate the act of writing. Mitchell sees a loss of immediacy, of contact between author and audience, in the child's disappearance at the mere mention of a "book," a loss of immediacy paralleled by the distance between textual authors and their readers. This critique of bookishness is symbolically echoed in the Piper's "stain[ing]" of the water to create his ink, but the grammatical ambiguity of this line – does he stain the water *which was* clear or stain it, paradoxically, *until it is* clear? – has been seen to open the door to more positive notions of writing's value. Glen points to the unusual terminal verb, "hear," and the way it disturbs our notions of how the written text is received, suggesting that Blake hereby lays the ground for a different mode of textual production consisting of more than a mere passive reception of a silent text. Both Glen and Mitchell see the ambiguity in the stanzas – what Glen calls a "curiously double attitude towards the written word" (*Vision and Disenchantment*, 69) – but each narrativizes this doubleness differently, according to the demands of the argument: for Mitchell, Blake's suspicion of writing is an anticlimax to what is otherwise an unambiguous "celebratory emphasis on writing" ("Visible Language," 55); for Glen, the surprising last verb is a welcome interruption to the process throughout the poem "in which spontaneity steadily disappears" (*Vision and Disenchantment*, 66).

On one level, of course, these interpretive differences represent a lesson on the fate of poetic ambiguity as it enters the realm of critical argument: what was unstable, undecidable between the two moments of textuality and atextuality, is tamed along a narrative line drawing one concept victoriously from the demise of another. The very fact that two quite different critical narratives can be supported by this one poem suggests, however, that the ambiguity in the text is perhaps more radical than either argument acknowledges, representing a real and lasting uncertainty about the poem's (and the entire volume's) participation in the apparatus of writing and print. The poem as it exists does not allow for the linear logic of Glen's and Mitchell's arguments, does not trace a line of transmission by which writing is delivered from bondage in speech or vice versa. To do justice to the plate, we must enter the state of in-betweenness which it radically initiates: a cursive script precariously in between writing and print, an unusual textual presentation in between pictorial and verbal production, as well as the pervasive in-betweenness by which written texts are always "heard" even if only in the voice of consciousness[26] (these are, after all, the *Songs* of Innocence & of Experience), not to mention the unusual situation of children's literature as it activates reading, seeing, and listening simultaneously. By its concluding stanzas, this poem which opens Blake's unusual children's book suggests not only its own uneasy relation to the simple inculcation of dominant values in the training of literacy, but the instability at the very heart of literacy itself, the ghost of orality which is always present in the written text and the unreliability of any simple reproduction in the written text's relation to its author's intentions.[27]

This same frustration of any straightforward reproducibility is rehearsed in the opening stanzas of the poem, which are usually read simply as Blake's description of a happy pastoral scene:

> Piping down the valley's wild
> Piping songs of pleasant glee
> On a cloud I saw a child.
> And he laughing said to me.
>
> Pipe a song about a Lamb;
> So I piped with merry chear,
> Piper pipe that song again –
> So I piped, he wept to hear.
>
> Drop thy pipe thy happy pipe
> Sing thy songs of happy chear,
> So I sung the same again
> While he wept with joy to hear.   (1–12)

The scene looks like a tutorial, and perhaps in particular like a Rousseauian tutorial where the initiative comes from the student rather than the teacher. But unlike Rousseau, this egalitarian pedagogy does not seem a mere cover for the actual power of the teacher: if we see Blake's Piper as a would-be Rousseauian tutor, who so controls his student's environment that the least stimulus can be counted upon to deliver the expected result, then the outcomes of his "lesson" would seem almost comically unsuccessful. Piped to an initially "laughing" child, the song is performed three times in these initial stanzas (and is perhaps among the "happy songs" written in the final stanza). For Glen, as noted above, this process represents a descent into print, the establishment of "a definition which enables repetition, so that something of the emotion felt in the original experience can be transmitted and reproduced" (*Vision and Disenchantment*, 66). But Blake's song actually mitigates against any such notion of "originals" and "reproductions," of the "sameness" which underwrites the process of transmission. Not only do we have the instability of form and content by which the "original" is a nonverbal "piped" song "about a Lamb," and the instability of medium by which the second "repetition" of the song is "sung" rather than "piped," but also the instability of reception, variously left undescribed (lines 5 and 6) or figured both as weeping (8) or weeping with joy (12). If Blake's Piper harbors any desire for simple transmission, we might imagine him, like Rousseau's frustrated traditional teacher, extremely troubled by the various responses his stimulus provokes in the child. The repetition of "again" in the text – "Piper pipe that song again . . . So I sung the same again" – evokes, not the reduction to uniformity traced by Glen, but the ingenuity of the childish listener who never tires of hearing and transforming the "same" story, and the comic persistence of the tutor whose efforts to teach by rote can never yield the "same" lesson. This rich Introduction to an equally rich collection of uniquely self-conscious children's rhymes ultimately exploits a feature of the situation of children's reading which had formerly been used only for the purposes of ideological indoctrination: the child's repetition of adult intonation of the text. Although the overt rationale of learning by repetition might be the establishment of a bourgeois self for the child, a reproduction in the child of the adult self, Blake's poem reveals a reconstituted reading scene where the shifting "I," moving from Piper to textual child, from adult to actual child, breaks down the absolute distinctions between authors and audiences, between readers and hearers. The child emerges from this Introduction not a stable subject, with desires and powers carefully balanced according to Rousseau's formula, but a joyous hearer/reader who possesses the power to change both the text and her reactions to it by acting on her desires.

The "stain" remains on the last stanza of this poem, however, and has implications for the volume as a whole. But rather than seeing it as the pessimistic acknowledgement of the work's implication in a reproductive ideology, as Blake's critics have tended to do, we might rather see it as the precondition for all "seeing" whatsoever. Mitchell's claim that "the hollow reed and the stained water suggest that a kind of emptiness, darkness, and loss of innocence accompanies the very attempt to spread the message of innocence" ("Visible Language," 55–6), finally remains implicated within and reproduces the very system of values it attempts to critique. In particular, the equation of "emptiness" and "darkness" represents a conventional schematization of values which, however unintentional, ignores the ways in which the Piper's "stain" actually fills the space of the page, whether we conceive of it as the ink which allows him to "write / In a book that all may read" or the colors which stain the pages of Blake's illuminated works. The stain clearly seems related to the "cloud" of the first stanza, which bears the child into the world of the poem and also initiates the movement from the aural imagery of the first two lines to sight – "I saw a child" – in the third. Beyond merely establishing a pleasing poetic closure, these parallel images suggest that the song is "stained" from the first stanza rather than simply descending into the stain of print in the last. The omnipresent staining of this poem also has something to say about the controlling concepts of the volume as a whole – the Innocence and Experience which compose the "Two Contrary States of the Human Soul" mentioned on the general title page (E7) – and more broadly about the educative value of these two concepts. Indeed, much ink has been spilt and many pages stained over the question of how we are to understand Blake's positing of the "Contrary States." There are those, Harold Bloom in *Blake's Apocalypse*, for instance, who generally see Innocence as a state of ideologically clouded consciousness corrected by the more clear-sighted Experience ("The Chimney Sweeper" and "Holy Thursday" poems, as well as the pair of "The Divine Image" and "The Human Abstract," can easily fit this pattern).[28] Some more recent treatments, Zachary Leader's and Heather Glen's prominent among them, grant more strength to the redemptive visions of Innocence, emphasizing the limitations of Experienced cynicism. And, of course, one can read Blake's concepts as fully dialectical, each undercutting or completing the other. But what all of these perspectives have in common is their quite sharp differentiation between the two states, this despite the fact that a number of the poems migrated from one section of the volume to the other over the course of Blake's lifelong reissuing of the text.

The staining or omnipresent "clouding" of the song which introduces perhaps not only Innocence but the volume as a whole suggests that maintaining this distinction may be a mistake, however. Blake hints as much in a note which appears on a manuscript page of *The Four Zoas*, claiming that "Innocence dwells with Wisdom but never with Ignorance" (E697). All of these general concepts – Innocence, Experience, Wisdom – undoubtedly beg for further elucidation, but we can, at the least, note the way in which even the "introduction" to Innocence opens itself to experience of a kind, to the mutually educative experience of a confrontation between Piper and child. The general title page, on which appears the problematic claim regarding the "Contrary States," makes much the same point pictorially (figure 4). Beneath the motto, cowering amidst flames, are a man and a woman, wrapped about their waists with fig leaves. The identification seems unavoidable, but the significance of these figures bears reemphasis: from the very first page of this volume, we are already, by one definition of the word, in a world of experience. Like Rousseau's Nature, Blake's Innocence is a term which possesses conceptual value, but is never directly accessible, obscured as it is by the Covering Cherub of the social world. But where Rousseau attempts to reintroduce Nature into the social world, by an ideologically motivated emphasis on the "naturalness" of maternal breast-feeding, Blake's volume much more resolutely sets to work in the mixed post-lapsarian world. The stain or cloud of the Introduction, like the stain of print or design on the page, is not a cause of despair in the Songs, but rather an acknowledgement that educative experience has always already begun.[29] This is not to say that Blake sees all educative systems as equal, does not acknowledge the need to resist the dominant reproductive model, but rather that the work of education is always under way and that further work is always at hand. Such a description of Blake's project seems better to account for the famous pronouncement from the letter to Dr. Trussler, himself an author (although a poor one, in Blake's opinion) of children's books: "The wisest of the Ancients considered what is not too Explicit as the fittest for Instruction because it rouzes the faculties to act" (E702). It is along these lines that we can begin to account for the seeming contradictions of an author who simultaneously praises the understanding of "Ignorant & Simple Minds" and also advocates a nonexplicit course of "Instruction."

"Innocence" and "Experience" perhaps finally name, not so much the state of individual Songs or their speakers, but rather states of reading. As noted in the previous section, a poem like "The Human Abstract" seems susceptible to widely various readings, depending on whether one rests with the pronouncement of the text that the Tree of Mystery grows "in the Human Brain," or rouses one's faculties to contemplate the discontinuity between this description and the externalization of bondage in the accompanying illustration. Which of these readings is innocent and which is

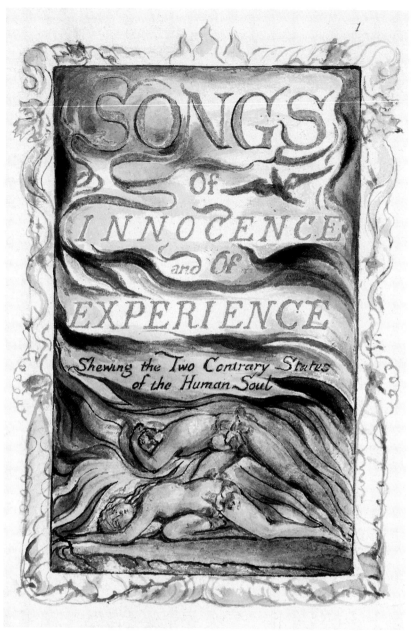

4 Title page for *Songs of Innocence and of Experience.*

experienced it is difficult to say: if one associates Innocence with liberative values, then the second reading would conform to that possibility, but such a reading only emerges after one has *experienced* the confining limitations of the text. If such a reading is to be characterized as "Innocent," then it is only as a stained or clouded innocence. But what is important about Blake's concepts, and about that even more confounding and crucial notion of "Contraries," is the way they break down any easy isolation of unique and inviolable states or selves. While Blake's critics have generally appreciated his multi-perspectival intention in dividing his volume into an Innocent and an Experienced section, they have reasserted a dubious unity of perspective when looking at individual Songs in the context of their placement in either section. But perhaps the point of the "Contrary States" is better reflected in the notion that each speaker and each Song migrates undecidably between Innocence and Experience, and that each plate is subject to "contrary" readings in its interactions with an audience. The effect of the Songs is not to reproduce a stable subject, either in their recording of specific speakers (Chimney Sweeper, Nurse, Little Vagabond) or in their educative interactions with various audiences. We should not be surprised, then, if the notion of "States" can be understood not only in the monolithic psychological sense of a unified cast of consciousness, but also in the sense peculiar to artists and bookmakers of the various treatments and techniques undergone by any "single" print or design.

A poem that activates many of these themes, the themes of education and reproduction, of clouds and stains, and which can perhaps stand in for the educative rousing of the rest, is "The Little Black Boy." The text, which depicts an educational scene more explicitly than any of the other Songs, also possesses some intriguing ties to Rousseau's *Emile.* For Rousseau reveals the limitations of his educational theory not only in its renaturalization of maternity, but also in its reproduction of dominant national and racial ideologies. In order for instruction to succeed, according to Rousseau, the student must be chosen as carefully as the teacher, both for individual good health and for a "naturally" constituted physical disposition. The climatological theory that Rousseau uses to support this latter criterion is certainly not peculiar to him, but it takes on additional significance in the context of a book that was enlisted in the service of egalitarian political movements:

The birthplace is not a matter of indifference in the education of man; it is only in temperate climes that he comes to his full growth. The disadvantages of extremes are easily seen. A man is not planted in one place like a tree, to stay there the rest of his life, and to pass from one extreme to another you must travel twice as far as he who starts half-way . . . A Frenchman can live in New Guinea or in Lapland, but a Negroe cannot live in Tornea nor a Samoyed in Benin. It seems almost as if the brain were less perfectly organized in the two extremes. Neither the negroes nor the Laps are as wise as Europeans. So if I want my pupil to be a citizen of the world I will choose him in the temperate zone, in France for example, rather than elsewhere. (*Emile*, 22)

Putting aside the Panglossian logic by which France unsurprisingly comes to produce the best of all possible students, we might note the way in which Rousseau's selective invocation of Nature serves particular ideological ends. Human beings, as described here, are not merely a product of Nature, "not planted in one place like a tree," but instead capable of the education which Rousseau had earlier identified as a necessary supplement to Nature. But despite this initial general definition, Nature reenters Rousseau's analysis as a way to distinguish the Frenchman from the "negroes" and "Laps" who are doubly limited by nature, both in their "less perfectly organised" brains and in their confinement to their regions of origin. The nonorganicism of Rousseau's generally conceived "man" finally seems only an ideological prelude to a "natural" theory of imperialism, by which French mobility dominates the organic rootedness of the inferior races. Rousseau's educative mobility, the power to move about like a man and to move to a new mental state, is thus itself finally rooted in the vegetative immobility of intemperate climes, the only soil where such a theory of education could come to "full growth."

Despite Rousseau's claims for the more perfectly organized French mind, we might thus be tempted to say of this racial ideology that "there grows one in the human brain." The relation to Blake becomes even clearer, however, in Rousseau's later development of his climatological thesis:

It seems certain from a comparison of northern and southern races that we become stronger by bearing extreme cold rather than excessive heat. But as the child's body grows bigger and his muscles get stronger, train him gradually to bear the rays of the sun. Little by little you will harden him till he can face the burning heat of the tropics without danger. (*Emile*, 110)

This passage, of course, continues Rousseau's invidious racial comparisons, now more starkly conceived as a northern/southern opposition rather than in terms of a temperate middle, and the teacher still seems to be training his student for a career of colonizing mobility, to "face the burning heat of the tropics without danger." The new note in this passage, and the one of most relevance to Blake's poem, is the idea here of an education of bearing, learning "to bear [*"braver"*] the rays of the sun." The creation of children who could "bear" various privations and extremities is no aberration in Rousseau's system, however, but rather one of its central tenets. Rousseau recommends, in a manner perhaps more shocking for a modern reader than for someone who lived in an age with an alarmingly high infant mortality rate, that children be exposed to harsh environments in order to strengthen them and improve their chances of survival into adulthood. Alluding to the legend of Thetis's immersion of the infant Achilles in order to render him invulnerable, Rousseau says of children, "Dip them in the waters of Styx," meaning, for him, "extremes of temperature, climate, and condition, hunger, thirst and weariness" (*Emile*, 17). Central to Rousseau's theory, this sentence became almost a motto for *Emile*, sometimes appearing beneath a pictorial representation of Thetis and Achilles on the title page of the volume.

This peculiar constellation of issues – the notion of education as a learning to bear, and its broader context in a system of racial distinctions – emerges again in Blake's poem, a text which also figures education as "learn[ing] the heat to bear" (17, E9). But rather than being a mere reproduction of Rousseau's racial ideology, "The Little Black Boy" seems to call into question the very notion of such easy transmissibility from one generation of educators to another, as well as the reliability of an education which compels its students to "bear" instruction. Like the Introduction to Innocence, the poem depicts a setting which might easily be understood as the prototypical scene of reproductive education. Both the first line – "My mother bore me in the southern wild" – and the seeming coincidence of textual description – "My mother taught me underneath a tree" (5) – with pictorial design (figure 5) suggest an education which will be literally reproductive in its Rousseauian emphasis on maternal instruction and reproductive also in its presentation of a seemingly stable text. Indeed, both text and illustration project an idyllic naturalized scene of education, admin-

5 First plate of "The Little Black Boy" from *Songs of Innocence and of Experience*.

istered by the child's "real nurse" (in Rousseau's terms) in a setting womb-like both in its protective sheltering of the pair "underneath a tree" and in the suggestive location of the "lap" as the primary space of educational transfer. The central lesson conveyed by this maternal teacher – a kind of "just so" story designed to explain his own blackness to the boy – equally spins out the logic of reproductive education, assigning means to ends, proposing providential wisdom as a way of justifying earthly circumstances:

> Look on the rising sun: there God does live
> And gives his light, and gives his heat away.
> And flowers and trees and beasts and men receive
> Comfort in morning joy in noon day.
>
> And we are put on earth a little space,
> That we may learn to bear the beams of love,
> And these black bodies and this sun-burnt face
> Is but a cloud and like a shady grove.
>
> For when our souls have learn'd the heat to bear
> The cloud will vanish we shall hear his voice.
> Saying: come out from the grove my love & care,
> And round my golden tent like lambs rejoice.   (9–20)

Just as the mother is here the "real nurse," "giving" her child this lesson on the rightness of things, we might see something of Rousseau's "real teacher" in the God whose tutorial is paradoxically conceived as a free "giving," but a giving which must be borne by its recipients. Like Rousseau's tutor, God subjects his students to a temporary pain, dips them in the waters of Styx, in order to reward them in a projected future. Under God's manipulative hand, the environment becomes itself a womb, whose fully formed subjects are brought forth in sorrow.

The linchpin of the mother's lesson, an explanation of blackness as "but a cloud, and like a shady grove," shows yet another reproductive feature of her instruction of the boy, her effort to seek out comforting likenesses in the world around her. Given the centrality of this education by likeness, we are perhaps the less surprised by the conclusion of the poem, in which the boy, "freed" from the cloud of blackness which covered him on earth and united with the white English boy who had spurned him previously, nevertheless still yearns to "be like him" (28) in the projected afterlife. It might be possible, indeed, to see some educational success in the process traced by the poem, in the distance between the boy's initial interpretation of racial difference – "White as an angel is the English child: / But I am black as if bereav'd of light" (3–4) – and the imagined scene of reconciliation which follows the mother's tutorial:

> Thus did my mother say and kissed me,
> And thus I say to little English boy.
> When I from black and he from white cloud free,
> And round the tent of God like lambs we joy:

> I'll shade him from the heat till he can bear,
> To lean in joy upon our fathers knee.
> And then I'll stand and stroke his silver hair,
> And be like him and he will then love me.   (21–8)

The poem seems to trace a course directly opposite to that traced by the Introduction to Innocence: where the earlier poem had gone from the unmediated community of Piper and child to the mediated distance of a relationship centered on the "stained" book, the current text seems to leave behind the differentiating "white" and "black" clouds of the opening for an undifferentiated communion in the final stanza.[30] But just as the Introduction had more to say about typography then simply positing it as a fall from innocence, so might we come to see the heavenly scene at the end of "The Little Black Boy" as a doubtful transcendence of the black on white of earthly literacy.

One place to begin is to differentiate the scene of education as it is depicted in the text and design from the education that is enacted by a creative interplay between the plates and their readers/viewers. The text depicts education as a series of reproductive transfers, a "bearing" not only in the sense of enduring the heat of the sun, but also in the literally reproductive sense which the boy significantly invokes in the very first line. The central, explicit instruction occurs beneath the tree as a transaction between mother and son. That scene is then projected forward to a heavenly future where the boy's education is itself borne across the divide of racial difference to educate the little English boy: "Thus did my mother say and kissed me. / And thus I say to little English boy . . . " Continuity in the passage of this educational content from generation to generation and from race to race is seemingly guaranteed by the summative

"thus," which promises likeness both in what the black boy is taught
and what he teaches. But the more closely we look at the poem, the
more we might see gaps in its closed circuit of reproductive transfer.
Several readers have noted, for instance, the pressures at work in the
first stanza –

> My mother bore me in the southern wild,
> And I am black, but O! my soul is white;
> White as an angel is the English child:
> But I am black as if bereav'd of light –

in which what looks like consecutive reasoning joined by "ands" and
"buts" and by a nascent logic of color, actually forces together *non
sequiturs*, facts, suppositions, and figures of speech.[31] But perhaps
more important for our purposes are the gaps discernible in the
educational transfer from mother to little black boy to little English
boy. Alan Richardson has convincingly pointed out that the Man-
ichean color scheme of the first stanza suggests that the speaker has
already attended more than a few racist colonial tutorials, administered most likely by the missionary schools common at the time in
African colonies (*Literature, Education, and Romanticism*, 162). But what
Richardson has failed to note is the way in which the mother's
education, with its submission to "bearing" and its providential
history, also seems to be the product of Christian schools.[32] Thus
while making the primary claim of being born of his mother, a claim
which then justifies him in figuratively "bearing" the little English
boy in the final transfer of the poem, the little black boy's initial
statement already bears the marks of colonial education. Although
professing to teach the little English boy, the little black boy is
already "taught" by Englishness before the poem begins. Progressive
linearity thus gives way to mere reproductive circularity, the "same
dull round," as the little black boy is born of the same Englishness
which he anticipates bearing in the last two stanzas. Alternatives to
this narrow colonial education will not come from any continuation
of the cycle which originates in the colonial school, but instead in a
disruption of the logic of reproductive education, an occupation of
literacy for different purposes.

Further disruptions of the reproductive circuit are evident in a
comparison of the last three stanzas with the illustration which
accompanies them (figure 6). This plate has borne as much if not
more commentary as any other in the *Songs*, if only because of

6 Second plate of "The Little Black Boy" from *Songs of Innocence and of Experience*.

Blake's various methods of coloring it throughout his career. In some copies (as in the King's College copy depicted here), the boy to the rear is quite obviously black, while the boy at Christ's knees is pinkish white. In other copies, the boys are colored a fairly indistinguishable dark shade, seeming to emphasize their "likeness" in this imaginary scene. While Joseph Viscomi has recently cautioned against any readings which take as their basis a comparison of different copies (a reading situation Blake almost certainly could not have anticipated),[33] we can at the very least note the ways in which *any* illustration would qualify the claims of the text. The text imagines the solution to color differentiation to lie in the erasing of all color whatsoever: "When I from black and he from white cloud free . . . " In making visible the claim to invisibility in the text, the full illuminated plate, rather than completing or reproducing the text, fatally undercuts it. The scene putatively imagined in the text is thereby relegated to the realm of the unimaginable, in that any attempt to realize it is unavoidably clouded by the colors of that realization. Even if the black boy's wish to "be like" the white boy could be realized, it would only be realized under the cloud of color, only within the stain of print. These discontinuities between text and design then drive the reader educated in Blake's school back to the text itself, to evidence, now visible even in this seemingly cloudless realm, that the proposed heaven still bears the marks of the colonial earth it seeks to transcend. Thus, while peace in heaven is supposed to be the reward for "bearing" on earth, we learn that the white boy still has some "bearing" to do (line 25) and that the black boy is still "like a shady grove" in the service he imagines himself providing in the afterlife. The close weaving of puns and contradictions finally suggests that the "bearing" praised by the boy's mother can only bear more of the same, and that the "shade" the boy imagines providing for his white English cohort actually implicates him in the "thickest shade" of ideological consciousness.

This might well be called an Experienced reading of a fairly unassuming Innocent poem. But, as I have suggested, the significance of Blake's innovative reworking of children's literature is to bring both of these concepts into play in the reading of any single poem and the assessment of any single poetic voice. The black boy's "innocence" is rooted in the same ground as his "experience": taught in the colonial schools of the English colonies, his mind has been clouded by a vision of a cloudless realm of freedom, the reward for his "bearing" on earth. But if Blake definitively rejects the reproductive education which produces only more of the same while holding out visions of freedom, it is only by the means of retaining the cloud and the stain of social existence, of making fully visible the world in which we live so that we might make it otherwise. If the black boy is the student *in* the text, then we must also imagine (or become) the students *of* the text, for whom the cloud of the boy's argument is itself a lesson in the various routes to social transformation. In Blake's transformed children's book, the final lesson is perhaps the realization that the Covering Cherub *is* the pillar of cloud which leads to a fully social Promised Land.

If "The Little Black Boy" thus raises the issue of how we are to interpret the utopian scenes which figure so prominently in Blake's texts, and suggests that the boy's colorless heaven is perhaps achieved too easily, then some of the same issues will have to be raised in connection with the poems he wrote concurrently, especially those which feature a strong female consciousness. *Visions of the Daughters of Albion*, in particular, has, as we shall see, been criticized for its facile depiction of a liberated female consciousness, in the absence of any specific political program for achieving that liberation. On the other hand, Blake's portrayal of Enitharmon in *Europe: A Prophecy*, and of the "Female Will" in general, in the late prophetic works, has been convincingly accused of falling into the dominant misogynist stereotypes of his time. I have suggested that a genuinely, "concretely," utopian interpretation of the *Songs* lies largely in the ability of its reader to evade the standardizing routines of a dominant literacy. But for *Europe* and *Visions*, the key to understanding Blake's depiction of women will come from an understanding of his ties to his acquaintance and fellow radical, Mary Wollstonecraft. The vision of utopian liberation available in the parallel works of these two early ideology critics will come, not from an escapist fantasy, but from a careful examination of the unequal gender relations which prevailed in late eighteenth-century England. The test of Oothoon's utopian discourse will thus be the extent to which it speaks from an understanding of the pervasive ideological implications of sexualized existence.

CHAPTER 3

The discourse of women's liberation in Vindication of the Rights of Woman, Europe, *and* Visions of the Daughters of Albion

I

As numerous commentators have noted, a central element of Blake's vision of the redeemed world is his notion of the liberation of the body and of human sexuality.[1] And because fallen sexuality is portrayed as the endless battle of the sexes, each vying for domination over the other, Blake's liberation of the body necessarily involves the liberation of women. The emancipation of women thus manifests itself in the final utopian chapter of *Jerusalem* as the elimination of contentious sexual difference in favor of a fully human existence, for "Humanity is far above / Sexual organization" (*J*79:73–4, E236). In the utopian movement of Blake's final epic, he abandons his previous notion of the female as mere secondary "Emanation" of the primary creative male, and substitutes for it the idea of a genderless "Man" who uses both male and female emanations to communicate with his "brothers":

When in Eternity Man converses with Man they enter
Into each other's Bosom (which are Universes of Delight)
In mutual interchange. and first their Emanations meet
Surrounded by their Children. if they embrace & comingle
The Human Four-fold Forms mingle also in thunders of Intellect
But if the Emanations mingle not; with storms & agitations
Of earthquakes & consuming fires they roll apart in fear
For Man cannot unite with Man but by their Emanations
Which stand both Male & Female at the Gates of each Humanity
How then can I ever again be united as Man with Man
While thou my Emanation refusest my Fibres of dominion.
When Souls mingle & join thro all the Fibres of Brotherhood
Can there be any secret joy on Earth greater than this?

(*J*88:3–15, E246)

71

One might point, indeed, to the remnants of misogynistic ideology which persist in this description – Los's "fibres of dominion" – but perhaps it is appropriate that this speech still contains traditional gender distinctions, for Los speaks it at a time before the final apocalypse, as a kind of proleptic vision of the utopian world. As Enitharmon's answer clearly shows – "This is Woman's World, nor need she any Spectre to defend her from Man" (88:16–17, E247) – we are still a long way from the elimination of sexual difference at this point in the poem. Fallen language, as Blake notes elsewhere, is a "Stubborn Structure" (*J*36:59, E183) which becomes genderless only when worked into its utopian form. But if the medium is still the inescapably gendered language of the fallen world ("Man," "Brotherhood"), within the limits of this ideological language a genderless utopia is struggling to express itself.

Odd as it may seem, however, the most formidable challenge to Blake's sexual utopia occurs within the context of the only modern utopian discourse, feminism.[2] Feminism's critique of Blake's utopia strikes at three elements of the Blakean text in particular. First of all, there is Blake's portrayal of the Female Will, explicitly named as such for the first time in the texts of *Jerusalem* and *A Vision of the Last Judgment*, but recognizably portrayed as early as the writing of *Europe*. "Female Will" is Blake's term for a tyrannical domination of man by the feminine, expressing itself through both sexual domination (Tirzah) and violent quasi-religious domination (Rahab). Many feminist critics are understandably disturbed by portrayals of the feminine as coquettishly demure or, conversely, insanely shrewish and emasculating, as well as by Blake's claim that "In Eternity Woman is the Emanation of Man she has No Will of her own There is no such thing in Eternity as a Female Will" (*VLJ*85, E562). Clearly, Blake's equation of the feminine with the monstrously domineering threatens the status of his genderless sexual utopia.

The second point at which Blake's feminist critics often balk is his tendency to subsume the female under the male, even in the context of *Jerusalem*'s utopian vision. As we have seen, a sympathetic reading of *Jerusalem*'s gendered language is possible because, as feminist theory has taught us, language is gendered. But one might also view Blake's celebration of the "One Man," Albion, as symptomatic of deeper misogynistic beliefs. Comparing Blake unfavorably with the feminist utopias of Marge Piercy and Ursula K. LeGuin, Anne Mellor notes that, "[b]y continuing to use the sexist language of the patriarchal culture into which he was born, Blake failed to develop an image of human perfection that was completely gender-free. A writer who wished to portray a truly androgynous creature or society would have to transform the language."[3] Not only distrusting the language which he uses to portray it, Mellor also distrusts the androgyny which is Blake's poetic goal: "[S]uch mutual inter-dependence should not obscure the fact that in Blake's metaphorical system the masculine is both logically and physically prior to the feminine" ("Blake's Portrayal", 153). Indeed, Blake is open to the criticism that, although his utopia treats both sexes as equal, one is "more equal" than the other.

Finally, some feminist critics take Blake to task for his use of traditional metaphors and valuations of the feminine. The poet who could be so contemptuous of literary tradition as to parody it ruthlessly in *Poetical Sketches* is also the poet who assigns the traditional lunar symbolism to the lower, or feminine, paradise of Beulah. Susan Fox, the most cogent critic of this aspect of Blake's symbolism, notes the persistence of traditional standards in Blake's assessment of feminine power: "Throughout the poem [*Milton*] females are either passive or pernicious. Females presented positively are passive . . . Active females are pernicious."[4] Blake's metaphoric structure, Fox claims, makes it impossible for him to conceive of a feminine power which is not inherently evil. But while it would be easy to excuse Blake's deployment of the feminine as harmlessly metaphorical, not to be taken literally, Fox insists that metaphors exist within a social and political context: "One cannot apologize away Blake's occasional shrillness towards women by calling it merely metaphoric, because to do so is both to ignore the richness and aptness of his social observations and to beg the questions of what a metaphor is anyway and why one chooses it" ("Female as Metaphor", 509).

This last point – "why one chooses [a metaphor]" – is particularly important because it reveals the basis of most feminist critiques of Blake and the substance of the most lethal challenge to Blake's utopia: that it is ideological, basely subservient to the repressive interests of a patriarchal society. The feminist critiques of Blake's sexual utopia, after sympathetically surveying his progressive views on female sexuality and political liberation, usually return to just this point, that Blake remained within the ideological circle of his time, trapped by its horizon (Urizen) as much as the most explicitly misogynistic writer.[5] Such a critique, however, reflective as it is of scientific Marxism, threatens the status of utopian thought alto-gether, feminist or otherwise. The boundary between ideology and utopia, whose establishment, as we have seen, is so important to the foundation of social critique, is again being collapsed, the utopian being reduced to the ideological. The feminist critique of Blake raises the question of whether such a mental progression is inevitable in the analysis of a utopia, that is, can one do otherwise, in the reading of a utopia, than conclude that the utopian is ideological? Or is there an element of the utopian which resists reincorporation into the "wishful thinking" of ideology?

It is with such questions in mind that we turn to Blake's representation of the Female Will in *Europe* and his idea of a utopian liberation of woman in *Visions of the Daughters of Albion*, examining both in the looking glass of that other utopian work of the period, Mary Wollstonecraft's *Vindication of the Rights of Woman*, which many have taken to be the inaugurating text of the modern utopian discourse of feminism. Although Blake's dating indicates that *Visions* was written one year prior to *Europe*, I have chosen to treat *Europe* first in order to lay out more clearly the complexities of the ideological and the utopian perspectives on the feminine. The place of woman in society, as torn in Blake's day as it is in our own between ideological and utopian formulations, represents an ideal testing ground for the authenticity of Blake's utopia, of utopian thought in general, and of that particular manifestation of utopian thought, feminism, which promises women's eventual participation in the fullness of humanity.

II

The influence of Mary Wollstonecraft upon the work of William Blake has by now been invoked so frequently as to have become a critical truism.[6] For the most part, comparisons have focused on the similarities between Blake's *Visions of the Daughters of Albion* and Wollstonecraft's *Vindication of the Rights of Woman*, with specific parallels between Wollstonecraft's critique of hypocritical feminine "modesty" and Blake's critique of the pernicious effects of "chastity" upon human relations.[7] In addition, biographical speculators have toyed with the idea that Blake may have known Wollstonecraft quite well from their mutual affiliation with the Joseph Johnson circle.[8] Besides Blake's illustrations for Wollstonecraft's *Original Stories from*

Real Life, this relationship has been taken to have fostered literary fruit as various as the Pickering Manuscript's "Mary" (a possible portrait of Wollstonecraft) to *Visions* itself (as a *poème a clef* depicting Wollstonecraft's love for Henry Fuseli).[9] Whatever the case may be as to the closeness of their relationship, thus far critics have largely ignored the deeper similarities between the two which mark them as coinhabitants of a particular point in history, newly open to radical analyses of their society.

The first and probably the most important of these similarities is their mutual discovery of the concept of ideology as a device for the critique and the explanation of their social situations. We have already traced the outlines of this idea in Blake, but we must also recognize that a central element of Wollstonecraft's brilliant achievement lies in her development of a concept of ideology. Early in her literary career, Wollstonecraft had authored books which differed very little from the dominant genres of the day: *Mary, A Fiction* bears close resemblance to sentimental novels, *Thoughts on the Education of Daughters* to that perennial favorite of the eighteenth century, the conduct book.[10] With her later works, however, Wollstonecraft shows the effects of an epistemic break which ultimately marks her as a thinker of the nineteenth, rather than the eighteenth, century. Mary Poovey, in *The Proper Lady and the Woman Writer,* identifies the turning point in Wollstonecraft's thinking as her consideration of the place of women in English society, first occurring within the context of *A Vindication of the Rights of Men* (1790):

Here [Wollstonecraft] is beginning to see both what complicated connections exist between the interests of women and those of the aspiring middle classes and how thoroughly the categories by which women are taught to estimate their worth emerge from the special needs of those who rule. She is beginning, in other words, to identify ideology at work in her society and in herself. (*Proper Lady,* 63)

One can imagine the process by which Wollstonecraft begins to compose a rational document of the Enlightenment, focusing upon the abstract basis of the rights of men (and which would be seconded one year later by Thomas Paine's *Rights of Man*), but is then drawn, by the sheer weight of her experience and knowledge, to explain the strange nonparticipation of her own sex in those same rights, an explanation which would eventually force her to a vindication of a much more particular, and less rationalistic, kind. The thesis of ideology, as Wollstonecraft would discover in her later vindication, is peculiarly suited to such particularized ends, analyzing as it does the dynamics of power and the systemic nature of human behavior. What Wollstonecraft is effecting in her evolution from the rights of "men" (in the abstract, genderless sense) to the rights of women (as gendered members of an historic situation) is the evolution from eighteenth-century political philosophy (as in Hobbes, Locke, and Smith) to nineteenth-century ideology-critique. The tone and language are often strikingly similar, but the method and conclusions are worlds apart.

The central thesis of Wollstonecraft's next book, the deservedly more famous *Vindication of the Rights of Woman*, is that women have failed to perform a productive function in English society not because they are inherently deficient, but because they have been trained from birth to behave as if they were the mental and moral inferiors of men. While this analysis might seem rather mundane in retrospect, it represents several substantive improvements over the social criticism of the day, improvements which mark it as an inaugural document in the tradition of ideology-critique. Of first importance in Wollstonecraft's analysis is her acknowledgement of the role of education and literature in the creation and perpetuation of female stereotypes. In her critiques of Rousseau and Milton, Wollstonecraft is recognizing, while not naming it as such, the role of ideology in literary production:

[W]hen [Milton] tells us that women are formed for softness and sweet attractive grace, I cannot comprehend his meaning, unless, in the true Mahometan strain, he means to deprive us of souls, and insinuate that we were beings only designed by sweet attractive grace and docile blind obedience, to gratify the senses of man when he can no longer soar on the wing of contemplation. (*Vindication*, 100–1)

Wollstonecraft hits upon the central tenet of the ideological critique of literature: that it represents, or can represent, the interests of one class or group (for example, a sexual group) in their maintenance of control over another. Literary criticism, in a very important sense, has here entered the nineteenth century.

Perhaps the easiest way to illustrate Wollstonecraft's radical difference from eighteenth-century philosophy is to note the changes she wrought upon a particular mainstay of that philosophy, associationism. As other commentators have observed, Wollstonecraft in many ways – in her rationalism, progressivism and, I would add, her associationism – differs very little from her philosophical forbears. Like so many of her contemporaries, Wollstonecraft, when discussing the typical education of English womanhood, introduces the associationist vocabulary of Hume, Smith, and Hartley:

Everything that [females] see or hear serves to fix impressions, call forth emotions, and associate ideas, that give a sexual character to the mind. False notions of beauty and delicacy stop the growth of their limbs and produce a sickly soreness, rather than delicacy of organs; and thus weakened by being employed in unfolding instead of examining the first associations, forced on them by every surrounding object, how can they attain the vigour necessary to enable them to throw off their factitious character? – where find strength to recur to reason and rise superior to a system of oppression, that blasts the fair promises of spring? (*Vindication*, 221)

Certainly the language – "fix[ing] impressions," "associat[ing] ideas" – is familiar, but the differences with associationism are just as numerous and ultimately more telling. The sequence of the quotation places it among the more interesting sections of Wollstonecraft's book. She begins by conceding that the associationist theory is correct, that girls are made women by a constellation of sense impressions and resultant ideas peculiar to their experience of the world. But the sequel to this concession contains ideas foreign to traditional associationist theory: the conventional notions of feminine beauty and delicacy are "false," "factitious," and destructive of women's bodies; the associations inculcated by patriarchal education should not simply be "unfolded," but should be "examined" and eventually "thrown off"; associations are not simply the product of a neutral experience of the world (as the associationists would seem to imply), but are the result of "a system of oppression." What we are witnessing in Wollstonecraft's confrontation with her intellectual past is the intersection of associationism with ideology-critique, the juxtaposition of a neutral theory of psychological development with an analysis of political and sexual power. While associationism might seem the most universal of all theories of ideology – representing as it does the closed circle of sense impressions which can never be escaped – Wollstonecraft supplies the necessary element of power, identifying the interests which perpetuate the cycle of oppression and indicting what she calls in her very next sentence, "[t]his cruel association of ideas" (*Vindication*, 221). Getting ahead of ourselves somewhat, we might even wish to examine the utopian potential of that "spring" whose "fair promises" are blasted by the blight of ideology and which serves as the distant stage from which Wollstonecraft performs her critique of English society. Whatever the case may be, all the elements of ideology-critique are present in what at first glance appears only an inferior mouthing of established philosophy.

Although the *content* of ideology-critique suffices to establish a parallel between the works of Wollstonecraft and Blake as a whole, I believe that the parallel with his concept of Female Will in general and with *Europe* in particular is to be found in the *tone* of ideology-critique. This observation goes some way towards explaining what can be a somewhat troubling feature of *Vindication of the Rights of Woman*: that Wollstonecraft's scathing attacks on feminine stupidity, hypocrisy, and lasciviousness are often indistinguishable from the attacks of the leading misogynists of the day. We begin to understand the virulence of these attacks only when we put them in the context of Wollstonecraft's analysis of female power. Having acknowledged that women's place within English society is the result of their manipulation by the forces of male domination, Wollstonecraft yet allows for a species of female power which expresses itself through cunning and strategies of displacement:

> Women . . . sometimes boast of their weakness, cunningly obtaining power by playing on the *weakness* of men; and they may well glory in their illicit sway, for, like Turkish bashaws, they have more real power than their masters . . . Women, as well as despots, have now perhaps more power than they would have if the world, divided and subdivided into kingdoms and families, were governed by laws deduced from the exercise of reason. (*Vindication* 125–6, Wollstonecraft's italics)

Wollstonecraft's description of the mechanics of female power bears many similarities to Blake's description of Female Will: it manifests itself as a "romantic species of modesty" (*Vindication*, 125) which yet allows for the indulgence of a degraded sexual appetite (Blake's Tirzah), or as that "despotic" power which establishes women as the "Turkish bashaws" in actual control of their merely nominal "masters" (Blake's Rahab). Like Wollstonecraft, Blake sees the actual power hidden beneath a mask of feminine weakness: as he has the lawyer Steelyard say in *An Island in the Moon*, "They call women the weakest vessel but I think they are the strongest" (E457). And just as does Blake, Wollstonecraft reserves all of her anger and contempt for this exercise of underhanded power, the degree of her anger an index of her horror in the face of the ideological world.[11]

Blake's *Europe, a Prophecy*, representing as it does his most pessimistic portrait of the ideological world, benefits substantially when considered in the light of Wollstonecraft's analysis. His portrayal of the eighteen-hundred year "female dream" (9:5, E63) which occupies the fallen world during the period between the birth of Christ and the English counterrevolutionary war of the 1790s, reads very much like Wollstonecraft's description of cunning female power. Before she settles down for her ideological nap, Enitharmon (not yet the redemptive character of the later prophecies) issues a challenge to her children to deceive and dominate the human race:

> Now comes the night of Enitharmons joy!
> Who shall I call? Who shall I send?
> That Woman, lovely Woman! may have dominion?
> Arise O Rintrah thee I call! & Palamabron thee!
> Go! tell the human race that Womans love is Sin!
> That an Eternal life awaits the worms of sixty winters
> In an allegorical abode where existence hath never come:
> Forbid all joy, & from her childhood shall the little female
> Spread nets in every secret path.   (5:1–9, E62)

As Michael J. Tolley has convincingly argued in his article on the poem, Palamabron and Rintrah represent respectively the priest and king whose approval is necessary for the legitimation of sexual union on the fallen earth.[12] Enitharmon's summoning of the brides of Palamabron and Rintrah – "silent Elynittria the silent bowed queen" (8:4) and "the lovely jealous Ocalythron" (8:7) – a few lines later invokes the peculiar machinations of the Female Will even more clearly: the regal Elynittria represents the violent, domineering face of the Female Will (Rahab), the "jealous" Ocalythron the modest, chaste sexual tease (Tirzah). It is important to make the connection between this relatively early poem and the later concept of the Female Will[13] because it serves to debunk one of the leading theories of Blake's attitude towards women, that is, that Blake, in his later career, underwent a radical reversal in his opinion of women, whether due to problems with his wife Catherine or for other reasons, which led him to the negative portrayals of *Jerusalem*.[14] Confirmation of *Europe* as an early, loosely formulated version of Female Will discredits such facile biographical speculation.

Enitharmon's challenge contains the ideological formulations of many ideas that will emerge in their utopian fullness only in other poems, among them the idea of utopia itself. The utopia which Enitharmon here envisions for fallen humanity – "an Eternal life . . . / In an allegorical abode where existence hath never come" – truly *is* wishful thinking, not a utopia at all, but the form which utopia takes in a wholly ideological world. The idea of such a bloodless utopia is merely one more trick in the ideological repertoire of the Female Will and its priestly representative, for it is designed to dispel the discontent of "the worms of sixty winters" much as the hope of "pie in the sky by and by when you die" (as Tolley notes [*"Europe*," 122]) was intended to quell the passions of angry laborers. Similarly, Enitharmon's pronouncement that "Woman's love is Sin" represents the ideological formulation of what emerges in others of Blake's poems as a utopian liberation of sexuality. This particular ideological ruse is intended to establish man's religious awe of chaste womanhood, a primary technique of the Female Will's dominion over fallen minds. Finally, we might note the similarity between Enitharmon's prediction that "from her childhood shall the little female / Spread nets in every secret path" and Wollstonecraft's analysis of female power. Just as Wollstonecraft suggested that female power was the product of cunning and deception, so does Blake here offer a portrait of fallen female power as indirect ("secret") and nonconfrontational in its use of nets rather than open strength. (The image of the female casting a net has utopian significations in Blake also, as we shall see in our reading of *Visions of the Daughters of Albion.*)

    This last image speaks to one of the major concerns of the feminist critique of Blake: if Blake intends merely a portrait of the fallen world, why does he insist on portraying it in exclusively feminine terms? In other words, why is the period of humanity's worst nightmare, the eighteen-hundred years from Christ to the counterrevolutionary fulminations of William Pitt,[15] a specifically *female* dream? Enitharmon's last prediction, that the little female "shall . . . spread nets in every secret path," might initially seem merely another of Blake's negative portrayals of manipulative woman, always lying in wait for the unsuspecting male. The context of the image, however, suggests that the female portion of humanity is as much the object of Enitharmon's ideological dream as is the male portion: the "little female" is merely one item on Enitharmon's list of ideological fiats. Indeed, the very content of the female's ideological consciousness is the mistaken notion that she has absolute agency in her dominion over man: to herself she seems to be throwing the net over man, but in reality she is already herself "netted" in the wider web of Enitharmon's nightmare. Wollstonecraft makes much the same point in her insistence that cunning female power is actually only a degraded substitute for real power: virtue, the source of real power for Wollstonecraft, is sacrificed for cunning, whose dreamlike rewards are only "temporary gratifications" and "the triumph of an hour" (*Vindication*, 125).

The objection might still be made: although the little female's dream of agency is merely a delusion, why does Blake assign such power to the mythical female figure of Enitharmon? If the little female is only a pawn in a larger game, Enitharmon, from Blake's portrayal, would appear to be the agent of all that occurs in the poem. Telling as this criticism might initially seem, given Blake's later elaborate portraits of Female Will in *Jerusalem*, where it often seems the only force for evil in a world otherwise ready for redemption, Enitharmon's power is called significantly into question in the text of *Europe*. As Tolley (*"Europe"*, 126–9, 141) and Erdman (*Prophet*, 265) have noted, Enitharmon's action in *Europe* is characterized by a consistent misreading of the course of history. When Christ's initial arrival is announced in the opening lines of the prophecy proper – "The deep of winter came; / What time the secret child, / Descended thro' the orient gates of the eternal day" (3:1–3, E61) – Enitharmon mistakenly takes this as a sign for the beginning of her dominion on earth. Although dawn is clearly announced in these opening lines, Enitharmon imagines that Christ's arrival initiates "the *night* of Enitharmon's joy!" In a typical literalization of metaphor, Blake is here portraying an Enitharmon who is truly "benighted." When she is awakened from her eighteen-hundred-year sleep by Newton's blast on the Trump of the last doom, she commits further errors of judgment. Awake, she is not aware that she has ever been asleep or that any time has passed (13:9–10, E65). Deceived by this initial error, she misjudges the situation and mistakenly assumes that Orc will retain his filial piety and endorse her reign on earth: "Orc! smile upon my children! / Smile son of my afflictions. / Arise O Orc and give our mountains joy of thy red light" (14:29–31, E66). But the time is no longer propitious for Enitharmon's schemes and the red light which is Orc's earthly avatar operates in ways completely unexpected by Her Royal

Highness[16]: "But terrible Orc, when he beheld the morning in the east, / Shot from the heights of Enitharmon; / And in the vineyards of red France appear'd the light of his fury" (14:37–15:2, E66). By one of those providential mistakes the oppressor never fails to commit, the ideological forces of counterrevolution have themselves, through their own ignorance of the workings of human society, called up the forces of violent revolution which will overthrow them. Ultimately, the "female dream" which comprises fallen history in Blake's view is not to be characterized primarily by its femaleness, but by the fact that it is merely a dream: Enitharmon's dream of agency is as misinformed and as short-lived as the most pitiful exercise of cunning female power.

Although we will return briefly to *Europe* in our consideration of Blake's theory of history in chapter 4, some questions yet remain for our observations on the place of woman in Blake's poetry: If *Europe* portrays the feminine as inescapably trapped in the ideological circle of late eighteenth-century England, is there any place for a conception of the feminine which escapes the limitations of this narrowly ideological portrait? If cunning female power is merely the expression of a fallen consciousness, merely the dream of female agency in a fallen world, is there yet any form of female power which is not fallen? Is there any cunning use of the cunning in Blake, any utopian fulfillment of the cunning power whose idea of its own agency is mere wishful thinking? The answers to these questions will require us to turn back to *Visions of the Daughters of Albion*, a work written the year previous to *Europe*'s composition, both to investigate Blake's specific differences with the model of ideology-critique Wollstonecraft develops in *Vindication of the Rights of Woman* and to interrogate the role of a utopian discourse in modern feminist theory.

III

Rousseau exerts himself to prove that all *was* right originally: a crowd of authors that all *is* now right: and I, that all will *be* right. (*Vindication of the Rights of Woman* 9; Wollstonecraft's emphasis)

As it has reemerged in the last thirty years, the discourse of modern feminism has been torn between an ideological and a utopian formulation. These contradictory formulations revolve around the question of feminine power and can most usefully be interrogated within the context of the feminist critique of pornography, a focus of feminist activism in the 1970s and eighties. A body of radical feminist thought, culminating perhaps in Andrea Dworkin's *Pornography: Men Possessing Women*, has been built around a central thesis drawn from the study of pornography and its psychological effects on both the women who are its objects and the men who are its subjects: that women, in the context of a patriarchal society, are completely powerless. Pornography, and its correspondent action, rape, are understood not as exceptions to the rule of human sexuality, but rather as its fundamental case and essence, expressing as they do the absolute powerlessness of women in the sexual situation. Theorists such as Catherine MacKinnon, identifying themselves with Dworkin's analysis, are thus led to characterize female power as "a contradiction in terms" or "a misnomer" and female sexuality as "self-annihilation" (not in the Blakean sense) or "how we come to want male dominance, which most emphatically is not in our interest."[17]

Far afield as these issues might seem from our discussion of the place of the female in Blake's poetry and its relation to the emerging discourse of women's liberation, I believe that the seeds of this modern formulation of the female as absolute powerlessness are already sown in the work of Mary Wollstonecraft and represent the greatest difference between her thought and Blake's. Besides Mary Poovey's perceptive observation that "Wollstonecraft is generally *not* challenging women to *act*" (*Proper Lady*, 79; Poovey's italics), we are faced with her abjuration of female sexuality and emotion. Although we have already stressed her difference from the prevalent modes of thought in the eighteenth century, Wollstonecraft seems to return to conservative patterns in her description of the ideal "rational" marriage:

In order to fulfil the duties of life, and to be able to pursue with vigour the various employments which form the moral character, a master and mistress of a family ought not to continue to love each other with passion. I mean to say that they ought not to indulge those emotions which disturb the order of society, and engross the thoughts that should be otherwise employed. (*Vindication*, 114)

In spite of signs of stress here evident in Wollstonecraft's authorial voice ("I mean to say"), the fact remains that a large gap separates the author of this passage, fearful of "disturb[ing] the order of society," from the author who called for women to "throw off" the injurious associations of patriarchal society and to "rise superior to a system of oppression" (*Vindication*, 221).

The repetition of the word *vigour* – "to be able to pursue with *vigour* the various employments which form the moral character"; "how can they attain the *vigour* necessary to enable them to throw off their factitious character?" (both my emphasis) – serves to indicate some of the complexities involved in distinguishing the ideological and the utopian formulation of the feminine. For "vigour" in the first sense – vigour^1, we might say – refers to the self-discipline required to perpetuate the ideological forms of the dominant class, to preserve "the order of society." Vigour^2, on the other hand, is that utopian sense of women's power which resists their confinement within an ideological order. The later passage seems to stress the existence of a female power which the earlier passage denies: it is woman's "vigour" which will throw off the factitious character of ideology, their "strength" which will "rise superior to a system of oppression . . . that blasts the fair promises of spring." But the beginnings of an ideological definition of the female, stressing women's powerlessness, continually interrupt these more utopian formulations. In short, there is some danger that Wollstonecraft's "REVOLUTION in female manners" (*Vindication*, 317) will not spell real change, but will only be a revolution in the fallen sense that Blake indicates in *Europe*:

> Thought chang'd the infinite to a serpent; that which pitieth:
> To a devouring flame; and man fled from its face and hid
> In forests of night; then all the eternal forests were divided
> Into earths rolling in circles of space, that like an ocean rush'd
> And overwhelmed all except this finite wall of flesh.
> Then was the serpent temple form'd, image of infinite
> Shut up in finite revolutions, and man became an Angel;
> Heaven a mighty circle turning; God a tyrant crown'd. (10:16–23, E63)

But this is not to discredit what real utopianism exists in Wollstonecraft's work, for despite her appeals to a rational social order and the maintenance of the status quo, her thought does thrust itself toward the future in a manner which can only be described as utopian. After imagining a future in which the place of woman would be determined by a rational standard rather than an absurd prejudice, Wollstonecraft herself acknowledges the utopian nature of her thinking:

These may be termed Utopian dreams. Thanks to that Being who impressed them on my soul, and gave me sufficient strength of mind to dare to exert my own reason, till, becoming dependent only on Him for the support of my virtue, I view, with indignation, the mistaken notions that enslave my sex. (*Vindication*, 121)

The rhetoric of this passage bears close analysis: Wollstonecraft half-heartedly acknowledges the dubious status of utopian thought within rational analysis by characterizing her visions of the future as "Utopian *dreams*," that is to say, mere wishful thinking. As a means of escape from this dilemma, she invokes the only authority available to the eighteenth-century empiricist who wished to speak of something beyond the senses, that virtuous "Being" who serves as the unmoved Mover of the eighteenth-century rational mind, the "invisible hand" which puts into motion the systems of both Adam Smith and Isaac Newton. But the comparison with Smith and Newton can be deceptive, for Wollstonecraft invokes the Deity not to establish the pedigree of industrial capitalism or linear physics, but to find a point from which to criticize, "with indignation, the mistaken notions that enslave my sex." Wollstonecraft's use of the "Deity" in this sense reveals religion as a site of considerable contestation in the late eighteenth century. Although not usually placed in their company, Wollstonecraft in her use of religious authority bears some similarity to the antinomian thinkers and millennial preachers who invoked God to legitimate a revolutionary critique of contemporary social conditions.[18] The tension and interest of Wollstonecraft's analysis thus lies partly in its double pedigree from both eighteenth-century rationalism and from the radical antinomianism of the seventeenth century and earlier, which provided such a rich seedbed for English revolutionary thought, Blake's included.

The quotation which begins this section – in which Wollstonecraft distinguishes herself from those who declare that all *was* right (Rousseau) or all *is* right – seems a more convenient link between Wollstonecraft's utopianism in *Vindication of the Rights of Woman* and Blake's utopianism in *Visions of the Daughters of Albion*, for in many ways Blake's poem depicts the possible victory of the "will be" over the "is" and the "was." Catherine MacKinnon can once again serve as a representative for the modern feminist anti-utopian position:

Now I want to say something about the use of the verb "to be" in feminist theory . . . Feminists say women are not individuals. To retort that we "are" will not make it so. It will obscure the need to *make change* so that it can be so . . . It acts as if the purpose of speech is to say what we want reality to be like as if it already is that way, as if that will help move reality to that place. This may be true in fiction but it won't work in theory. ("Desire and Power", 114; MacKinnon's emphasis)

Besides casting some doubt on MacKinnon's desire that women become "individuals," Blake's and Wollstonecraft's future-directed- ness suggests some of the limitations of MacKinnon's position. Most essentially, they ask a question regarding strategy: If the purpose is, as MacKinnon says, to make change, how can the change from "is" to "will be" be effected when woman is compelled by her own theory of liberation to continually repeat what is? This is the basis of the challenge posed by Oothoon's radical, seemingly nonfactual statement, "I am pure" (2:28, E47). This utopian statement and Wollstonecraft's "Utopian dreams" suggest the usefulness of a utopian "purpose of speech" even when it does not conform to a narrow definition of reality. In this context, *Visions of the Daughters of Albion* emerges as the battlefield on which will be fought the battle between the "is" and the "will be," the ideological and the utopian.

The plot of the poem is simply told: Oothoon, languishing in Leutha's vale, plucks the marigold of sexual experience. She rushes to consummate her love with Theotormon, but is raped by the thunder god Bromion before she can reach him. The remainder of the poem is occupied by long speeches in which the three principals argue their respective philosophies and evaluations of events: Bromion argues that Oothoon is a harlot by the standards of the monolithic code he endorses for all mankind; Theotormon alternates between agreement with Bromion and anguished self-pity; Oothoon gradually dares to affirm that she is free of all taint and that sexual liberation is there for the taking. It is appropriate that most of the poem is occupied with reflection on past action rather than action itself, for reflection, as several commentators have noted,[19] is one of the dominant images of the poem. The usefulness of *Visions of the Daughters of Albion* as a document of utopian thought and the status of utopianism in general will ultimately depend upon whether the "reflection" that the poem depicts is merely a repetition of the same (Blake's fallen "revolution") or a foundation for real change.

The motto of the poem – "The Eye sees more than the Heart knows" (E45) – would itself seem to suggest a radical discontinuity between the two poles of reflection, one constituted by the ideolo- gical framework which translates the image for the "knowing"

Heart, the other expressive of a utopian surplus which escapes the limits of that Heart and threatens to reveal "more." In his characteristic manner of extreme condensation, Blake reinforces this discontinuity in the first stanza of the Argument:

> I loved Theotormon
> And I was not ashamed
> I trembled in my virgin fears
> And I hid in Leutha's vale! (iii:1–4, E45)

Why has not this impossible stanza caused Blake's critics greater anguish? Harold Bloom overcomes the grammatical and logical caesura between the first two and the second two lines by narrativizing their relationship: "Though she loved Theotormon . . . and had pride in her love, nevertheless Oothoon confesses that her lack of sexual experience resulted in ambiguous fears, so that she hid herself in the vales of a female sub-deity called Leutha."[20] But no such continuity, no such "nevertheless," exists in the text: narrative continuity is posited for this text only at the price of the radical disjuncture between two contradictory perspectives which Blake evidently intends to portray. Even the seeming unity of the title falls apart when investigated more closely: Are these the "visions" which the daughters had of Albion? Are they the visions had by a community known as "the Daughters of Albion?" Or are we being privileged, from, as we might say, the peeping-tom's perspective, with a few visions of the Daughters of Albion themselves? While these matters might seem superfluous in the consideration of other texts, in a text as concerned with questions of perspective as *Visions of the Daughters of Albion* they are entirely relevant and perhaps crucial.

The focus of all this perspectival speculation falls, of course, on the central action of the poem, which is described in simple (although metaphoric) language: "Bromion rent her with his thunders" (1:16, E46). With typical Blakean coyness, the Argument actually reveals more about this event than its depiction in the poem proper:

> I plucked Leutha's flower,
> And I rose up from the vale;
> But the terrible thunders tore
> My virgin mantle in twain. (iii:5–8, E45)

Oothoon herself suggests later in the poem that the "twain"-ness into which her mantle is torn might only be the physical manifesta-

tion of a double perspective on the event itself. She offers Theotormon two alternatives, starkly juxtaposed, torn from one another
as much as the ideological is from the utopian:

> Then is Oothoon a whore indeed! and all the virgin joys
> Of life are harlots: and Theotormon is a sick mans dream
> And Oothoon is the crafty slave of selfish holiness.

> But Oothoon is not so, a virgin fill'd with virgin fancies
> Open to joy and to delight where ever beauty appears
> If in the morning sun I find it: there my eyes are fix'd
> In happy copulation; if in evening mild. wearied with work
> Sit on a bank and draw the pleasures of this free born joy.

$$(6:18-7:2, E50)$$

The gap in the text, given Blake's general concern with manuscript
design as a significant element of poetic meaning, represents the gap
between the ideological and the utopian perspectives on Oothoon's
status, a gap which has been forced open by the intrusion of
Bromion's "thunder." Oothoon is offering Theotormon the world of
the later *Europe*, except that instead of a "female dream," he is
offered a "sick mans dream" and the "crafty" power of the
manipulative Female Will. Alternatively, she is offering him the
utopian perspective of her as a "virgin fill'd with virgin fancies /
Open to joy and delight." To any reader familiar with Blake, the
word "virgin" must set off alarms, for virginity is usually cast in
Blake as an artifice of the Female Will. But we must recognize
Oothoon's doubling of the concept of virginity itself, for Oothoon is
speaking here of a paradoxical "open virginity," able to maintain
itself while at the same time copulating in the very act of seeing or, in
the more usual sense, while "[s]it[ting] on a bank and draw[ing] the
pleasures of this free born joy." In distinction to Wollstonecraft, the
progress to utopia in Blake is not effected by the elimination of any
element of the fallen world, whether sexuality, labor, or war, but
instead by the "copula" which will join fallen signifiers to their
utopian meanings.

Are we, however, by stressing the utopian perspective, leaving the
strength of the ideological perspective itself behind? Are we ne-
glecting to acknowledge the real status of real women in real sexual
situations? Are we, as MacKinnon would suggest, leaving behind the
ugliness of the "is" for rose-colored visions of the "will be?"

Oothoon's anguished portrait of fallen sexuality and woman's situation in ideology would suggest otherwise:

> [S]he who burns with youth. and knows no fixed lot; is bound
> In spells of law to one she loaths: and must she drag the chain
> Of life, in weary lust! must chilling murderous thoughts. obscure
> The clear heaven of her eternal spring? to bear the wintry rage
> Of a harsh terror driv'n to madness, bound to hold a rod
> Over her shrinking shoulders all the day; & all the night
> To turn the wheel of false desire: and longings that wake her womb
> To the abhorred birth of cherubs in the human form
> That live a pestilence & die a meteor & are no more. (5:21-9, E49)

It is passages like this that have encouraged commentators such as Alicia Ostriker to characterize Blake as a proto-feminist, having "created a heroine unequalled in English poetry before or since" who "attacks ideology root and branch" ("Desire", 158). Yet even here we see the stage of utopianism from which Oothoon speaks, the "eternal spring" which, as we have seen, was such a potent utopian image for both Wollstonecraft and Blake as well as other eighteenth-century thinkers. Yet how do the utopian and the ideological coexist? Or are they to be forever separated by Bromion's intrusive thunder?

A new wave of critical revisionists has tended to negotiate the gap between ideology and utopia in *Visions* very much to the detriment of utopianism. Citing the naive complicitous readings of earlier Blake criticism, Thomas A. Vogler stresses the need to understand *Visions of the Daughters of Albion* as a text about "the production of Truth," rather than as "a direct assertion of Truth."[21] By this he means to say that Blake's critics have tended to accept Oothoon's utopian statements at face value, without questioning their place within the poem and within Blake's work as a whole. Vogler suggests a reading of the poem which understands Oothoon's claims for "happy happy Love! free as the mountain wind" (7:16, E50) not as a call for change but for "accommodation in the service of stability" ("An Un-Reading", 299). He justifies this reading by noting the workings of a discursive system which represses disruptive energy by allowing it expression through carefully controlled channels:

How ironic, if the most effective means of neutralizing the potentially disruptive voice were to celebrate and affirm it, to give it a place in the economy of discourse where it can speak all it wants, or where what it wants can be spoken for it and through it by the ventriloquating male. ("An Un-Reading", 300)

This Foucauldian reading is complimented by the more traditionally Marxist reading of David Aers. In distinction to Vogler, Aers suggests that the naivety of utopian readings of *Visions* is not to be laid at the door of Blake's critics but at the door of the poet himself. Aers praises Blake's depictions of the (ideological) female as possessive and power-hungry, but he dismisses the idealistic portrayal of Oothoon as a utopian (in the pejorative sense) failure:

Blake presents Oothoon as able to transcend the consciousness of her fellow woman *absolutely*: but how this can be so, how she has attained so clear a revolutionary critique of sexual and social exploitation, and of their interaction, how she had reached so full an understanding of the psychological effects and perverted indulgences of repressed sexuality . . . this remains a mystery.[22]

The strategies are ones we have seen before: the utopian is reduced to the ideological either by the claim that Blake is consciously representing the workings of ideology (Vogler) or is ideology's unconscious victim (Aers). The gap that Bromion forcefully opened is thus effectively closed, but not to any advantage of the utopian, merely as part of the closing of the ideological circle.

A different way of conceiving of the relation between utopia and ideology will require a different way of thinking of power, of sexuality, of the feminine, and finally of reading itself. Because the solution to this problem involves cunning, it would perhaps not be inappropriate to use Foucault in a manner precisely opposite to the way Vogler uses him – "piercing Apollyon with his own bow" (*J*12:14, E155), as Blake might have said – in that we are required to think of power in a new way:

It seems to me that power is "always already there," that one is never "outside" it, that there are no "margins" for those who break with the system to gambol in. But this does not entail the necessity of accepting an inescapable form of domination or an absolute privilege on the side of the law. To say that one can never be "outside" power does not mean that one is trapped and condemned to defeat no matter what.[23]

This formulation has three important consequences for a utopian theory of sexuality and the feminine: (1) it dismisses as essentialist the idea of an absolute powerlessness, that is, it dismisses what we have been calling the ideological theory of the feminine; (2) it grounds utopia in the very real world of power dynamics; and (3) while grounding utopianism in the ideological world, it does not reduce utopia to ideology, but allows for the possibility of escape.

Since we have already discussed the place of the ideological female in Blake's poetry – the Enitharmon whose dream of agency is merely an ideological cover for her powerlessness – it is necessary to understand the ways in which Blake grounds Oothoon's utopian vision in the real world. In the first place, we must recognize a central element of Oothoon's vision which several of Blake's commentators have not neglected to point out: its complete inefficacy. Not only does the tyrant Bromion refuse to acknowledge Oothoon's calls for sexual liberation; even Theotormon, in whose interest Oothoon is speaking, refuses to listen. After the high excitement of Oothoon's daring rhetoric, the poem ends on a bleak note: "Thus every morning wails Oothoon. but Theotormon sits / Upon the margind ocean conversing with shadows dire" (8:11–12, E51). One must also regard cautiously the reaction of the Daughters of Albion, recorded in the refrain which ends each movement of the poem: "The Daughters of Albion hear her woes, & eccho back her sighs" (2:20, 5:2, 8:13). Certainly the Daughters hear her, but perhaps the point in this poem which questions the perspectival nature of reality is that the only things which they hear are her "woes" and the only things they "eccho" (the idea of a disjunctive reflection is here invoked again) are her "sighs." Properly understood, Oothoon's message is not a sigh and its burden is not a series of woes, but instead, "Love! Love! Love! happy happy Love! free as the mountain wind!" (7:16, E50). The "reflection" of Oothoon's speech by the Daughters of Albion says more about the reception of utopia in an ideological world than it does about the utopia itself. In this sense, Blake is allowing us a vision of the Daughters of Albion as the *object* of ideology, rather than recording their utopian visions from within ideology. Blake illustrates the place of utopia in an ideological world in the illumination to plate 4, where Oothoon is floating above the mourning Theotormon but with her ankle securely chained to the stones of the ideological world (figure 7). Oothoon's vision is thus grounded, in a very literal sense, in the very world she strives to escape.

Given the intimate relationship between utopia and ideology, this escape will only be effected, as Foucault notes, from "inside" the boundaries of ideology and repressive power. Liberation is not

7 *Visions of the Daughters of Albion.*

achieved by a renunciation of power (as MacKinnon suggests), nor by a renunciation of female sexuality (as Wollstonecraft sometimes advocates), but by an "inside job" which will raise these ideological elements to their utopian level. In regard to the question of female sexuality, we have already discussed the cunning power which women possessed in a culture which established them as the gate-keepers of sexuality. But perhaps this cunning power is also a proleptic figuration of a fuller utopian power. In the terms of the master/slave dialectic, does not the slave possess the unique power of being the "reflection" through which the master mediates his consciousness? And is it not possible for the slave to reflect something other than the face of her ideological master? Oothoon originally desires to "reflect / The image of Theotormon on my pure transparent breast" (2:15–16, E46), but the lesson of *Visions of the Daughters of Albion* is that sexuality's utopian potential eventually takes Oothoon beyond a mere one-to-one reflection, to the point where she represents Theotormon's contrary, engaged in the struggle to wrench him from his ideological gloom. Theotormon sees a defiled Oothoon, bearing the stamp of Bromion's signet, and because she is the mediator of his consciousness, he sees himself defiled also. But Oothoon, in her vision of utopian purity, holds out to Theotormon a reflection of his own purity: "How can I be defiled when I reflect thy image pure?" (3:16, E47). In short, Oothoon exploits her position within the power dynamics of the fallen world, which is not a position of absolute powerlessness but rather power of a particular kind, to voice the demands of utopian sexuality.

Finally, our new vision of the utopian face of cunning power will require us to adopt a new way of reading, a new way of seeing Blake's images. The tendency in the synoptic readings of Blake's symbolic language has been to read Blake's repetition of images as an attempt to express equivalent meanings in different contexts. That is to say, when, for example, Blake uses the image of a snake in *Jerusalem*, he must mean very much the same thing as he meant when he used a snake in *America*, because, after all, a snake is a snake. In other words, the attempt has been made to establish a one-to-one reflection across Blake's entire corpus, with identical images serenely contemplating each other across the space of thirty years. A cunning hermeneutic, on the other hand, would emphasize the difference in reflections, and, in particular, that difference in the image between its ideological and its utopian reflection. Let us take as an example the use of the net and trap as an image in *Visions of the Daughters of Albion*. Blake uses this image three times in the text of the poem. It first appears in the context of Oothoon's speech on the difference between the perceptions of every person on earth:

> How different their eye and ear! how different the world to them!
> With what sense does the parson claim the labour of the farmer?
> What are his nets & gins & traps. & how does he surround him
> With cold floods of abstraction, and with forests of solitude,
> To build him castles and high spires. where kings & priests may dwell.
>
> (5:16–20, E49)

On the next plate, it occurs within Oothoon's description of the creation of the female personality, in a context which can't help but remind us of Enitharmon's invocation of "the little female / Spread[ing] nets in every secret path":

> Who taught thee modesty, subtil modesty! child of night & sleep
> When thou awakest. wilt thou dissemble all thy secret joys
> Or wert thou not awake when all this mystery was disclos'd!
> Then com'st thou forth a modest virgin knowing to dissemble
> With nets found under thy night pillow, to catch virgin joy,
> And brand it with the name of whore; & sell it in the night,
> In silence. ev'n without a whisper, and in seeming sleep.   (6:7–13, E49)

Finally, it occurs in the context of Oothoon's utopian promise to Theotormon:

> But silken nets and traps of adament will Oothoon spread,
> And catch for thee girls of mild silver, or of furious gold;
> I'll lie beside thee on a bank & view their wanton play
> In lovely copulation bliss on bliss with Theotormon.   (7:23–6, E50)

Critics such as Vogler have used the repetition of this central image to cast doubt upon Oothoon's utopian vision and to suggest that by it Blake means to indicate that Oothoon's supposed escape from the ideological world will only result in more of the same, a Urizenic "revolution."[24] Even its first appearance, however, would suggest that we are not to accept this image as a stable signifier: if the eye and ear of the parson and the farmer, the industrious citizen and the husbandman (5:13), the giver of gifts and the merchant (5:12), are themselves so different that they perceive different worlds, we cannot expect that the net, the gin, and the trap will be the same in every manifestation. To do so would be to surround the image "with cold floods of abstraction" and would violate the meaning of

Blake's text every bit as much as the parson violates the farmer by requisitioning his product. The second appearance of the image bears scrutiny too. As we have said, its setting reminds us of *Europe* not only because Enitharmon dictates the use of nets by the "little female," but also because the virgin which Oothoon describes is a "child of night & sleep," much as the little female is merely one part of the "female dream" of "the night of Enitharmons joy." But Oothoon's virgin employs her cunning nets only in "seeming sleep," in a state which seems to be oddly between sleep and wakefulness itself. The power Oothoon describes is still the illusionary fallen power of the ideological world, but the door is being opened to a utopian fulfillment of this partial power. Finally, Oothoon announces the redeemed vision of this fallen image in the "silken nets and traps of adament" which will catch "girls of mild silver, or of furious gold." What might be taken as a repetition of the ideological trap is really its utopian fulfillment, for these are, paradoxically, the nets of generosity and openness, not of jealousy and secrecy. The strength of Blake's utopian vision lies precisely in his refusal to leave behind even his symbol of jealous love, which is here redeemed for the purposes of utopian sexual liberation. A cunning hermeneutic thus formulates the "reflection" of images not as a return of the same, but as a mirroring which reveals the utopian content within the ideological form.

At first glance, this last scene – Oothoon viewing the "wanton play" of Theotormon and the "girls of mild silver, or of furious gold" – would seem to return us to the locus of pornography, but we must notice the subtle changes which are here rung upon the pornographic scene. The artificiality of the scene – the fact that the girls are "silver" and "gold" – would itself suggest that we are witnessing a pornography with a difference, a self-conscious, reconceived pornography. But the most telling difference with the ideological pornographic scene depicted and universalized by Andrea Dworkin and Catherine MacKinnon is the fact that the sexual positions have here been reversed: Oothoon is now the subject of a utopian pornography (if we can retain that word) for which she had formerly been the universal object. Blake's cunning is to have worked inside the ideological forms of pornography, to have changed them from within. What Foucault has said of power is true of ideology, that there is no "outside" from which to position one's writing and thinking. But the absence of an outside does not preclude the escape to a "nowhere" which refigures, while not abandoning, the forms of the fallen world. It is only by means of the "nowhere" that we can understand powerlessness against the background of power, rape against the background of fulfilled sexuality, sexual domination against the background of sexual liberation. The female which appears as the reflection of male dominance "is" an object which mediates male consciousness, but she is also more, a "more" which the utopian eye sees: she is always the possibility of her own subjecthood. It is not a question of abandoning the ideological world, but of teasing utopian significations out of ideological forms. To do anything less would be to trap Oothoon within the ideological nets of cold abstraction.

Like "The Little Black Boy," then, *Visions of the Daughters of Albion* raises issues about the status of utopian discourse, issues that are raised throughout the works of the early 1790s, Blake's first period of great literary creativity. Indeed, the Blakean contraries of Innocence and Experience, important throughout this period and not just in the volume which takes its name from them, might usefully be seen in the light of the concepts of ideology and utopia, even if the pairs cannot precisely be mapped on to each other. Throughout this period, Blake is concerned to ask questions about the nature of statements and feelings of what we might call a "radical hopefulness," a sense that the degradations and deprivations of the present are temporary, susceptible to remedy. The question raised in the *Songs*, in *Visions* and in the other works of this period, can be roughly put as follows: Is radical hopefulness merely another expression of ideology's dominion, a sedative for potentially unruly subjects, or can it, as I have suggested is the case with Oothoon, be seen to have some actual disruptive relation to the dominant discourse?

As noted above, whatever its status, utopian discourse in *Visions* remains, even in the representational world of the poem, precisely at the level of discourse, not yet a part of any actual reconfiguration of social constructions. But in the historical poems written during these years – in *America*, particularly – and in the prophetic works which would follow in the decades to come, Blake increasingly turns his attention to the larger role played by utopian formulations in the structure of society as a whole. Utopia becomes less a matter merely of what people might say and more a matter of how a liberative, equitable society might emerge from the current situation. The solutions which Blake derives for this largely social problem differ widely, as we shall see, but the interest in transformational change remains constant throughout.

CHAPTER 4

Edmund Burke and models of history in America, The Song of Los, *and* The Four Zoas

I

Morality, religion, metaphysics, all the rest of ideology and their corresponding forms of consciousness . . . no longer retain the semblance of independence. *They have no history, no development;* but men, developing their material production and their material intercourse, alter, along with this their real existence, their thinking and the products of their thinking.

Marx and Engels, *The German Ideology*[1]

Distinguish therefore States from Individuals in those States. States Change: but Individual Identities never change nor cease.

(*M*32: 22–3, E132)

Man Passes on but States remain for Ever he passes thro them like a traveller who may as well suppose that the places he has passed thro exist no more as a Man may suppose that the States he has passd thro exist no more Every Thing is Eternal.

(*VLJ*, E556)

In the section of *Ideology and Utopia* entitled "The Utopian Mentality," Karl Mannheim distinguishes between the four types of utopian consciousness: (1) orgiastic chiliasm, (2) liberal-humanitarianism, (3) conservatism, and (4) socialist-communism. The four are most easily distinguished by their sense of time and by the temporal configurations of their respective utopias. Chiliasm – exemplified for Mannheim by Thomas Münzer, the sixteenth-century Anabaptist – posits a complete break with the historical world in which utopia is realized as an ahistorical Eternal Present:

[F]rom the point of view of Chiliastic experience, the [spatial and temporal] position that we occupy is only incidental. For the real Chiliast, the present becomes the breach through which what was previously inward bursts out suddenly, takes hold of the outer world and transforms it.[2]

Liberal humanitarianism, on the other hand, accepts the course of history by positing a utopia at its end, thus ordering all of history as a narrative of progress or evolution towards a final goal: "[W]ith the liberal-humanitarian idea the utopian element receives a definite location in the historical process – it is the culminating point of historical evolution" (*Ideology and Utopia*, 224). Conservatism, while seeming wholly anti-utopian, valorizes the past in such a way as to render the present order of things utopian: "Conservative experience merges the spirit, which at one time came to us from beyond and to which we gave expression, with what already is, allowing that to become objective, to expand in all dimensions and thereby endowing every event with an immanent, intrinsic value" (*Ideology and Utopia*, 237). These three utopian mentalities thus project themselves each into a single temporal direction, into, respectively, the present (chiliasm), the future (liberal-humanitarianism), and the past (conservatism). Socialist communism – the culmination, in Mannheim's view, of all previous utopian visions – synthesizes the partial views of the other utopias and asserts the place of the past and the future within the historical present: "It is not only the past but the future as well which has virtual existence in the present" (*Ideology and Utopia*, 246). For the socialist-communist, then, time is not a narrative leading towards a predetermined end, as it is for the liberal-humanitarian, but is a series of "strategical points" (*Ideology and Utopia*, 244) in which the opposing claims of past and future must continually be negotiated and through which the posited utopia must continually be revised.

While Mannheim, in a curiously liberal-humanitarian fashion, proposes a narrative of progress for these four mentalities, by which the errors of chiliasm, liberal-humanitarianism, and conservatism are erased in the emergence of socialist-communism, it is nevertheless possible to see all or some of these four elements at work in any single historical period. For example, in the period which is the subject of the present study a persistent topic of political debate involved the conflict between what Mannheim would identify as a liberal-humanitarian and a chiliastic point of view. The best representatives of this debate are Edmund Burke and Thomas Paine, not only because their war of pamphlets constituted the most successful publishing venture of the decade (Paine's *Rights of Man* presumably sold 250,000 copies in two years), but because the liberal-humanitarian and the chiliastic mentalities are represented at their most pure in the works of these two opposing titans. Certainly, by labeling Burke a "liberal-humanitarian" one is swimming against the flood-tide of commentary which has placed him (either jubilantly or accusingly) amongst the conservatives.[3] But the fact remains that, despite his contempt for reason and radical change, Burke advocated "improvement" throughout his career and even in that bible of conservative thought, the *Reflections on the Revolution in France*.[4] Paine's credentials as a radical revolutionary are less difficult to establish, but the relation between his thought and Mannheim's chiliastic utopian mentality requires a closer analysis of his formulations and their implied historical model. At this point we need merely note that the Burke–Paine debate represents a central conflict between divergent utopian mentalities and that the complexities of that debate shed light on two distinct periods of Blake's poetic career: the period of historically referential poetry (the subject of this chapter) and the period of inward-turning chiliastic poetry (the subject of chapter 5, below). Burke and Paine might thus stand as the contrasting emblems of Blake's poetic development in the decade beginning in 1793 (with the engraving of *America*) and ending in 1804 (with the composition of *Milton*).[5]

However, as the epigraphs for this chapter indicate, the progressivist utopia remained a concern for Blake throughout his career – in *Milton* and *A Vision of the Last Judgment* as well as the more explicitly historical works – and took many forms in its different contexts. The similarities between Marx's landmark formulation in *The German Ideology* and Blake's apparently contradictory statements in the later works indicate the basic strategy of the liberal-humanitarian mentality, its place in the tradition of ideology-critique and the complexities which plague any progressivist definition of history. The strategy, baldly stated, of a utopian theory of progress revolves around the realization that stands at the center of both Blake's and Marx's theory of history, that ideology has no history, or, as Blake puts it, that "States remain for Ever." Marx assigns the motive force of history to the nonideological modes of production, which themselves serve as the base for ideology but which carry no ideological legacy as they change over time. Marx's normative model of history, expressed in *The Communist Manifesto* and elsewhere, thus emerges as a progressive series of modes of production which shed ideologies like so many dead skins on their path to the utopian communist state.[6] In proposing that "Man Passes on but States remain for Ever," Blake also posits a theory of progress in which history is the vehicle of escape from fallen ideology. By a kind of Nietzschian will to forget, the "traveller" through history can "suppose that the States he has passed thro exist no more," because, for all their effect on the course of time, they might as well be nonexistent. Although "Every Thing is Eternal" in Blake's estimation in *A Vision*, one must assume that the eternity of States is here a "bad" Eternity, like the bad Eternity which Nietzsche assigns to moments which do not recur but remain trapped in their temporal position.[7] Bad Eternity, in short, is the characteristic of ideology, which, in the formula of progressivist historicism, is left behind as "the dust of creeds outworn."[8] The traveler, like the "traveller thro Eternity" in *Milton* (15:21–35, E109), thus escapes the trap ("vortex") of ideology by progressing through history to its utopian conclusion, the apocalyptic fulfillment of fallen time.

But, as one might expect, Blake's and Marx's formulations are not identical. The differences between them begin to indicate the distinction between a truly humanistic and a socialist theory of progress. For, although Marx's formulation in *The German Ideology* does not yet reflect the antihumanism of the later works, the place of man has already become problematic. "Man" is the subject of the sentence – "men, developing their material production and their material intercourse, alter, along with this their real existence, their thinking and the products of their thinking" – but the focus on "material production" is already quite strong. "Material production" [*materielle Produktion*] is man's "real existence" [*Wirklichkeit*]; thinking seems merely supplementary. The changes of material production and thinking could be seen as occurring simultaneously – man alters ideology "along with" material production [*Menschen ändern mit dieser ihrer Wirklichkeit auch ihr Denken und die Produkte ihres Denkens*] – but the hint of a causal relationship persists: thinking, at least in the order of the sentence, changes only *after* material production changes and perhaps only as a result of those material changes. Finally, in claiming that ideology has no history, Marx, given his definition of ideology in *The German Ideology*, is denying the validity of the single characteristic which has set humans apart from the animals throughout the history of Western philosophy: the capacity for thought.[9] Although not the economism of the later Marx and later Marxists, the formulation of ideology and history in *The German Ideology* is a prelude to those antihumanist formulae. Blake, on the other hand, in a manner consistent with the late eighteenth-century focus on human consciousness, locates the power of historical progress squarely in "Man," in "Individual Identities." If he is expressly concerned with history in these formulations, it is a phenomenological history, a history of the consciousness of Man: Blake thus addresses himself to the human historical organ which "supposes," supposes, in this case, that the States which "remain for ever" may as well "exist no more." For Blake, the human ability to "suppose" is not a by-product of history (as it is for Marx), but is history itself: "Every thing possible to be believ'd is an image of truth" (*MHH*8:38, E37).

But Blake, perhaps not surprisingly, seems even to disagree with himself. Efforts have been made to regularize the differences between the two statements – "States Change: but Individual Identities never change nor cease"; "Man Passes on but States remain for Ever" – themselves separated by perhaps as little as six years in date of composition. But the radical disunity of the two, in what ironically appears to be Blake's attempt to restate an earlier position, points to a radical contradiction at the center of the progressive hypothesis itself. For if the theory of progress is at heart a theory of change, it is also a theory of continuity, of changelessness. Consider the structure of progress, which is in many ways the structure of a sentence: the subject, a substantive, has substance in itself, but also as it is directed towards its own fulfillment in the predicate, that which comes after. The predicate exists as the culmination of the sentence but not as its destruction; in its very name, the predicate makes reference to the continued existence of what was "before said." The predicate, the object of the sentence's progress, thus wavers between the transformation and the reproduction of its originary subject.[10] Who is to say whether the principal achievement of the narrative of progress is its ability to preserve its beginnings or to change them, to retain "Individual Identities" which "never change nor cease" or to shrug off "States" which "remain for Ever?" Hegel's solution to this problem, as can be seen in his analysis of the sample sentence "God is being,"[11] is to develop the concept of sublation, the simultaneous dissolution, transformation, and reproduction of what has come before. Blake, at least in these two instances, seems rather to alternate between the two faces of the progressive thesis, its continuation of the past and its realization of the future. Whatever the solution, it is clear that the problems posed by the theory of progress are inherent in that theory, inescapable components of a model of history which posits a utopian future as the culmination and completion of the ideological present. Thus it is to the inherent limitations of the theory of progress that we can assign Blake's ultimate willingness to progress beyond it. Although initially useful as a model for describing historical events on their path to utopian fulfillment, even the theory of progress, as we shall see, is eventually left behind as a "state" whose uselessness is such that it may as well exist no more.

II

When seen from the perspective of the present, the onset of the "Age of Revolution" can often seem to be signaled by its definitive rejection of the historical past. What else could possibly motivate or legitimate the nascent democratic movements of the time, with their suggestion that privilege should not be inherited along with land and title, but a denial of the very forces of history that surrounded them in practically every institution, every grand building, every de-grading custom? But as recent commentators of the period have suggested, history served as a useful concept not only for the reactionary opponents of democratic "leveling," but also for many of the radicals themselves. If Thomas Paine's rejection of historical precedent and its "manuscript-assumed authority" sounds the clarion note of the period, it should not deafen us to the many radical uses of history and the argument from precedent at work in the period. Jon Mee and Michael Ferber have identified a crucial strain of "radical antiquarianism" in the late eighteenth century, important to Blake in both his professional development, as an apprentice engraver, but also for his political thought. And James Epstein, in *Radical Expression*, has inventoried the radical uses of a number of historical rhetorics, including the appeal to the elusive precedent of the English Constitution.[12] It is in the spirit of this strain of radical historicism, and especially in relation to its use of a constitutionalist rhetoric, that we might undertake an illustrative comparison of Blake's thought to the work of a writer with whom he might initially seem to have nothing in common, Edmund Burke.

Although the two might be said to inhabit different ends of the political spectrum, at least in regard to their opinions of the French Revolution, Burke can stand, particularly in his status as the leading constitutionalist thinker of his day,[13] as an unusually useful parallel for Blake's developments in the history poems of the mid-1790s. But before that link can be made directly, we need to reflect on the peculiar nature of Burke's ideas on history and their implications for an historicist notion of ideology and its overcoming.

The Burke/Blake connection must be established delicately because Burke inspires, as perhaps no other English historical figure can, strong partisan feeling, both admiring and condemnatory. This state of affairs has come to exist at least partly because Burke has not been allowed to be only an "historical" figure, but has been enlisted as a founding father of modern political movements, of both the "right" and the "left." Conor Cruise O'Brien, in the survey of Burke's reputation which introduces his biography *The Great Melody*, identifies the Whigs and their inheritors, the Liberal Party, as the main intellectual descendants of Burke and "the Rockinghams," for

[t]heir commitment to political and constitutional issues, as distinct from the politics of place and preferment; their determination to act in a body; their willingness to make a stand on issues which they believed to be right, even when their stand was unpopular with parliamentary majorities, with the Court and with the country as over the American War; and their resolute defence of the Constitution against the encroachment of George III. (*Great Melody*, xxxiii)

For conservatives also, of course, in both Britain and the United States, Burke has the status of an originary figure, largely for his advocacy of traditionalism and his seeming distrust for any concept of change whatsoever: "A spirit of innovation is generally the result of a selfish temper and confined views" (*Reflections*, 37–8). But if the contentiousness of Burke's valuation thus emerges in part from the way he has been revived in modern political contexts, it also springs from the way he has been frozen in a particular historical moment, a moment of great contentiousness in its own right. The Burke remembered today is not usually the young aesthetician, author of the *Philosophical Enquiry into the Origins of Our Ideas of the Sublime and the Beautiful* (1757) and major influence on Kant's *Critique of Judgment*; nor so much the radical pamphleteer who criticized the Court in *Thoughts on the Cause of the Present Discontents* (1770); nor yet the parliamentary dynamo who took on himself the crusade against British abuses in

India under the administration of Governor-General Warren Hastings; but instead, almost singly and monumentally, the Burke who authored *Reflections on the Revolution in France* (1790). In the statuary hall of historical memory, then, Burke is almost always seen as locked in struggle, most prominently with Thomas Paine, but also with the other numerous respondents to *Reflections* who contributed to the "pamphlet war" of the 1790s. By a strange sort of historical deflation, Burke becomes the site of political controversy itself, as more than a few modern political arguments have been fought out on the ground of allegiances to Burke or Paine, the two positioned as irreconcilable "sides" of a titanic battle.

However powerful this polemical figure of Burke may be – and, indeed, the current study will partly participate in it by proposing contrasting views of revolution in this chapter and the next, which draws on parallels with Paine – it nevertheless blinds us to the most interesting aspects of Burke's thought. Commentators on Burke's career, in his own time and ours, have registered this difficulty in their inability to reconcile the polemical Burke of the *Reflections* with the Burke of the Hastings impeachment or of the resistance to George III's policies in America. Not surprisingly, it is an American, Thomas Jefferson, who expresses this difficulty most succinctly when, after reading *Reflections*, he wrote to a friend that "the Revolution in France does not astonish me so much as the revolution in Mr. Burke" (quoted in O'Brien, *Great Melody*, lxxi). Although clearly intended as a piece of wit on Jefferson's part, the statement summarizes the parallels between a crisis in Burke's career, a crisis in the policy of nations, and, fundamentally, a crisis in any notion of continuation whatsoever. What ultimately makes Burke a useful analogue for Blake – two writers who might be said to be divided by an absolute difference in their attitudes to the French Revolution – is precisely the effort to historicize, to narrativize, this revolution, both in the political events of their time and in their own experiences.[14] Or, to use Blake's own language for historical continuity, we might very well see the polemical Burke of the *Reflections* as a "State" which changes, but the historical Burke who underwrites him in the same work as an "Individual" who "never change[s] nor cease[s]." Each of these formulations, clearly, is an attempt to distinguish between those elements of individuals or societies which "have no history," what Marx would call ideology, and those parts which do possess the historical momentum to make a continuous story of their own pasts.

One effect of freezing Burke at the moment of his antirevolutionary polemic has been to cast him as the "traditionalist" in every sense of the word, both in his defense of the *ancien régime* and in his intellectual allegiances. But if we place him more carefully in the context of the Enlightenment thinkers who immediately precede him, we will see that he participates, as much as the other figures discussed in this book, in the construction of a notion of ideology which will continue to be used in the emerging *episteme*. Of particular interest, and one element which marks Burke as more than just a traditional thinker, is the peculiar turn he gives to the Enlightenment notion of "prejudice." Jorge Larrain, in *The Concept of Ideology*, has outlined the role played by the notion of prejudice in the development of a concept of ideology *avant la lettre*, in the work of Condillac, Holbach, Helvitius, and others.[15] For the most part, "prejudice" in these thinkers referred to religious conceptions, the identification of which stood as the first step in the Enlightenment project of clearing away all impediments to rational thought. We might formalize these early versions of a concept of ideology by considering, first, the nature of the temporality which they assign to the notion of prejudice, and, second, the amount and kind of work they propose in the elimination of prejudice. The fact that religion is identified as the prime example of "prejudice" reveals the extent to which these thinkers are antihistorical in their approach to ideology and its critique, for "religion" in this context stands as the representative of "traditional knowledge" generally and for a species of thought that can be discarded primarily for its irredeemable pastness. The identification and critique of prejudice thus stands as part of a more general temporal consciousness, one which rejects the legitimacy of the past in favor of an enlightened present whose epistemologically privileged status is at least partly due to its ability to claim the "now." The nature of the rejection of *prejudice* (a word which refers in its prefix to its own pastness), of the work which is required to dispel the effects of prejudice, is intimately bound to its relegation to the past. In the absence of any more thorough theoretical distinction between "superstition" and "reason," the necessary work of identifying these two mentalities, prefatory to eliminating the former, can be performed by an analysis which separates the thought of the past from the thought of the present. This preliminary distinction also motivates the ease with which prejudice is discarded in the Enlightenment framework, since the path to right reason now consists in nothing more than leaving the past to the past. The Enlightenment elimination of prejudice is a mental operation which can always be undertaken "now."

It is within this broad context that Burke's use of "prejudice," so disarming for a modern reader, needs to be understood. The most powerful discussion of Burke's idea of prejudice in the *Reflections* comes after his dramatic condemnation of the events of 1789, including the famous apotheosis of Marie Antoinette, during a broad comparison between French "Enlightenment" and British "tradition":

> You see, Sir, that in this enlightened age I am bold enough to confess that we are generally men of untaught feelings, that, instead of casting away all our old prejudices, we cherish them to a very considerable degree, and, to take more shame to ourselves, we cherish them because they are prejudices; and the longer they have prevailed, the more we cherish them . . . Many of our own men of speculation, instead of exploding general prejudices, employ their sagacity to discover the latent wisdom which prevails in them. If they find what they seek, and they seldom fail, they think it more wise to continue the prejudice, with the reason involved, than to cast away the coat of prejudice and to leave nothing but the naked reason; because prejudice, with its reason, has a motive to give action to that reason, and an affection which will give it permanence. Prejudice is of ready application in the emergency; it previously engages the mind in a steady course of wisdom and virtue and does not leave the man hesitating in the moment of decision skeptical, puzzled, and unresolved. Prejudice renders a man's virtues his habit, and not a series of unconnected acts. Through just prejudice, his duty becomes a part of his nature. (*Reflections*, 98–9)

I quote this passage at length because it raises so many of the questions which are crucial to an assessment of Burke's historical thought, regardless of one's opinion of the particular polemic in the service of which he here writes (although we shall consider the connection between "tradition" and actual politics below).[16] Burke's most striking transvaluation of Enlightenment philosophy, which he here explicitly rejects, is, of course, his general approbation of Enlightenment's greatest enemy, prejudice. Although partly assuming the voice and tone of an Enlightenment *philosophe* in calling the British love for prejudice their "shame," Burke is ultimately quite clear in his preferences for prejudice over "naked reason." His rationale for this preference goes beyond mere jingoism or simple "conservatism," however. In relation to the Enlightenment development of ideology-critique, his notion of prejudice represents some crucial corrections and, I would argue, developments. First of all, Burke's "prejudice" makes possible the idea of development itself: if the temporal consciousness of the Enlightened debunker of prejudice is in an eternal now, cut off from the past, then Burke's notion of a "redeemed" prejudice seems expressly to forge the links between past and present, to ensure that individual lives and social systems are more than just "a series of unconnected acts." But if Burke has deviated from the temporality of Enlightenment thought, he would not, at least initially, seem to differ in his assessment of the work needed to dispel prejudice. For him, as much as for the *philosophes*, it seems always a possibility for the British "men of speculation" to "cast away the coat of prejudice and to leave nothing but the naked reason." If prejudice is retained, it is from a choice to "cherish" it rather than an acknowledgement of its inescapability. Could this merely be another bit of Burkean irony, another example of the willingness to assume his opponent's voice which often renders the text of *Reflections* an interpretive tangle? The answer to this question will perhaps grow clearer as we proceed, but at the very least we can note the way in which Burke empties out the Enlightenment "now" of reason. Even if Enlightenment's elimination of prejudice is possible, the present which issues from this purifying process is, in Burke's view, incapable of stirring any further action. It is prejudice, with its ties to the past, that "has a motive to give action to that reason, and an affection which will give it permanence." The price of Enlightened ideology-critique, from this perspective, is to be divorced from history in every sense, not only to free oneself from the shackles of the past, but to ensure complete ineffectiveness in shaping the future.

Burke's emphasis on both "action" and "permanence," on a principle of change as well as a principle of continuity, would seem to accord well with Blake's formulations, differently stated, as we have seen, in different places, of a portion of humanity which "Passes on" and a portion which "remain[s] for Ever." The dialectic of change and continuity at work in both thinkers is the basis of a concept of history. But what of that reference to "nature" in the last sentence quoted above ("Through just prejudice, [a man's] duty becomes a part of his nature")? Surely nothing would more clearly distinguish Burke from a poet who excoriated the notion of both an external nature and a human nature in the character of "Vala," one of the most substantial impediments to Edenic renewal. James

Chandler has already thoughtfully discussed the implications of Burke's notion of nature in this passage – in particular, its status as a human-created "second nature" – and the influence of this idea in the development of Wordsworth's poetic philosophy.[17] What remains for us is to consider the effect of Burke's notion of nature on Blake, a poet far less disposed to approve of "natures" of any kind than Wordsworth was, and the relation between Burke's "nature" and a nascent concept of ideology. To begin with, one must simply acknowledge the importance of the reference to nature for Burke, and the considerable argumentative weight it is forced to bear, as in his rejection, early in the *Reflections*, of Richard Price's doctrine of "leveling":

Believe me, Sir, those who attempt to level, never equalize. In all societies, consisting of various descriptions of citizens, some description must be uppermost. The levelers, therefore, only change and pervert *the nature of things*; they load the edifice of society by setting up in the air what the solidity of the structure requires to be on the ground. The association of tailors and carpenters, of which the republic . . . is composed, cannot be equal to the situation into which by the worst of usurpations – an usurpation on *the prerogative of nature* – you attempt to force them. (*Reflections*, 55–6; my emphasis)

Clearly, however flexible we may find Burke's notion of nature elsewhere, it also can possess a degree of rigidity. The invocation of nature here possesses all of the characteristics which have made it a mainstay of ideological argumentation: inevitability, moral rectitude, and scientific verifiability. In the structural metaphor by which he links the class system with an "edifice," Burke seems paradoxically to clear his notion of social degree of any figurative content whatsoever: just as a building cannot stand without its bottom floor, so does a social order depend on the existence of an underclass. The necessity of the class structure thus acquires the strength of natural law. The order of society knows a gravitational force every bit as powerful as that in nature, which will inevitably bring down the airy structure of universal equality just as it would bring down a foundationless building. By appealing to this natural metaphor, Burke is thus able to dismiss any political innovation whatsoever. As he says elsewhere, the new democratic political philosophy requires "a revolution in nature" (*Reflections*, 237); that revolution, like the revolution in France, is impossible for Burke to imagine.

But if Burke's use of a metaphor drawn from nature would seem to grant his political positions the force of natural law, there are moments where the figurativeness, the artfulness, of the reference to nature is highlighted instead. Even in the passage just quoted, as strong an example as can be found in *Reflections* of a reified notion of nature, a discontinuity persists between a physical nature, given and unchangeable, and a social, "second" nature, created by human beings. The "perversity" of the levelers, while attributing a moral value to Burke's natural order, rests uncomfortably beside the structural metaphor, as if Burke were torn between telling the levelers that they *cannot* do something or that they *should not* do something. The figurative character of Burke's reference to nature returns at this point of metaphorical instability, as the "perversion" of the levelers reveals, negatively, the active role of human imagination in the construction of any idea of nature (or of history) whatsoever, thus bringing Burke's metaphor of reified nature crashing to the ground. But lest this example be taken merely as an attempt to read Burke perversely, we might note other Burkean uses of the reference to nature. Of particular interest, both for Burke's general use of a concept of nature and for a consideration of his relation to Blake, is his first work of any importance, *A Vindication of Natural Society* (1756). A first glance at its title would seem to indicate that this book is the sheer opposite of Blake's early illuminated pamphlet "There is No Natural Religion," but closer examination reveals deep similarities between these two career "preludes." Burke's title is ironic, another instance of his willingness to speak in the voice of his opponent, and in addition to placing Burke and Blake on the same side of the issue regarding nature in these two works, it also indicates a similarity of strategy. Blake too, in the "No Natural Religion" pamphlets as well as in "All Religions are One," is willing to use the propositional logic of his philosophic opponents to serve an end far different from theirs. The titles to Blake's pamphlets represent his conclusions, but his means of reaching these conclusions are a combination of serious and mock-logical axioms, each numbered in a manner to satisfy (superficially, at least) the strictest rationalist. Blake's propositions, especially in the [b] version of "No Natural Religion," have a strange way of transmuting into proto-Proverbs of Hell – "The bounded is loathed by its possessor" (E2) – and that indeed is the point, to activate a rationalist discourse of deductive logic until it comes to the point of exceeding itself, of indicating something beyond the boundaries of "natural" reason.

Such is also the case in Burke's *Vindication*, an impersonation of Bolingbroke's natural philosophy for the purpose of revealing its limitations, and, in particular, of discrediting the rationalist dependence on a standard drawn from "nature." The effect of *Vindication*'s "infernal method" of philosophical impersonation, perverse as it may seem as a strategy of argumentation, is to reveal "nature" as itself a figure of speech. The perverse denaturing of nature is, indeed, one measure of Burke's much-contested consistency over the course of his career, a consistency best indicated by his own gnomic proverb from *An Appeal from the New to the Old Whigs*, written the year after the *Reflections* (1791): "Art is man's nature."[18] The similarities between this statement and Blake's early formulation, in "All Religions are One," that "the Poetic Genius is the True Man" (E1), should not be underestimated.

Given the metaphorical quality of Burke's reference to nature, which David Bromwich has characterized as "a strong figure of speech,"[19] we are now in a position to think about what Burke's notion of history has to offer a radical poet such as Blake. First of all, we might turn back to Burke's notion of prejudice which was, as we will remember, the means of transforming "duty" to "a part of . . . nature." The process of establishing and "cherishing" a prejudice now appears more artful than ever:

Many of our men of speculation, instead of exploding general prejudices, employ their sagacity to discover the latent wisdom which prevails in them. If they find what they seek, and they seldom fail, they think it more wise to continue the prejudice, with the reason involved, than to cast away the coat of prejudice and to leave nothing but the naked reason. (*Reflections*, 99)

O'Brien, Bromwich, and others have pointed out the predominance of a quality of "fantasia" in Burke's construction of history, and it applies equally to this discussion of prejudice.[20] The "wisdom" of prejudice, rather than being self-evident, requires "sagacity" to discover. More than a hint of "fantasia" persists in Burke's conditional clause also: "If they find what they seek, and they seldom fail . . ." In short, the figurative quality of Burke's idea of prejudice involves more than his method of expression, his constant recourse to metaphors ("coat of prejudice . . . naked reason"); it also involves the very identification of a line of history by which something of the past is carried over into the present and the future. Burke's dominant metaphor for history in the *Reflections*, that of inheritance, would seem to suggest a reified history, but beneath this figure lies the essential figurativeness of history itself, the extent to which it also is created by a sagacious artist, a "Poetic Genius" who seldom fails to find what he seeks.[21] A full understanding of Burke's "nature" thus makes available a much more "artful" history for the construction of a line of continuity.

The question remains of the relation between this notion of prejudice and a theory of ideology, a concept which, as we have seen, is predeveloped, so to speak, in the Enlightenment critique of prejudice. Burke, however, clearly does not simply critique prejudice, but rather, in his transvaluation of the term, seeks to discover the "latent wisdom" in it. Is this merely the definitive mark of Burke's ideological consciousness, as his critics would have it, that he has learned to stop worrying and love his prejudices? It is rather, I would suggest, the mark of Burke's development of a more thorough-going concept of ideology, one which goes beyond the Enlightenment notion of an easily-dispelled "illusion" confined to the abstractions of religious consciousness. In this context, we might speak of Burke's predevelopment of a notion of "hegemony," because it is this term, particularly in its use by the Italian socialist Antonio Gramsci, which best encapsulates the shift in thinking about ideology here attempted. For Gramsci also, hegemony arises from a sense of dissatisfaction with a concept of ideology which, like the Enlightenment concept of prejudice, grants it only an ephemeral, supplementary existence. Assessing the place of ideology in the classical Marxist framework of base ("structure") and superstructure, Gramsci notes the propositions that lead to a mistaken notion of ideology:

1.   ideology is identified as distinct from the structure, and it is asserted that it is not ideology that changes the structure but vice versa
2.   it is asserted that a given political solution is "ideological" – i.e., that it is not sufficient to change the structure, although it thinks that it can do so; it is asserted that it is useless, stupid, etc.
3.   one then passes to the assertion that every ideology is "pure" appearance, useless, stupid, etc.[22]

In contrast to this "stupid" ideology, Gramsci then imagines an ideology which, like Burke's prejudice, gains stability from its place in an historical tradition:

One must therefore distinguish between historically organic ideologies, those, that is, which are necessary to a given structure, and ideologies that are arbitrary, rationalistic, or "willed." To the extent that ideologies are historically necessary they have a validity which is "psychological"; they "organise" human masses, and create the terrain on which men move, acquire consciousness of their position, struggle, etc. (*Selections*, 376–7)

It is this "historically organic" ideology which, like Burke's prejudice, gives reason its motive force, which Gramsci will elsewhere call, distinguishing it more carefully from the classical formulation of ideology, *hegemony.* Like prejudice, it possesses neither positive nor negative value in the abstract, but only as it forms the basis of organization for a particular historical group, in which case, of course, it carries a great positive or negative charge, depending on whether or not one belongs to that group. Also, like Burke's prejudice, hegemony names much more than a simple illusion of erroneous thinking, an excrescence of consciousness easily dispelled, but instead a deep structure of culture, an ideology "to the bone," which organizes an entire way of life from the ground up. And the source of hegemony's authority, its principle of existence in the absence of any theoretical rationale, is precisely in its historical preexistence, its dependence on the "prejudice" of its bearers.

A final point of similarity between Burke's prejudice and Gramsci's notion of hegemony, their opposition to a merely "rationalistic" notion of ideology, can help us to move towards a fuller consideration of Blake's historical poems and can help us to locate him more precisely in the Revolution controversy in which they participate. Jon Mee has already suggested the dangers in imagining a united Jacobin front in the debates of the 1790s, when in reality there existed a wide spectrum of radical political opinion split, on one axis, along rationalistic and antirationalistic lines.[23] A still more complex picture of the debate can emerge from a comparison of Gramsci's antirationalistic "hegemony," Burke's antitheoretical "prejudice," and Blake's antirational "Poetic Genius." At the very least it can suggest that, in spite of Blake's sympathies with the immediate political goals of the Jacobins during the Revolution controversy, he does not reach his conclusions due to any abstractly deduced notion of the "rights of man," but instead from his allegiance to a principle of continuity much like Burke's notion of prejudice.[24] As the Conclusion to "There is No Natural Religion" [b] has it, "If it were not for the Poetic or Prophetic character. the Philosophic & Experimental would soon be at the ratio of all things

& stand still" (E3). Like the conception of "Individual Identities [which] never change nor cease," the idea of "Poetic or Prophetic character" is a principle of continuity which itself underwrites the potential for coherent change. In contrast, Enlightenment reason ("the Philosophic & Experimental"), which had billed itself and had been commonly accepted as the engine of dramatic Historical change, is revealed as a static concept, unable to do more than "stand still." By means of a typically pregnant pun, Blake reduces Enlightenment *ratio* to a simple fraction, a sterile equation obeying only the rule, as the computer programmers put it, of "garbage in, garbage out." Gramsci's notion of hegemony also must be seen as the moment where the hitherto transparent and causative relation between an economic base and an ideological superstructure reveals itself as inadequate to the explanation of the workings of social movements.[25] Such considerations might also cause us to rethink Burke's pervasive "antitheoreticalism," a trait which has too frequently been taken as merely another indication of his political conservatism.[26] At a fundamental level, these conceptual ties across conventional political lines reveal that a rejection of an undeveloped Enlightenment notion of ideology as "illusion" does not have to express itself only as political conservatism, but instead displays a key insight, common to Burke, Blake and Gramsci alike, as well as to the constitutionalist radicals of the period, that the engine of political change is contained in history itself, that the potential for constructive growth comes not from the denial of cultural heritage, but from its deepening and development.

One last objection might be considered before we turn to a consideration of Blake's own prehistory of revolution, *America: A Prophecy*: the idea that not all traditions are equivalent and that Burke's notion of history does not allow for the kind of transformative change that Blake and Gramsci anticipated under the name of revolution. This is a telling criticism and one that must be squarely faced, but an initial indication that Burke's notion of history is not merely static or, in Mannheim's terms, that his utopian mentality amounts to more than just a conservative valuation of what already exists, emerges from Burke's statement, in the midst of a defence of civil society, that "without . . . civil society man could not by any possibility arrive at the perfection of which his nature is capable, nor even make a remote and faint approach to it" (*Reflections*, 112). While much remains to separate this statement from many of the radical

theories of the 1790s – from William Godwin's call for the elimination of governmental structures in the *Enquiry Concerning Political
Justice* (1793), for instance – it still contains a belief in "perfectibility"
which casts it towards a utopian future and thus towards a conception of the change which will collapse the distance between the
present and that future. We must still consider the limits of Burke's
notions of change and of history as we open them to the challenges
of Blake's poetry, but these limits must not blind us to the broad
similarities of approach between these distinct thinkers. To begin
with, we might note the strange temporal placement of *America*, a
poem seemingly written in apocalyptic urgency and which, indeed,
titles its main section "A Prophecy," but which refers to events some
twenty years before the time of composition. Blake might have found
ample precedent for this writing strategy in both of the biblical
genres to which the poem makes reference: historical scholarship of
the Bible has suggested that Ezekiel, Isaiah, and the other prophets
frequently "predated" their prophecies so that events which had
already happened were "foretold" in detail; and apocalypse,
although usually understood as a record of the last days, also served,
as in the most prominent example of the Book of Revelation as a
commentary on contemporary political events, on, in John's case,
the abuses of Nero's Rome. What both of these biblical precedents
indicate is a concern to establish a history for the present moment,
to lay a line of continuous development which can project society
towards the future. It is, in the terms of yet another type of biblical
writing, to establish a "saving history," a traditional story in which
the deliverances of the past are commemorated in order to connect
them to the crises of the present.[27] And it is this backward turn to
historical precedent in a time of crisis which most profoundly links
the counterrevolutionary Burke of the *Reflections* with the revolutionary Blake of *America*.

Burke's recourse to history in the *Reflections*, to the Glorious
Revolution of 1688, is, of course, undertaken as a cautionary tale, in
order to suggest the ways in which the French Revolution deviates
from the earlier example and to resist Richard Price's invocation of
that precedent for events in France. What is most important for
Burke in the history of the Succession Crisis is precisely the way it
managed to avoid a break with the past, the way it kept history
whole. The effect of the engineers of the Protestant succession was to
preserve the continuity of a line (a metaphor which persists in

Burke), to avert the crisis (the "turning-point") which would take the line in a new direction:

> At no time, perhaps, did the sovereign legislature manifest a more tender regard to [the] fundamental principle of British constitutional policy than at the time of the Revolution, when it deviated from the direct line of hereditary succession. The crown was carried somewhat out of the line in which it had before moved, but the new line was derived from the same stock. It was still a line of hereditary descent, still an hereditary descent in the same blood, though an hereditary descent qualified with Protestantism. (*Reflections*, 24–5)

Burke's metaphor, a geometric one, is once again instructive: the line of William and Mary is both a deviation and not a deviation. It begins "somewhat out of the line" of previous succession, but ultimately derives itself from that line by drawing its continuation "from the same stock." Continuing the geometric metaphor, we might say that the chief accomplishment of the revolution, as Burke sees it, was its ability to establish a new justification of the hereditary line by some skillful constitutional triangulation: that is, the line of succession was henceforth maintained by virtue of two points of reference, hereditary descent and Protestantism. The continuity of the line is thus insured, its future course mapped as an undeviating loyalty to its dual points of origin. The Glorious Revolution is not a revolution as such, in Burke's eyes, but the most subtle of course corrections. For Blake also, writing at a time when the French Revolution had already taken the life of Louis XVI and many others, it is equally important to have recourse to an earlier revolution, not this time in order to dismiss the idea of revolution altogether, but to provide it with a "line" and a saving history. In understanding the backward turn of *America*, we must first recognize that it is written in the knowledge that America's revolution has not spread – despite the predictions – to all the nations of the world. Although Blake has the British soldiers throw down their weapons in the face of Orc's anger (13:5–9, E56), he also knows that Britain's defeat at the hands of her colony has not resulted in the pacification of her foreign policy. In Blake's 1793, despite the "prophecies" of *America*, prisons are not empty in Britain (nor in the US), slaves continue to be traded (in and between both nations), and the franchise has not been extended to the propertyless (in Britain) nor to women (in either country). The apocalyptic joy of the poem must always be read in the light of this historical disconfirmation, not indeed as an exercise in pessimism but as a way of suggesting that the promises of that earlier struggle have yet to be fulfilled, a fulfillment they will find only in the medium of history, as Blake's continuation of the line from America to Europe and eventually to Asia serves to show.

Blake's historical turn to the American Revolution can thus be understood in its relation to Burke, not only because in so doing Blake has reverted to a struggle with which Burke sympathized, but also because the poem represents an attempt to historicize, to narrativize, the explosive revolutionary energies of the past, to channel them for use in the present, however differently the two thinkers may have interpreted that present. Such a view of *America* requires a more complex interpretation of the poem's representation of revolution, however, not necessarily positing a Burkean rejection but rather a critique of some revolutionary premises.[28] First among these premises is the notion that revolution represents an end to history itself, that like Orc, Blake's fiery spirit of revolution, the revolutionist can claim that "the times are ended" (8:2, E54). The effect of *America* is to put this declamation in a narrative context, to project the point of revolutionary decision into a line of historical renewal extending even to Blake's present. But if Orc's catastrophic notion of revolution is qualified, so also is the view of Albion's Angel who, in his excoriation of Orc, suggests that revolution is merely a stagnant "renewal" of what has already existed:

> Ah vision from afar! Ah rebel form that rent the ancient
> Heavens; Eternal Viper self-renew'd, rolling in clouds
> I see thee in thick clouds and darkness on America's shore.
> Writhing in pangs of abhorred birth; red flames the crest rebellious
> And eyes of death; the harlot womb oft opened in vain
> Heaves in enormous circles, now the times are return'd upon thee,
> Devourer of thy parent, now thy unutterable torment renews.
> (9:14–20, E54)[29]

Against Orc's notion of a unique event, an end to history in revolution, is posed this other view of the impossibility of uniqueness, that, in the world of politics at least, there is nothing new under the sun. Each of these views represents one of the etymological strands of the word *revolution*, which, as Raymond Williams has traced it, has referred both to the circular movements of planets revolving around a fixed center and to the cataclysmic rebellion of one class (or group) against another.[30] Blake's punning imagination is no doubt aware of

these multiple meanings, but his effort in *America* is to critique both
of them as antihistorical, to show how each falls short of a saving
history which allows for coherent change. In each case, the idea of
revolution being proposed seems to have as much to do with the
mentality of the proposer as it does with revolution itself. The case of
Orc will be considered momentarily, but in regards to the more
obvious villain of the piece, one might note that the Angel of
Albion's views on revolution are here implicated in a more general
misogynistic perspective, in that fear of sex and the body which
characterizes Orc's appearance as "the harlot womb oft open[ing] in
vain / Heav[ing] in enormous circles." Albion's Angel is, in other
words, an early version of the neurotic patriarch, the Noboddaddy
whom Blake imagined ruling the orthodox world, and he thus sees
every new arrival on the scene as a potential "Devourer of [his]
parent." Even more telling for a critique of this broadly counterrevolutionary perspective is the fact that this indictment of revolution as compulsive repetition occurs in a speech which itself uses a
single line – "Sound! sound! my loud war-trumpets & alarm my
Thirteen Angels!" – four times in one plate (lines 1, 13, 21, 26).
Whether or not the Angel of Albion is fighting the "same" Orc he
has faced before is left undetermined in the poem, but we can be
relatively sure that the Angel's hysterical reaction, the reflex response
of a blinkered autocrat, has occurred before and will occur again.

But what are we to make of the presentation of Orc, who, in most
accounts of the poem, is taken as Blake's apotheosis of the spirit of
revolution? Surely there is something sublimely heroic and cathartic
in his sudden appearance over a "sick" Albion and a "faint[ing]"
America:

> [I]n the red clouds rose a Wonder o'er the Atlantic sea;
> Intense! naked! a Human fire fierce glowing, as the wedge
> Of iron heated in the furnace; his terrible limbs were fire
> With myriads of cloudy terrors banners dark & towers
> Surrounded; heat but not light went thro' the murky atmosphere.
>
> (4:7–11, E53)

In bold outlines, Orc emerges as the spirit of action, appearing
without precedent on the scene, characterizable only as "a Wonder,"
and thus, from the perspective of the Earthly wonderers, seemingly
outside of the categories of causation and continuity. But that last
descriptor, of Orc's bringing "heat but not light," suggests an

incompleteness about Blake's revolutionary representative, a sense in which Orc's titanic interruption of British colonial tyranny must be extended and developed in order to be fully realized. That theme of heat's supplement in light becomes even more important in the imagery of Orc's first speech:

> The morning comes, the night decays, the watchmen leave their stations;
> The grave is burst, the spices shed, the linen wrapped up;
> The bones of death, the cov'ring clay, the sinews shrunk & dry'd.
> Reviving shake, inspiring move, breathing! awakening!
> Spring like redeemed captives when their bonds & bars are burst
> Let the slave grinding at the mill, run out into the field
> Let him look up into the heavens & laugh in the bright air;
> Let the inchained soul shut up in darkness and in sighing,
> Whose face has never seen a smile in thirty weary years;
> Rise and look out, his chains are loose, his dungeon doors are open.
>
> (6:1–10, E53)

This bracing speech has been convincingly called (by David Erdman) "Blake's poetic paraphrase of the Declaration of Independence,"[31] and it stands as a high point in Blake's poetic retelling of history. But it is important not to lose track of the genre of speech to which it belongs in the impressive vigor of its imagery. It is indeed a "declaration" and, like the historical document to which it refers, it stands as the *beginning* of the process of independence rather than its end. It is tempting to close the gap between this representation of political independence and its fulfillment in historical time, if not least for the way the verbal tense of the passage seems to assume such an equivalence, going from an ecstatic present – "The morning comes" – to a triumphant retrospective – "The Sun has left his blackness, & has found a fresher morning." We must understand such utterances as special cases of what we might call the "prophetic tense," a speech genre which attempts to make something so in the saying of it. But we must also not be surprised if the performatives of this being who sheds "heat but not light" – "Let the slave grinding at the mill . . . ," "Let the inchained soul . . . ," "let his wife and children . . ." – lack the divine power of an earlier *Fiat lux*. In fact, as we shall discover in comparing the "divine" and the human levels of this mythic poem, one thing which is particularly called into question is the relevance of divine performatives for human history. A declaration (of independence or of anything else) is indeed a kind of performative utterance, but not one which enacts itself in its speaking; it is, rather, a promise for the future, a commitment on the part of the declarers to create a history for themselves and their posterity. Not only do Orc's forecasts of incipient light fail to be followed by their immediate enactment in the larger narrative context of the poem, but the other predictions, of liberty, of joy, even of resurrection, can only be fulfilled with the participation of their human actors. Orc's divine performative, seemingly outside the frame of history as much as Elohim's creative word, will have to enter the stream of human history before it can be fulfilled.

A similar qualification of Orc's ability to reconstitute society in a single revolutionary gesture is suggested by the larger structure of the poem, its division into a "Preludium" (plates 1–2) and "A Prophecy" (plates 3–16). Readers of Blake are familiar with his "Arguments" which do not argue, but the relation between the two sections of the poem is particularly telling for a consideration of Blake's view of historical change. The "Preludium," a difficult mythic set piece, tells the "story" of Orc's imprisonment, subsequent bursting of his chains, and, finally, his rape/liberation of "the shadowy daughter of Urthona." Clearly, such a rendering of revolutionary energy, despite its earthly references to "Africa," the "American plains," "Canada," "Mexico," "Peru" and "the South-sea," is of dubious usefulness as an explanation of the historical emergence of revolutionary movements. The ambiguous status of Orc's congress with the daughter of Urthona itself suggests some of the shortcomings of the passage, her response to his "seiz[ing] the panting struggling womb" (2:3, E52) beginning with joyful recognition – "I know thee, I have found thee & I will not let thee go" (2:7) – but ending with despair – "This is eternal death; and this the torment long foretold" (2:17). An indication of Blake's own ambiguous feelings towards the scene of the Preludium can be found in the four lines which, in some copies, appear beneath the picture of Orc's emergence from the ground, but in other copies have been erased:

The stern bard ceas'd, asham'd of his own song; enrag'd he swung
His harp aloft sounding, then dash'd its shining frame against
A ruin'd pillar in glittring fragments; silent he turn'd away,
And wander'd down the vales of Kent in sick & drear lamentings.

(2:18–21, E52)

Erdman dates these lines to 1795, claiming they express Blake's "despair in the prophecy,"[32] but might they not rather express a despair in the Preludium, since that is where they occur? An equivalence between Preludium and Prophecy must not be presumed, but rather, even if they are taken to represent roughly parallel events of revolutionary liberation, we must pay heed to the differences in the manner of presentation. Against the mythic, static atemporal rendering of the Preludium, where Orc's breaking of his chains is rendered as a causeless primary act of violence against the female, we must pose the more narrative, earthly references of the Prophecy, its reference to the recognizable human agents of "Washington, Franklin, Paine & Warren, Gates, Hancock & Green" (3:4, E52). Rather than regarding the Preludium as an introduction to what follows, we might better think of it as a first draft, whose stationary, ahistorical approach to political events – well represented by the frozen sculpture of the frontispiece (figure 8) – is rejected in favor of the temporal, historical approach of the Prophecy.

The Prophecy of *America*, the main body of this poetic text, represents some of Blake's most narrative verse, the closest he comes (except perhaps for the unilluminated *The French Revolution*) to a novel-in-verse. Compared, for example, to the operatic *Visions of the Daughters of Albion*, *America* seems quite full of the events and twists of fate that constitute the narrative, the historical, aesthetic: the "Guardian Prince of Albion" arises as "a dragon form" over England (3:13–4:1); Orc, in response, arises as a gathering of red clouds over the Atlantic (4:2–11); after exchanged speeches, the scene shifts to a sub-Atlantic meeting place, where the Angel of Boston repudiates his symbols of office and joins the rebellion, inspiring the other angels to do likewise (10:5–12:12); the royalists in America surrender to Washington, British soldiers throwing down their swords and muskets (13:1–9). But although this summary possesses some of the ins and outs we have come to associate with narrative, it also raises questions about just how important the human level of action is in *America*. In spite of the somewhat startling effect of Blake's inclusion of that string of historical names immediately after the Preludium, there are moments in the poem when these characters seem to be standing stiffly beneath the scene of the real action, the sulphurous heavens where Orc and Albion's Angel exchange charge and countercharge. In more general terms, this disjunction between the earthly and the heavenly scene raises the same questions we were compelled to raise for Burke's notion of history, questions which involve whether the source of historical change resides in

8 Plate 1 of *America: A Prophecy.*

human agency or whether it must be assigned to some motive power beyond the human sphere. As we saw in connection to Burke, these questions involve the very character of the historical line also, whether it is to be conceived of as a natural, and therefore inevitable, course of events or whether it possesses a figurative, malleable existence, created by its human agents and actors. And although we have already observed some connections between Burke's historical "fantasia," his figurative construction of history, and Blake's notion of the centrality of "Poetic Genius" to human affairs, it is precisely here, in the matter of the degree of human activity involved in the creation of history, where they ultimately part company. For if Burke does allow some role for human "prejudice" in the creation and maintenance of an historical line, he does not seem to grant every sector of human society the same historical force. Historical "fantasia," like property, is, in Burke's view, the prerogative of a certain class, and if he manages to undermine the structured difference between a "natural" and a figurative history, between a level of divine and of human causation, he nonetheless recreates these distinctions in maintaining an hierarchical relation between what we might call the "historical" and the "non-historical" classes. Raymond Williams has suggested something similar when he notes that Burke's thought shifts from an "essential reverence for society," as the cultural world created by human beings, to a misplaced respect for the state in its administrative capacity.[33] But we might make the same point by saying that, although Burke can claim an early notion of ideology as hegemony, he possesses no idea of "counterhegemony," of that alternative cultural construct which, as Gramsci outlined, is always locked in combat with the dominant culture for control of everyday life and its history. Blake participates in the counterhegemonic discourse of his time by suggesting, along with, for instance, Joseph Ritson and the other radical invokers of historical precedent, that more than one history can be at work in the development of social changes, and that the sphere of human-created history is a contested one, the ground of "revolution" itself.[34]

From this perspective, *America* traces not so much the exchanges of the two superhuman actors, but the gradual "becoming-human" of history, the descent from the clouds to the ground of an historical agency which, in its appearance as Orc, is initially described as "a Human fire" (4:8, E53), but which requires the work of the poem to be fully humanized. The figure of fire, and the later figure of pestilence, themselves indicate Blake's transvaluation of Burke's notion of human agency, for Burke also had used these figures in speaking of revolution, although the French Revolution in his case. In opening his criticism of Richard Price's public praise for the French Revolution, Burke justifies his writing of the *Reflections* in a typically figurative manner: "Whenever our neighbor's house is on fire, it cannot be amiss for the engines to play a little on our own" (*Reflections*, 10). Earlier in the same year he wrote the *Reflections*, in the speech he gave to Parliament on 9 February, he uses an alternative figure to describe current events in France, as compared to their past propensity for excess authoritarianism:

This day the evil is totally changed in France: but there is an evil there. The disease is altered; but the vicinity of the two countries remains, and must remain, and the natural mental habits of mankind are such, that the present distemper of France is far more likely to be contagious than the old one.[35]

Fire and plague, interestingly enough, are the figures Blake uses for revolution also, but in an entirely reconfigured way. The pages of *America* are singed with "the fires of Orc," spreading from his initial appearance to the general conflagration which covers the scene by the end, but disease, contagion, plague, has a more specific role. In one of the poem's many apocalyptic tropes, plague enters the poem with the Angel of Albion's plan to defeat the revolutionists with the "diseases of the earth" (13:14, E56). But in the central narrative event of the poem, the key revolutionary peripeteia, the plagues are turned back upon their originator:

Then had America been lost, o'erwhelm'd by the Atlantic,
And Earth had lost another portion of the infinite,
But all rush together in the night in wrath and raging fire
The red fires rag'd! the plagues recoil'd! then rolld they back with fury
On Albion's Angels; then the Pestilence began in streaks of red
Across the limbs of Albion's Guardian.   (14:17–15:2, E56)

Erdman identifies Blake's use of plague imagery with the Great Pestilence of 1348,[36] but might not its historical significance also lie in the way it changes contemporary images of revolution? Pursuing the practice that Jon Mee has labeled, following Claude Levi-Strauss, Blake's "*bricolage*,"[37] his effect here is to do in discourse much the same thing the revolutionists do in the poem: to use the imagery of the dominant culture against it, to "recoil" the image of plague in order to create a counterhegemony, an alternative histor- ical use of imagery already at large in the revolution controversy.[38]

A comparison of Burke's and Blake's alternative uses of plague and fire imagery, beyond simply revealing their differing opinions of contemporary events in France, ultimately distinguishes between their ideas of history itself. It is surely not coincidental that when Burke turns to criticism of French political innovations his rhetorical figures take on a quasi-natural reference. Where the historical line of the British Constitution can be characterized as a "legacy" or an "inheritance," the conscious passing of privileges and responsibilities from one generation to the next, the spreading of revolutionary ideas can only be compared to a natural firestorm or to the unwilled spread of contagion. Blake's *bricolage* not only transvalues these negative images for revolution, but reveals that they have been all along, even in Burke, figures of continuity and transmission, images of cultural hegemony, although here in the form of a counter- hegemony resistant to dominant practices. What is finally important about fire and plague is not that they burn or blight, but that they *spread*, that each figures a human-created consensus, an historical moment, which projects itself towards both the past and the future. Fittingly enough, it is with the recoiling of the plagues that the human actors of Blake's poem take the initiative away from their divine counterparts. No longer is the drama confined to the supernatural agents, not even to the named historical figures of plate 3, but instead to the "all" who "rush together in the night in wrath and raging fire," an "all" glossed in the preceding lines as "[t]he citizens of New York," "[t]he mariners of Boston," "[t]he scribe of Pennsylvania," "[t]he builder of Virginia" (14:13–16, E56).[39] The remainder of plate 15, with its descriptions of the spread of plague in England and the spread of fiery revolution in America, is dominated by unnamed human actors ("the millions," "the fierce Americans," "the Priests," "the females"), ending definitively only with Urizen's counterrevolutionary appearance on the last plate of the poem. What this penultimate movement of the poem indicates is a huma- nizing of history, a grasping of the motive force of history in human hands, and the contravention of this movement in the last plate of the poem, as Urizen's snows begin to fall on the revolutionary scene, represents not only the end of revolutionary hope, but the reimposi- tion of a superhuman, quasi-natural agent of history. The Urizen who thus dismally closes the poem could indeed be a figure for Burke, not simply the Burke who opposed the French Revolution, but the Burke who withdrew historical agency from the unnamed masses, who dismissed revolutionary activity as a natural event as unpredictable as fire or plague, or here, as snow. But the Burke of historical "fantasia," of human-created history (and, not coincidentally, of support for the American cause), might also be glossed in the figure of Boston's Angel, who, in a gesture much like Burke's rejection of George III's position in America, declares "no more I follow, no more obedience pay" (11:15, E55).[40] Burke's legacy to Blake, like his legacy to liberal politics generally, is fully complex enough to allow for these opposed alternatives.

The importance of history for revolutionary activity, and in Blake's continuing cycle of historical poems, is indicated by Washington's speech to his fellows at the opening of *America*:

> Friends of America look over the Atlantic sea;
> A bended bow is lifted in heaven, & a heavy iron chain
> Descends link by link from Albions cliffs across the sea to bind
> Brothers & sons of America, till our faces pale and yellow;
> Heads deprest, voices weak, eyes downcast, hands work- bruis'd,
> Feet bleeding on the sultry sands, and the furrows of the whip
> Descend to generations that in future times forget.   (3:6–12, E52)

The choice, as Blake here poses it, is not between the burden of history and the freedom of transcendent revolutionary action, but between two forms of continuity: the line of the whip and the chain, and the line of historical memory here advocated by Washington. Although both are versions of continuity, the former oppressive line is characterized specifically by unconsciousness, by a "forgetting" which it is Washington's purpose to resist. It is then to the conscious, humanly willed history of memory, the fantasia which provides revolution with a line of continuity, that we must turn to understand Blake's poetic projects after *America*, in *The Song of Los* and later in the unilluminated manuscript of *The Four Zoas*. For Blake's widening of his continental scheme to include not only America and Europe, but also Africa and Asia, represents his effort to make the "all" of *America* extend even to peoples who had previously been denied a history-making function. Blake's early and continual intent to have *America* stand as only one element of a larger historical narrative is indicated most powerfully by an engraving he executed for John

9 *Europe Supported by Africa and America*

Stedman's *Narrative of a Five Years' expedition . . . on the Wild Coast of South America* (figure 9). *Europe Supported by Africa and America*, engraved one year before the publication of *America*, pictures the shackled allegorical figures for the two colonized continents[41] supporting a feeble but seemingly content Europe. The garland which unites them, framing from below the composition of their three figures, could stand as the line of historical progress, beginning with Africa (Blake's constant point of origin), continuing to America (here an Amerindian maiden) and ending in the left hand of the weakened Europe. Africa and America are the historical precedents which will sustain Europe's progressive journey forward, a journey which concludes, as we shall soon see, in the fourth continent of Asia. For what seemed from the perspective of *America* to be the conclusion of Blake's historical narrative – the pan-European revolution predicted in that poem's last plate – seems, from the perspective of *Europe*, a year later, merely one more stage in the inexorable progress of man. *Europe* ends with a revolutionary call to "the strife of blood" (15:11, E66) even more ambivalent than *America*'s qualified revolutionism. More clearly than ever, Blake propels the reader's interest past the end of the *Europe* poem, past the bloody revolutionary wars about to beset that continent, and forward to a fuller realization in the passage of time. The engraving of 1792 thus serves as the ideal transition to a fuller consideration of the poems Blake would use to frame this historical narrative, the "Africa" and "Asia" of *The Song of Los* (1795).

The similarities between Blake's "four harp" song (*SongL*:1–3, E67) and the numerous progress poems of the eighteenth century are unmistakable, but the differences are perhaps even more instructive. We might take as the prototype of the genre James Thomson's *Liberty* (1736), for that poem follows the pattern that would be repeated in Thomas Gray's "The Progress of Poesy," William Collins's "Ode to Liberty" and even Shelley's "Ode to Liberty" of 1820. We should not be troubled by the mingling of poetry's and liberty's progresses in these poems, for the coexistence of the two had been established as a convention long before Shelley's political claims for drama in *A Defence of Poetry*. With minor variations, the narrative line of these poems traces the progress of poetry or liberty from its origin in Greece to its continuation in Rome to consummation in "blest BRITANNIA."[42] Admittedly, Gray's poem does make reference to "Chili's boundless forests" where Poesy "deigns to hear the savage

Youth repeat / In loose numbers wildly sweet / Their feather-cinctured Chiefs, and dusky Loves,"[43] but for the most part the pattern is a wholly European one, as Gray's "Progress" goes on to make clear:

> Till the sad Nine in Greece's evil hour
> Left their Parnassus for the Latian plains.
> Alike they scorn the pomp of tyrant-Power,
> And coward Vice, that revels in her chains.
> When Latium had her lofty spirit lost,
> They sought, oh Albion! next thy sea-encircled coast.
> ("Progress of Poesy" lines 77–82)

The appearance of Blake's characteristic name for England and for the "One Man" who would appear in the later poetry should immediately signal to us his participation in but radical difference from this poetic tradition. For the Blake of *America*, *Europe*, and *The Song of Los* in particular, the jingoistic celebration of England's liberty is entirely inappropriate. Blake distinguishes Tyranny rather than Liberty as the leading characteristic of "Albion's angel"; positive identifications with Albion and with the "green and pleasant land" of Blake's birth would await the composition of more personal, less outwardly political poems. But what is perhaps more telling in any account of Blake's differences with eighteenth-century progress poetry is his refusal to confine the narrative line to the European continent, his dual refusal to acknowledge Greece as the cradle of liberty and England as its final destination, its "last Abode."[44] Blake's relentless narrativity at this stage in his career pushes the origin of Liberty back beyond its supposed Grecian birthplace and its destination beyond the domestic environs of England.

Put in the language of contemporary academic politics, Blake's effect in positing Africa as the birthplace of liberty is to de-Europeanize the literary canon of the progress poem, or, in the terms we have been employing, to suggest a counterhegemonic version of the history of liberty. Although clearly following biblical precedent for this attribution – "Adam stood in the garden of Eden: / And Noah on the mountains of Ararat" (*SongL*3:6–7, E67)[45] – the political intent of such a gesture, in a time when abolition was being hotly debated, cannot be ignored. Supporting this claim is the persistence of Blake's interest in Africa as originally free and yet capable of restoring freedom worldwide, a concern for Blake as late as the composition of *Jerusalem*:

> When Africa in sleep
> Rose in the night of Beulah, and bound down the Sun & Moon
> His friends cut his strong chains, & overwhelm'd his dark
> Machines in fury & destruction, and the Man reviving repented
> He wept before his wrathful brethren, thankful & considerate
> For their well timed wrath. But Albions sleep is not
> Like Africa's: and his machines are woven with his life.
>
> (40:19–25, E187–8)

The African, by his unique historical position, has the power to make the "Man" of Europe repent. Like the biblical remnant saved from prophecies of destruction, the African is to be distinguished from the Englishman, whose sleep is "not like Africa's," and whose limitations are more than skin-deep, "woven with his life." The African, in Hegelian and Marxian terms, is a world-historical individual, and Blake recognizes his special place in the narrative of world progress.

However, although Africa is originally unfallen, the site of the Edenic garden and also of Los's retrospective song (3:2–3, E67), the story of "Africa" is that of the gradual diminution of the human: "The human race began to wither, for the healthy built / Secluded places, fearing the joys of Love / And the diseas'd only propogated" (3:25–7, E67). The main event of "Africa" is the Fall of Man, "[t]il like a dream Eternity was obliterated & erased" (4:4, E67). By a little geographical transplantation, Blake places "Newton & Locke . . . Rousseau & Voltaire" (4:17–18, E68) in Africa and consolidates that continent as a representation of all that occurs before man attempts to escape from the Fall. The articulation, then, between "Africa" and *America*, the site of man's first revolutionary gesture, is the line which ends the former poem and begins the latter: "The Guardian Prince of Albion burns in his nightly tent" (*SongL* 4:21, E68; *A*3:1, E52). But, as we have seen, Blake's narrative line finds no resting place in either *America* or *Europe*, and so the progression must be followed to "Asia." That poem begins with the Asiatic despots responding to Los's call to "the strife of blood" which ended *Europe*:

> The Kings of Asia heard
> The howl rise up from Europe!
> And each ran out from his Web;
> From his ancient woven Den;

> For the darkness of Asia was startled
> At the thick-flaming, thought-creating fires of Orc.
>   (*SongL*6:1–6, E68)

The spider-kings follow with a series of repressive proposals designed "[t]o turn man from his path" (6:23, E69), but the progress towards redemption continues as relentlessly as did the progress of degradation.

It is at this point, the point of conversion from fall to redemption, from ideology to utopia, that Blake's narrative meets its most profound difficulty, the difficulty, in effect, of positing a utopia within a theory of progress. The mark of this difficulty is the *suddenness*, the non-narrative, unarticulated shock of the point of conversion:

> For Adam, a mouldering skeleton
> Lay bleach'd on the garden of Eden;
> And Noah as white as snow
> On the mountains of Ararat.
>
> Then the thunders of Urizen bellow'd aloud
> From his woven darkness above.
>
> Orc raging in European darkness
> Arose like a pillar of fire above the Alps
> Like a serpent of fiery flame!   (7:20–8, E69)

Blake has here attempted to represent, on the continent of Asia, a revolutionary culmination of all of time that will not simply result in "more of the same": he has combined man's origin in "Africa" (Adam's skeleton in Eden, Noah on Mount Ararat), with the Urizenic snows that fall at the end of *America* and *Europe*'s Alpine scenery. This time, as the text goes on to relate, Orc's revolutionary fires will finally result in a resurrection of man's fallen abilities:

> Forth from the dead dust rattling bones to bones
> Join: shaking convuls'd the shivring clay breathes
> And all flesh naked stands: Fathers and Friends;
> Mothers and Infants; Kings and Warriors.   (7:31–4, E69)

But the mark of Blake's dissatisfaction with this utopian conclusion is the unexplained suddenness of Orc's appearance on the global revolutionary stage, "like a pillar of fire," a conscious or unconscious echo of Orc's emergence in *America* as "a Human fire fierce glowing," which, as we have seen, itself required narrative qualification. The narrative articulations between "Africa" and *America, America* and *Europe, Europe* and "Asia," are all for nought when the point arrives for utopia's conclusive arrival. The mute blank space between Urizen's ideological thunders and Orc's utopian raging stands as the symbol of Blake's inability to definitively narrativize the conversion from fall to redemption, his inability to maintain the narrative line of progress from ideology to utopia. Even this seemingly final "conclusion," leaving Blake no other continent on which to pursue his progressive narrative, elicits from the poet an ominous murmur which qualifies the certainty of "the end of time":

> The Song of Los is Ended.
> Urizen Wept.   (7:41–2, E70)

Unable to rest with the unsatisfactory ending of his utopian narrative, Blake recalls the Urizenic snows which fell as tears at the end of *America* and which necessitated Revolution's exodus to Europe. Africa–America–Europe–Asia: the narrative line is more expansive, more encompassing, than that of the traditional Greece–Rome–England progress poem of the eighteenth century, but, as Blake realized, that line of global progress finally traces the circle of fallen ideology, of "finite revolutions" circular and serpent-formed.

III

We must let ourselves be drawn into the circle and then we must try to make the circle a spiral. (Paul Ricoeur, *Lectures on Ideology and Utopia*[46])

By 1798, the American revolutionary spirit celebrated in *America* had been effectively squashed by the repressive Alien and Sedition Acts. In "the vineyards of red France" (*E*15:2, E66), looked to expectantly at the end of *Europe*, the Directory had buried any hopes of progress beneath a corrupt and self-interested bureaucracy. The *coup d'état* of 18 Brumaire was only a year away, the reimposition of empire only six years away. In short, the narrative of progress which informs Blake's optimistic historical poems had been revealed as the naive prelude to a tyrannic "circling back," mere wishful thinking which could in no way exceed the bounds of fallen ideology. It is important to note that Burke himself had anticipated this circular ending to the events in France as early as 1790, in the form of a dire warning of a return to monarchy, but a monarchy worsened by totalitarianism and cruelty:

[I]f the present project of a republic should fail, all securities to a moderated freedom fail along with it; all the indirect restraints which mitigate despotism are removed, insomuch that if monarchy should ever again obtain an entire ascendency in France, under this or any other dynasty, it will probably be, if not voluntarily tempered at setting out by the wise and virtuous counsels of the prince, the most completely arbitrary power that has ever appeared on earth. This is to play a most desperate game. (*Reflections*, 217)

In the warning of a circling back to monarchy, but a monarchy qualified by despotism, Burke provides a dystopian alternative to the utopian narrative of progress, a downward spiral which interprets history as the eternal fall of mankind. To interpret history in this manner is to look at the past with the eyes of Walter Benjamin's "Angelus Novus," eternally blown forward while the ruins of time accumulate: "This storm irresistibly propels him into the future to which his back is turned, while the pile of debris before him grows skyward. This storm is what we call progress."[47] Or, to adopt a Blakean analogue, it is to imagine the Mental Traveller as a mere tracer of circles, caught between the antinomies of young and old, male and female, the progressive reduced to the circular.

Blake's loss of faith in the narrative of progress is broadly indicated by the turn his writing takes after *The Song of Los*, by his deviation from the narrative line he had established in his quartet of historical pieces. The later Lambeth books, in their parodic re-shaping of the scriptural narrative of creation and deliverance, the saving histories of the Pentateuch, go so far as to undermine the fundamental narrative template of Judeo-Christian culture itself. We have already discussed in chapter 1, the universal ideology depicted in *The Book of Urizen*, a portrait of "arbitrary power" every bit as prescient as Burke's predictions for the tyrannical end of the French Revolution. The Genesis in Blake's "Bible of Hell," *Urizen* employs a narrative framework only more convincingly to discredit narrative altogether, to tell the story of a civilization whose only "progress" was, like Benjamin's, the progressive accumulation of ruins. *The Book of Ahania*, the Exodus of the infernal Bible, parodies its model's deliverance narrative by ironically delivering mankind up to "Ur-izen's slumbers of abstraction" (4:11, E87), to the fallen body and its fallen perceptions. *Ahania*'s only response to the degradation of the present is its title character's unabashed nostalgia for a vanished time of "golden palace[s]" and "ivory bed[s]" (5:3–4, E89), a recourse to the consolation of the "Daughters of Memory" which the later Blake would certainly have condemned. *The Book of Los*, the last of the Lambeth prophecies, completes the fallen circle of this part of Blake's career by leaving mankind in the grips of a seemingly inescapable "Human Illusion / In darkness and deep clouds involvd" (5:55–6, E94). The line of narrative progress would thus seem to have turned back upon itself in the form of a limiting circle, the "horizon" of mankind's perception, or, at best, a spiral progressing only downwards.

It is within this sphere of possibility – or, rather impossibility – that Blake undertook the writing of his unengraved epic *The Four Zoas*, more properly known in its original conception as *Vala or the Death and Judgement of the Ancient Man a Dream of Nine Nights*. It is important to retain this original title at least provisionally, for it contains within it the contradictory forms of imagining the fallen world which characterize both Blake's pessimistic vision in the *Vala* poem and the more optimistic formulation of its revision as *The Four Zoas*. Specifically, it imagines Albion's fall both as a conclusive and permanent fate – a "Death" to be followed only by "Judgement" – and as a preliminary and temporary state – a "Dream" from which Albion, we may well imagine, will awake. The persistence of a concept of death in *Vala*, of the inescapability of man's fallen condition, is consistent with the general spirit of Blake's "first draft" of the poem which would eventually become *The Four Zoas*. Blake portrays, in Burke's words, the "desperate game" of revolution's inevitable degeneration into despotism, Orc's transformation into the tyrannic Urizen. The middle Nights of the poem provide Frye with a standard text for his exposition of the Orc cycle: "the birth and binding of Orc, Urizen exploring his dens, and the crucifixion of Orc."[48] Even Urizen laments the necessity of the never-ending recurrence of the past, the circular repetition compulsion of ideology:

> Can I not leave this world of Cumbrous wheels
> Circle oer Circle nor on high attain a void
> Where self sustaining I may view all things beneath my feet
> Or sinking thro these Elemental wonders swift to fall
> I thought perhaps to find an End a world beneath of voidness
> Whence I might travel round the outside of this Dark confusion.
> (*FZ*72:22–7, E349)

Like his spiritual father in science, Archimedes, Urizen is searching for a point outside of the ideological earth from which to move it. But in this ideological world of "Circle oer Circle," the utopian point of leverage is truly "nowhere" to be found.

Confirmation of this sense of irredeemable fallenness in *Vala* is to be found in its discussion of time and, in particular, in its treatment of Blake's allegorical figure for time, Los. In *Vala*, the model of time as progress which had informed the historical poems has been dropped for a model of time as static and repressive, the metaphor for which is Los's "chains of sorrow" (*FZ*53:6, E335). This image from "Night the Fourth" partly recapitulates a similar element of *The Book of Urizen*, where Los the "Eternal Prophet" was pictured "forging chains new & new / Numb'ring with links. hours, days & years" (*BU*10:17–18, E75). Los's task in *Vala* is the same as in *The Book of Urizen* – the forging of a body for the chaotic Urizen – but superadded to the earlier descriptions are images of circularity which express the rejection of an idea of progress:

> Round him Los rolld furious
> His thunderous wheels from furnace to furnace. tending diligent
> The contemplative terror. frightend in his scornful sphere
> Frightend with cold infectious madness. in his hand the thundering
> Hammer of Urthona. forming under his heavy hand the hours
> The days & years. in chains of iron round the limbs of Urizen
> Linkd hour to hour & day to night & night to day & year to year
> In periods of pulsative furor. mills he formd & works
> Of many wheels resistless in the power of dark Urthona.
>
> (*FZ*52:25–53:4, E335)

Instead of a Burkean line of progress from Africa to America to Europe to Asia, time is now figured as "chains of iron" linking "hour to hour . . . & year to year" or as "mills . . . Of many wheels." The abandonment of an explicitly historical subject matter in *Vala* can at least partly be attributed to this transformation in Blake's idea of time: if ideologies cannot be surpassed by a fidelity to the line of progress, the progression of history, what is the point of depicting history at all? If the thesis that "ideology has no history" is replaced with the thesis that "all history is ideology," there remains no value in separating one moment from another. Indeed, the statement that "all history is ideology" is not far from saying that "there is no history," thereby justifying the lack of historical detail in *Vala*. Los's "chains of sorrow" threaten to bind fallen man to an "Eternal Death" which admits of no possibility for change.

A peculiar transformation of the "chains of sorrow," however, can equally stand as the transformation of the circular *Vala* into the newly progressive *The Four Zoas.* I refer to the Seven Eyes of God section from "Night the Eighth," the first appearance of an idea which would occupy Blake for the remainder of his poetic career.[49] Given the importance of this formulation, we do well to review what initially appears a needlessly obscure passage:

> [T]hose in Eden sent Lucifer for their Guard
> Lucifer refusd to die for Satan & in pride he forsook his charge
> Then they sent Molech Molech was impatient They sent
> Molech impatient They sent Elohim who created Adam
> To die for Satan Adam refusd but was compelld to die
> By Satans art. Then the Eternals Sent Shaddai
> Shaddai was angry Pachad descended Pachad was terrified
> And then they Sent Jehovah who leprous stretched his hand to Eternity
> Then Jesus Came & Died willing beneath Tirzah & Rahab.
>
> (*FZ*115:42–50, E381)

In an apparently late addition to "Night the First,"[50] Blake refers to these seven figures as "the Seven / Eyes of God & the Seven lamps of the Almighty," who surround the fallen Man "[t]ill the time of the End" (19:9–10, E312). The conjunction of the Seven Eyes with "Seven lamps of the Almighty" reminds us, not surprisingly, of the figure in the midst of the "seven golden candlesticks" in the first chapter of Saint John's Revelation, and of the recurrence there of sevenfold figures for heavenly dispensation – the seven seals, the seven trumpets, the seven thunders, the seven vials.[51] As such, it also reminds us of a tradition of biblical exegesis which interpreted the imagery of Revelation as an obscure account of earthly history. As Ernest Tuveson discusses it, the contribution of late seventeenth- and eighteenth-century historiographers was to recover history from the medieval and Renaissance doctrine of universal decline, supposedly shadowed forth in Revelation, and to replace it with a cyclical theory of historical progress.[52] Blake's strategy in "Night the Eighth" might thus be seen as his refiguring apocalyptic imagery as more than just an historical accumulation of plagues – the view of Revelation dominant in the Middle Ages – and to reorder it as a linear series of cycles, in which figures are consecutively "sent" from

Eden but "refuse to die for Satan," until "Jesus Came & Died willing."[53]

Historical parallels for the Seven Eyes have long since been well established by Northrop Frye,[54] but it is important to note the difference between the *shape* of history newly formulated in "Night the Eighth" and the historical model dominant in the *Vala* poem. It is not too much to imagine that Blake had conceived the biblical "eyes of the Lord" quite literally to signify a series of orbicular dispensations from Eden. The "chains of sorrow" forged by Los to represent the passage of earthly time would thus be cannily transformed into a similar series of circular movements, but this time linking not "hour to hour & day to night & night to day & year to year," but Lucifer to Molech to Elohim to Shaddai to Pachad to Jehovah to Jesus. This is a chain which, rather than binding man to the fallen world, represents the lifeline which will rescue him from Eternal Death. Frye discusses the Eyes in terms of "seven great periods" of history (*Fearful Symmetry,* 128), but perhaps a more accurate image is to be found in a parallel to Blake's theory of "States," also mentioned for the first time in the pivotal "Night the Eighth":

> There is a State namd Satan learn distinct to know O Rahab
> The Difference between States & Individuals of those States
> The State namd Satan never can be redeemd in all Eternity
> But when Luvah in Orc became a Serpent he des[c]ended into
> That State calld Satan.   (*FZ*115:23–7, E380)

This formulation is central to Blake's reassertion of a theory of historical progress. It contains both an element of continuity ("Individuals") and an element of superfluity ("States"): Individuality, as we have discussed in connection to a similar passage in *Milton*, is to be retained as the utopian goal of progress; "States," on the other hand, are to be shed as the ideological husks which "never can be redeemd in all Eternity." Blake indicates his disenchantment with the idea of revolution by noting that Orc, the sometime hero of his earlier "progress poem," has "des[c]ended into / That State calld Satan." We would be attributing to Blake only his usual allotment of textual ingenuity to suggest that the "O" which begins Orc's name recapitulates the serpentine circularity of fallen revolutions, both as a link in Los's "chains of sorrow" and as the orbicular hollow for an Eye of God.

The conjunction of the theory of States with the Seven Eyes of God, both broached for the first time on the breakthrough page 115 of *The Four Zoas*, represents a canny negotiation between the too-easy progressivism of *America*, *Europe*, and *The Song of Los* and the extreme pessimism of the unrevised *Vala*. States, as Blake here discusses them, possess an inertia highly resistant to historical change: Satan is the state which will "never . . . be redeemd in all Eternity." Similarly, the first six Eyes which Eden sends to die for Satan are reluctant to perform their utopian task: Lucifer through Jehovah refuses to die for Satan, each for reasons peculiar to his particular State, whether pride, impatience, irresponsibility, anger, fear, or disease. Blake thus expresses the ideological recalcitrance of history by periodizing its refusal for change. The "Eyes" of God seem blinded to their utopian future, content to trace out the same circular pattern of assignment and refusal, with only minor variations as to their respective motivations. But the act of periodization already shows the way to a newly progressive model of history. If history had been drained from *Vala* by the formulation of time as merely a succession of links in Los's "chains of sorrow," it is restored by Blake's attempt (spoken in the voice of a newly prophetic Los) to establish a determinate order of change over time. Blake's new theory of historical change is not the naive confidence in the "March of Mind" as voiced by Urizenic utilitarians; rather it is an awareness of the heterogeneity of the historical fabric and of the seeming self-sufficiency of ideological periods. The formulation of the Seven Eyes of God acknowledges that from the inside of history time appears circular, a "dull round" threatening to become, with Los's "chains of sorrow," "a mill with complicated wheels." But it also acknowledges that every cycle has its ending, that every planetary "revolution" (to borrow a sense of the word current in Blake's time) has its "period." The periodization of history not only allows for the *possibility* of change; it virtually insures change.

We have not yet treated the Seventh Eye, however, the Eye of Jesus, which does not refuse to die for Satan, but instead "Came & Died willing." The Seventh Eye, the satisfactory conclusion of Blake's miniature historical drama of repeated refusal, is ultimately what separates his account from a neutral historical account of the "rise and fall" of successive civilizations. While in *Milton*, after he has reevaluated the meaning of Christ's incarnation, Blake will have added an Eighth Eye in the person of Milton himself (*M*15:1–7,

E109), the implication remains the same: Blake must add a saving supplement, a utopian surplus, to the cyclic progression of history, so that the Eyes of God do not become the repressive "chains of sorrow." The circular Eyes of God are drawn towards an ending in Christ's utopian self-sacrifice, the circular made upwardly spiral. Pagan accounts of cyclical change and contemporary historical accounts of rise and fall are thus redeemed in Blake by an ultimate utopian "rise" which will know no subsequent "fall." But what, one might ask, separates Blake's account from the orthodox accounts of providential grace which he had seemed so to resist? The answer lies once again in the shape of Blake's model of history and its inclusion of both ideological and utopian elements. For if, as we have seen, the spiraling Eyes of God qualify the circular repetitiveness of fallen history, it is equally true that this same history qualifies the pretensions of an orthodox soteriology. As Ricoeur notes in his convincing discussion of the relation between utopia and ideology, "we must try to cure the illnesses of utopia by what is wholesome in ideology . . . and try to cure the rigidity, the petrification, of ideologies by the utopian element."[55] The saving grace of Jesus, Blake implies at this point in his career, will not be won by an ahistorical appeal to righteousness, but only by the steadfast unwinding of history. The path to utopian salvation is not the narrow line affirmed by orthodox churchmen, nor is the gate to Eden "strait," in either a literal or a punning sense. Instead, it is the spiral line of history, open to any "Individual" who will pass through its ideological "States" to its utopian conclusion. The path to Jesus lies through the circular Eyes of Lucifer, Molech, Elohim, Shaddai, Pachad, and Jehovah.

"Night the Eighth," however, is only the prelude to Blake's first extended utopian vision in "Night the Ninth," an autumnal pastoral which literalizes the biblical metaphor of the Eternal Harvest. Leaving aside the brilliant exuberance of this apocalyptic scene, we might raise the same question that we raised at the end of Blake's previous utopian progress poem, the "Asia" section of *The Song of Los*: How is the transition from fall to redemption, from Jehovah to Jesus, from ideology to utopia, depicted in the text? Even such an undeviating Blakean as Northrop Frye acknowledges the poet's deficiency in this regard. Frye laments that "there is little connection between [the] opening [of "Night the Ninth"] and the close of the preceding Night" and fears that the triumph of the Final Harvest belongs not to Los but to the circular Orc: "*The Four Zoas* . . . has not given us an imaginatively coherent account of how we can get from eighteenth century Deism to a Last Judgment through the power of Los, not Orc."[56] In effect, Frye is lamenting the fact that the model of redemption through time (Los) has been supplanted by the model of redemption through timeless revolution (Orc). The weakness of Blake's transfiguration of the "chains of sorrow" is not at the level of the links themselves, but at the articulation between the links, at the still point of transition from one Eye of God to the next. In particular, the weakness lies at the crucial point of transition from "Night the Eighth" to "Night the Ninth," from fall to redemption, from ideology to utopia. We are reminded of similar difficulties in that other grand historical narrative, the Marxian material dialectic, and of the tortured gap between prehistory and History proper, the realm of necessity and the realm of freedom. Perhaps Frye is right in saying that the inadequacy of that final articulation was the factor which led Blake finally to abandon *The Four Zoas.* Whatever the case may be, the triumph of Blake's next utopian move, as we shall see, lies precisely in his ability to occupy that gap between the successive Eyes of God, to see if perhaps, in the lack of connection between points of time, there might be "a Moment . . . that Satan cannot find" (*M*35:42, E136).

Blake's significant experiment with historical narrative, with liberal progressivism, to return to Mannheim's typology of utopian mentalities, thus ends at the point where moment cannot be joined to moment in any motivated way. The turn to an unmotivated moment of utopian insight, to the present-oriented chiliastic mentality, would almost seem necessitated by the ruin of Blake's historical structure. It is surely not entirely coincidental that the figure who can serve as the most useful analogue for Blake in this next stage of his career, the definitive debunker of the historical argument, is that writer forever locked in rhetorical struggle with Burke: Thomas Paine.

CHAPTER 5

The utopian moment in Rights of Man *and* Milton

I

There is an unequivocal *"epistemological break"* in Marx's work which does in fact occur at the point where Marx himself locates it, in the book, unpublished in his lifetime, which is a critique of his erstwhile philosophical (ideological) conscience: *The German Ideology.* (Louis Althusser, *For Marx*[1])

For a long time now, criticism of Blake's later prophetic poetry, of *Milton* and *Jerusalem*, has been organized around the figure of crisis. The nature of that crisis, however, the character of this transition in Blake's career, has been variously formulated. It has, for instance, been characterized as a retreat into esotericism after the relative clarities of the Lambeth books or, paradoxically, by E. D. Hirsch, as a "return to Innocence."[2] By Blake's socially oriented critics, the turn in his poetry has sometimes been interpreted as a betrayal of the revolutionary impulses of *America* and *Europe* for the piety that "each shall mutually / Annihilate himself for others good" (*M*38:35–6, E139). In a related vein, Blake's theologically oriented critics have traced the change from the human-centered theology of *The Marriage of Heaven and Hell* – "All deities reside in the human breast" (11, E38) – to the more orthodox soteriology of *Milton* and *Jerusalem*, reflected in the reprobate poet's anguished call for salvation, "O when Lord Jesus wilt thou come?" (*M*14:18, E108). The crisis in Blake's poetry has also been explained biographically, for his letters of this period seem to indicate a radical rejection of the past and a deeply felt need for reinvigoration: "I have traveld thro Perils & Darkness not unlike a Champion I have Conquerd and shall still Go on Conquering" (22 November 1802; Letter to Mr. Butts, E720).[3] The confrontation with Hayley alone would seem explanation enough of a crisis in Blake's conception of his vocation and of the form of his poetic vision.

But what all the formulations of Blake's crisis have thus far neglected to consider fully is the figure of crisis itself. If *Milton* is, as some claim, the "work of the break"[4] in the Blakean text, the problem yet remains of how to conceive of this break. As our invocation of Louis Althusser's designation for *The German Ideology* might indicate, the problem of a crisis in thought and literary production is more than just a Blakean issue: it is a problem for any interpreter who would propose a periodized schema for the work of a single author (e.g., Marx) or a national literature (e.g., the shift from eighteenth-century to Romantic British literature). For Althusser in particular, it is the problem of distinguishing Marx's ideological works (*The Economic and Philosophical Mannuscripts of 1844*, *The Holy Family*) from his properly "scientific" works (*Capital* and after). And as Althusser's comments on *The German Ideology* would indicate, the crisis in Marx's career marks the shift from an ideological position to a position from which "a critique of . . . ideological conscience" becomes possible, that is, the shift to the position we have been labeling the "utopian" position. The problem for Althusser is conceiving of this shift in other than ideological terms. He criticizes past efforts to periodize Marx's texts:

When eclectic [i.e., non-"scientific"] criticism is faced with the question, "how were Marx's growth to maturity and change possible," it is apt to give an answer which remains *within ideological history itself*. For example, it is said that Marx knew how to distinguish Hegel's *method* from his *content*, and that he proceeded to apply the former to history. (*For Marx*, 72; Althusser's emphasis)

For Althusser, the problem with this and similar explanations of Marx's crisis is that they posit science as a development within ideology, a natural progression by which Marxist science arises from the ideological Hegelian past. For Althusser, such progress is inconceivable, for, since "ideology has no history,"[5] the passage of time will never lead ideology out of itself. Consequently, the only way to imagine the emergence of Marxist science, "how . . . Marx's growth to maturity and change [were] possible," is by positing a radical rupture, an "epistemological break," which unconditionally separates the immature work of the early 1840s from the consummated scientific work of *Capital* and thereafter. In his rejection of any notion of "Marx's path" (*For Marx*, 74) from bondage in ideology to the promised land of Marxist science, in his rejection, therefore, of any progressive scheme of historical development, Althusser instead substitutes a cosmic portrait of the titanic Marx bursting through the Mundane Shell of ideology: "*The contingency of Marx's beginnings was this enormous layer of ideology* beneath which he was born, *this crushing layer* which he succeeded in breaking through" (*For Marx*, 74; Althusser's emphasis). The "march of mind" is thus refigured as the crisis of heroic thought.[6]

If, however, the "break" formed in the "crushing layer" of ideology by the revolutionary Marx bears some similarity to the "Breach" (34:42, E134) formed in the Mundane Shell by the descending Milton, there yet remain many differences between these two conceptions of utopian crisis. First, we must acknowledge that Althusser's notion of the "break" in Marx's text, the crisis in Marx's thought, remains a rather private affair. While having immense significance for the generations of materialist historians that were to succeed him, Marx's realization has little effect on the outside world: if the layer of ideology has been broken, it has been broken only for Marx. As Althusser puts it, "[T]his science [i.e., Marxist science] cannot be a science like any other, a science for 'everyone.' Precisely because it reveals the mechanisms of class exploitation, repression and domination, in the economy, in politics and in ideology, it cannot be recognized by *everyone*."[7] Blake's text, on the other hand, while remaining trapped in the language of a knowledgeable elite, expresses an intense desire to broadcast the moment of crisis widely. The poem as a whole, as much as the section which has come to be known as the "Bard's Song," speaks in words which Blake urges us to "Mark well . . . they are of your eternal salvation" (2:24, E96).[8] The seeming contradiction between Blake's rhetorical purposes and the private language in which he chooses to express them constitutes, as we shall see, a major problem in conceiving of his revolutionary crisis. An additional and perhaps related factor which distinguishes Blake's crisis from that in Althusser and Marx is its nonexclusivity within the poem, the fact that there is a "Moment *in each Day* that Satan cannot find" (35:42, E136; my emphasis). Both the crisis in the Marxian text as construed by Althusser, and the ultimate crisis in history proposed by Marx himself, are, conversely, unique historical events. The "work of the break" marks a definitive rupture between ideology and science in the Marxian text, after which, for Marx at least, there will be no going back. The crisis between prehistory and History proper is equally absolute and waits for its unique moment of realization: the Marxist critique of the utopian socialists, for example, revolves around the contention that they were premature in the establishment of a proto-communist state, that the time for achieved communism had not yet arrived.[9] Blake, on the other hand, by placing the moment of crisis "in each Day," speaks with the voice of Paul in his epistle to the Romans: "*[Now]* it is high time to awake out of sleep: for *now* is our salvation nearer than when we believed."[10] Blake thus places his faith in the "Moment" in which "the Poets Work is Done" (29:1, E127), the Eternal Now which might as well occur today as tomorrow, always capable of breaking through the Mundane Shell of the common day. And Blake, unlike the postideological Marx, must return to his "mortal state" after his moment of insight, to await a further "Resurrection & Judgment in the Vegetable Body" (42:26–7, E143).

Blake's faith in the Eternal Now places *Milton*, as numerous commentators have noted, in the tradition of the apocalyptic vision, but it also locates Blake in the utopian mentality that we have labeled, following Mannheim, "chiliasm," for which "the present becomes the breach through which what was previously inward bursts out suddenly, takes hold of the outer world and transforms it."[11] In many ways, this short description of chiliasm can serve as a precis for *Milton* itself, right down to the "breach" that is opened in the Mundane Shell of the present. It can also be taken as the basis for Blake's break with his own past, for, as I hope to show, Blake's mentality in *Milton* is as different from his mentality in *America*, *Europe*, and *The Four Zoas* as chiliasm is different from the liberal progressivism that we have seen informing those earlier works. The chiliastic utopian mentality also serves to distinguish those two polemic giants of the day, whose works we have taken as historical parallels for Blake's own strategies, Thomas Paine and Edmund Burke. Paine, after all, had his own theory of revolutionary crisis, and in the famous first sentence of the papers collected under the name of *The Crisis*, he declares, "These are the times that try men's souls: The summer soldier and the sunshine patriot will, in this crisis, shrink from the service of his country; but he that stands it NOW, deserves the love and thanks of man and woman."[12] Although more needs to be said to establish a parallel between Paine and the chiliastic utopian mentality, the initial similarity between Paine's work and Blake's innovations in *Milton* lies in their mutual reliance on the "NOW" as the site for revolutionary change. Paine's essential disagreement with the Burke of *Reflections on the Revolution in France* revolves around his rejection of the Burkean line of progress in favor of the crisis of revolutionary thought. Paine's strategy in the polemical *Rights of Man*, as we shall see, is to punctuate Burke's line of historical progress and to reveal how revolution emanates from a utopian crisis of thought. As such, the following section of this chapter deals with similarities in Blake's and Paine's treatment of history from the perspective of the moment of crisis. The final section will consider the questions of Blake's theory of classes and his idea of an audience for *Milton* in relation to a theory of revolutionary crisis.

II

To articulate the past historically does not mean to recognize "the way it really was" . . . It means to seize hold of a memory as it flashes up at a moment of danger. (Walter Benjamin[13])

As opposed to establishing a relation between Blake's thought and that of Edmund Burke, the idea of establishing a relation between Blake and Thomas Paine is initially distinguished by seeming entirely noncontroversial. Although Blake referred directly to Burke only three times throughout his entire life's work, all in the Annotations of Reynold's *Discourses*, he refers to Paine many times (twenty-six altogether) and displays an intimate knowledge of Paine's texts.[14] By far the majority of his references to Paine occur in the marginalia to Bishop Watson's *An Apology for the Bible*, a defense of revealed religion and an attack on Paine's "heretical" work, *The Age of Reason*. Blake there finds himself in the odd rhetorical position of siding with the representative of a philosophy he found abhorrent – rationalistic Deism – against the representative of a power he found equally abhorrent – the established Church. As such, the marginalia to this volume either search out sympathetic, sometimes radically revisionary, readings of Paine's critique of revealed religion, or seek to occupy the precarious middle ground between what Blake feels are two indefensible positions. Perhaps the key to Blake's reaction to this turn-of-the-century religious debate can be found in his summary note on Watson's fifth letter: "The Bishop never saw the Everlasting Gospel any more than Tom Paine" (E619). If, however, Blake's response to *The Age of Reason* was less than enthusiastic, his response to Paine's masterpiece, *Rights of Man*, knows no such qualifications. In the context of a discussion of miracles and the necessity of belief for their performance, Blake raises Paine's pamphlet to the status of a divine event: "Is it a greater miracle to feed five thousand men with five loaves than to overthrow all the armies of Europe with a small pamphlet" (E617). Blake refers, of course, to the enormous popular success of *Rights of Man*, a success which must be taken as a primary inspiration for the mass-market publishing efforts of the early nineteenth century.[15] But given Blake's own ambivalent interest in popularity and large-scale publishing, we might also surmise that he is expressing admiration for the enormous effect of a single man and a single book on the course of history. Unless we are to assume that Blake is here abandoning his antipopulist stance, we must conclude that it is in the stark contrast between "*all* the armies of Europe" and the "*small* pamphlet" which overthrew them that Paine's miracle lies. In effect, Blake is contemplating the revolution created by the smallest of books and the smallest of thoughts, the critical point of crisis upon which all change hinges.

This seemingly apolitical or asocial response is not, as one might first assume, entirely out of keeping with Paine's text. Paine, as well as Blake, is interested in the apparent immediacy of revolutionary change, the smallest point of time in which revolution is effected. Of the French Revolution, Paine writes, "It has apparently burst forth like a creation from a chaos."[16] But Paine rejects such creation *ab nihilo* as firmly as does Blake in his Genesis parody, *The Book of Urizen*, instead assigning the origin of revolution its rightful place in the mind of man: "[The Revolution] is no more than the consequence of a mental revolution priorily existing in France. The mind of the nation had changed beforehand, and the new order of things has naturally followed the new order of thoughts" (*Rights of Man*, 93). If this analysis of history sounds disturbingly like the proclamations of idealist thinkers such as Friedrich Schiller, who, in his *On the Aesthetic Education of Man*, suggested that the cause of political freedom should be subordinated to that of aesthetic and mental freedom, then perhaps the similarity is instructive. Blake also, as we have suggested, has been entered in the lists of the abstract and ahistorical, particularly after the crisis which preceded and, indeed, constituted the writing of *Milton*. The obscurities of that text, the assignment of all revolutionary action to the time of a "Pulsation of the Artery" (29:3, E127), has been harshly greeted by advocates of the more explicitly revolutionary *America* and *The French Revolution*. But Blake is confronting, as is Paine, the problem of conceiving of the revolution as an historic event, an event unprecedented in the course of time, though unthinkable as only "a creation from a chaos." The problem, as we shall see in both our reading of Paine and our reading of *Milton*, is in constructing the "Moment" of revolutionary crisis as a believable rupture in the fabric of historical time. The solution involves a radical rereading of the line of historical progress which had structured both Burke's historical analysis in *Reflections on the Revolution in France* and Blake's narrative of revolutionary progress in *America*, *Europe*, *The Song of Los*, and *The Four Zoas*.

The founding gesture of *Rights of Man*, its reason for existence, is Paine's rejection of Burke's model of the line of progress and his notion of a pedigree for freedom. Rejecting Burke's claim that the parliamentary action at the time of the Glorious Revolution had rectified, once and for all, the line of monarchical succession, Paine injects a sense of the crisis occurring at the point of any legislative decision:

> It requires but a very small glance of thought to perceive, that although laws made in one generation often continue in force through succeeding generations, yet that they continue to derive their force from the consent of the living. A law not repealed continues in force, not because it *cannot* be repealed, but because it *is not* repealed; and the non-repealing passes for consent. (*Rights of Man*, 44; Paine's emphasis)

In "contending for the rights of the *living*" (*Rights of Man*, 42; Paine's emphasis) against those of the dead, Paine contends for the ever-present moment of consent, either tacit or overt, which authorizes the continuation of the line. As opposed to Burke's linear geometrics, Paine's political theory is based on a geometry of the point, without extension or magnitude, but logically prior to the line and capable of causing its termination. Or to adopt a parallel from the literature of contemporary Marxism, Paine's emphasis is the equivalent of Althusser's in the article on Ideological State Apparatuses, focusing not on the continuous mode of production, but on the "reproduction of the conditions of production" which stands as the "ultimate condition of production."[17] "[E]very child knows," Althusser quotes Marx as saying, "that a social formation which did not reproduce the conditions of production at the same time as it produced would not last a year" ("Ideological State Apparatuses," 127). Equally evident to Paine, and the constant source of his revolutionary hope, is the fact that the line of progress must submit itself to the judgment of every generation, to continue or not at their discretion. What stands as Paine's most powerful contribution to the literature of revolution, however, and his most cogent critique of Burke, is the "revolution" in historiography made possible by his theorizing from the point, from the ever-present crisis in which history is constituted. For Paine exposes the "metaphysics" of Burke's positions precisely by tracing the line of his opponent's rhetoric to its point of origin, an exposé which inevitably involves a new way of seeing the past:

Although Mr. Burke has asserted the right of the parliament at the [Glorious] Revolution to bind and control the nation and posterity for *ever*, he denies, at the same time, that the parliament or the nation had any right to alter what he calls the succession of the crown, in anything but in part; or by a sort of modification. By his taking this ground, he throws the case back to the *Norman Conquest*; and by thus running a line of succession springing from William the Conqueror to the present day, he makes it necessary to inquire who and what William the Conqueror was, and where he came from; and into the origin, history, and nature of what are called prerogatives. Everything must have had a beginning, and the fog of time and antiquity should be penetrated to discover it. Let then Mr. Burke bring forward his William of Normandy, for it is to this origin that his argument goes. It also unfortunately happens, in running this line of succession, that another line, parallel thereto, presents itself, which is, that if the succession runs in the line of the conquest, the nation runs in the line of being conquered, and it ought to reserve itself from this approach. (*Rights of Man* 78, Paine's emphasis)

Paine's strategy is partly the perennial rhetoric of the *reductio ad absurdum*, allowing Burke's line to extend to the point of unraveling, or, allowing ourselves a slight paraphrase, giving Burke enough line to hang himself. But Paine is also expressing the priority of the point over the line, deducing that, since "[e]verything must have had a beginning," Burke's own line must find its point of origin in the Norman Conquest. However much Burke would wish to derive authority from the past, from the precedent of time immemorial, sinking his plumb line to assure the stability of the "ancient edifice"[18] of England, he must acknowledge that authority ultimately derives from a single point, from the point of the establishment, of the foundation, of the primitive state. And in what does this point of origin consist? Elsewhere Paine compares the Norman invasion to base thievery, calling William's force "a banditti of ruffians" who rudely disturbed the pastoral existence of the early English herders: "Their power being thus established, the chief of the band contrived to lose the name of Robber in that of Monarch; and hence the origin of Monarchy and Kings" (*Rights of Man*, 168). The final irony of Burke's polemic, as Paine sees it, is that the institution which Burke identifies as the only thing standing between England and wholesale violence – the established monarchy – was itself founded in an act of violence by the French against the English. The firebreak which Burke joyfully places between the burning French house and the ancient edifice of England, still intact in Burke's eyes, is itself the source of a fire which has been burning since 1066.

It is only with the parallel line that Paine projects from Burke's line of monarchical succession, however, that we can begin to see the more profound similarities between the historical vision of *Rights of Man* and Blake's view of the past in *Milton*. Paine is proposing nothing less than an alternative history of England in asserting that a line of conquest runs parallel to Burke's line of kings and nobles. In the words of Walter Benjamin, whose late Messianic writings, I would suggest, provide the most useful modern parallel to Blake's and Paine's historical visions, "There is no document of civilization which is not at the same time a document of barbarism."[19] Paine's parallel lines – one the orthodox history of serene succession, the 700-year peaceful transition of the crown from father to son and from house to house, the other the alternative history of violent conquest – are echoed by the parallel texts that Benjamin proposes be read into the evidence of the past, one the official account of history, the progress of civilization, the other a record of brutality and repression. Paine's task, as much as Benjamin's, is to recover the history of common people and their common sense, "to brush history against the grain" ("Theses," 257) of its orthodox custodians. But the similarities between Paine and Benjamin do not end with their sense of an alternative historiography; they extend also to a sense of crisis, of the crucial status of the Now as a theater for political action. The "tradition of the oppressed," Benjamin's name for the alternative to orthodox "historicism," teaches us, in his words, "that the 'state of emergency' in which we live is not the exception but the rule" ("Theses," 257). Fascism was only the latest avatar of a repressive force which had driven the oppressed and their alternative history underground since the beginning of recorded time. But if the present is always the moment of repression, "the times that try men's souls," it is also the ever-present potential for Messianic redemption from the burden of the past. In a phrase eerily reminiscent of Blake, Benjamin claims that "[F]or the Jews [a tradition Benjamin appeals to throughout "Theses on the Philosophy of History"] . . . every second of time was the strait gate through which the Messiah might enter" ("Theses," 264). It is in the combination, then, of a sense of crisis and a sense of the alternative history which emerges from the perspective of that crisis, that the visions of Paine and Benjamin find their most profound nexus. Along with Blake, those two thinkers are themselves monuments in the alternative history they tried so hard to record.

Blake's own connections to a theory of Messianic crisis and the alternative history emanating from it become evident from the very first plate of *Milton*, in a conjunction of ideas which initially seem completely contradictory. In a paraphrase of Milton's "The Reason of Church Government Urged Against Prelaty," Blake anticipates the time when "the Daughters of Memory shall become the Daughters of Inspiration," freeing the poets of the New Age from any desire to copy classical precedents, "[t]he Stolen and Perverted Writings of Homer & Ovid: of Plato & Cicero. which all Men ought to contemn" (E95). But shortly after rejecting the faculty of memory, the historical precedent of Greek literature, Blake himself, in those oft-quoted introductory verses, seems to hearken back to an earlier time, beside which the present seems entirely inadequate:

> And did those feet in ancient time,
> Walk upon Englands mountains green:
> And was the holy Lamb of God,
> On Englands pleasant pastures seen!   (1:1–4, E95)

As Nancy Goslee has noted,[20] in connection with Northrop Frye's discussion of Blake's historiography, this vision of England's "ancient time" owes much to both the myth of the Atlantic Golden Age and the Glastonbury legends that Christ had visited England to dedicate the church of Joseph of Arimathea. But why does Blake evoke a memory of England's past only lines after rejecting the services of the classical "Daughters of Memory?" The seeds of an answer can be found in the last of the stanzas, where it becomes evident that Blake invokes the legendary past not in the service of nostalgic jingoism, but rather to effect a renovation of England's repressive present:

> I will not cease from Mental Fight,
> Nor shall my Sword sleep in my hand:
> Till we have built Jerusalem,
> In Englands green & pleasant Land.   (1:13–16, E95–6)

From the perspective of a moment of crisis, the present of England's "dark Satanic Mills" (1:8), Blake is reflecting on a history which enables change for the future. The history which he appeals to is not the subject of serene contemplation, as it would be for orthodox historians, but is instead the stuff of "Mental Fight," forward-looking revolutionary action. Indeed, the "history" to which he appeals, the material of British and European legend, was not credited by the "serious" historians of either his time or ours. In a sense, this "memory" which Blake happens upon at the moment of beginning *Milton* is the offspring not of the "Daughters of Memory," but of the "Daughters of Inspiration": at the very least, it is an inspired memory, perhaps the inspiration for *Milton* itself. The subtle transition from the perspective of the individual to that of the group – from the "I" of line 13 to the "we" of line 15 (a transition which Goslee also treats) – will be the subject of my last section. It suffices for now to note that the introductory stanzas depict Blake's discovery of an alternative history in the legends of ancient Britain, a saving for which the country's dire condition calls out.

Commentators on *Milton* have long noted that the first book enacts the redemption of history,[21] but they have largely failed to identify the nature of that redemption and of the history which is thereby redeemed. Redemption comes, as it does for the speaker of Wordsworth's Immortality Ode, as a "timely utterance" giving relief to a "thought of grief"[22]:

> At last when desperation almost tore his heart in twain
> He recollected an old Prophecy in Eden recorded,
> And often sung to the loud harp at the immortal feasts
> That Milton of the Land of Albion should up ascend
> Forwards from Ulro from the Vale of Felpham; and set free
> Orc from his Chain of Jealousy.   (20:56–61, E115)

Los, the subject of this passage, has ample reason for despair before this inspired memory comes to his rescue: the willfully ignorant "Eternals" have just driven the "Shadowy Eight" (Milton's guardians) from their haven in Eden to Generation below, causing the Eternal Prophet to doubt whether Albion will ever rise from the Couch of Sleep. At this moment of crisis occurs Los's discovery of a hitherto neglected prophecy. What first impresses the reader about this turning point in the text is its seeming arbitrariness. Why have we never heard of this prophecy before? It is not, as with others of Blake's prophecies, an adaptation of biblical prophecy, unless it can be said to resemble Isaiah's description of the child who shall be born as a sign to the people of Judah and Jerusalem.[23] At the same time, it has no precedent in Blake's own text: indeed, Blake would seem to be confounding (with a typically Blakean lack of respect for overdrawn distinctions) his historical and his symbolic allegories in claiming that "Milton" shall "free Orc from his Chain of Jealousy." There lingers, in short, a suspicion that Los might simply have "made up" this prophecy and its salvational history. The accuracy of the prophecy – by the end of the poem, Milton shall indeed have "ascend[ed] from Ulro from the Vale of Felpham," although he will not, admittedly, have "set free Orc from his Chain of Jealousy" – does not mitigate against this suspicion. But for Blake the efficacy of prophecy does not depend upon a narrowly-defined concept of historical accuracy; instead, prophecy creates, in a moment of crisis, the alternative history which will effect the transition from the ideological to the utopian. "Man," as Paine says in the context of a discussion of the revolutionary spirit then sweeping through the world, "discovers . . . that, in order '*to be free, it is sufficient that he wills it*'" (*Rights of Man*, 210; Paine's emphasis).

The swiftness of this crisis in Blake's text, the seeming speed with which Los moves from despair to hope by the agency of timely recollection, is in keeping with the temporal configuration of *Milton*. Time is no longer the "chains of iron . . . Linkd hour to hour & day to night & night to day & year to year" (*FZ*53:1–2, E335) of *The Four Zoas*, but is instead "the swiftest of all things" (24:73, E121). In the terms of Leslie Brisman's appraisal of *Milton*, Blake is substituting "apocalyptic haste" for "prophetic patience": "We can use the term 'apocalyptic' . . . to refer to vision as instantaneous and atemporal; 'prophetic' implies the creation of new times, and more specifically of new deferrals."[24] Los's recollected "prophecy" is atypical to the extent that its purpose is not consolatory, but revolutionary, intended to begin the work of apocalypse NOW: instead of introducing "new deferrals" into history, Los claims three plates later that "the end approaches fast" (23:55, E119). In the terms of Roland Barthes's definition of the hermeneutic code of narrative as that which "must set up *delays* (obstacles, stoppages, deviations) in the flow of discourse,"[25] we might say that Blake is substituting a radical lyrical mode for the narrative mode of *The Four Zoas, America,* and *Europe.*[26] Even in personal and psychological terms, time has a different meaning for the Blake of *Milton* than it had for the Blake of those earlier poems. He writes to Thomas Butts on 11 September 1801 of his changed perception of time since settling in Felpham, lamenting his lack of productivity: "Time flies faster, (as seems to me), here than in London" (E716). But eventually even this faint nostalgia for time considered in orthodox terms will be expelled by a new sense of work-time considered as poetic work in the Moment:

I have written this Poem [*Milton*, presumably] from immediate Dictation twelve or sometimes twenty or thirty lines at a time without Premeditation & even against my Will. the Time it has taken in writing was thus rendered Non Existent. & an immense Poem Exists which seems to be the Labour of a long Life all producd without Labour or Study. (Letter to Butts, 25 April, 1803, E728–9)

The crisis of Blake's new poetic vision is thus both a theme of *Milton* and enacted in its very composition.

This new sense of the swiftness of time, the foreshortening of what had before seemed the expanse of time, informs the long culminating section of book 1, in which Los and his Sons rebuild and redeem the world of fallen time and space. In that paradoxical "moment" equal to 6,000 years (28:62–3, E127), the entirety of history presents itself to the architect Los:

I am that Shadowy Prophet who Six Thousand Years ago
Fell from my station in the Eternal bosom. Six Thousand Years
Are finishd. I return! both Time & Space obey my will.
I in Six Thousand Years walk up and down: for not one Moment
Of Time is lost, nor one Event of Space unpermanent
But all remain: every fabric of Six Thousand Years
Remains permanent: tho' on the Earth where Satan
Fell, and was cut off all things vanish & are seen no more
They vanish not from me & mine, we guard them first & last
The generations of men run on in the tide of Time
But leave their destind lineaments permanent for ever & ever.
(22:15–25, E117)

It is not inapposite to note the similarity between this formulation and Benjamin's in the "Theses on the Philosophy of History," where he writes that "only a redeemed mankind receives the fulness of its past – which is to say, only for a redeemed mankind has its past become citable in all its moments."[27] But for Benjamin, as well as for the Blake of *Milton*, this redemption can no longer be conceived as the end or goal of an historical progress. The most cogent characteristic of Los's description of his compendious "library" of Six Thousand Years is the fact that all time, all history, has been emptied out of it. Although Los even-handedly declares that now "both Time & Space obey my will," one cannot but think that Space has gotten somewhat better conditions of surrender. Blake attempts to balance the terms of "lost" and "unpermanent" against each other in the formula that "not one Moment / Of Time is lost, not one Event of Space unpermanent," but the effect of Los's description is precisely to spatialize the temporal. Besides the notion of Los's "walk[ing] up and down" throughout time, which notion itself involves a spatial metaphor, there are also the references to time as a "fabric" or as "lineaments." Blake's own characterization of the permanence of time is a visual, a spatial, metaphor: "They [i.e., every fabric of Six Thousand Years] *vanish not* from me & mine." In short, time has been excluded from the fabric of *Milton*, in favor of the timeless, spatialized Moment, not in the interests of abandoning the poem's relevance to the real historical world, but as a way of affirming that its relevance issues from a moment of crisis, rather than from a progressivist historicism. The revolutionary historian, Benjamin affirms, "cannot do without the notion of a present which is not a transition, but in which time stands still and has come to a stop" ("Theses," 262). From this perspective, a chiliastic theory of crisis would seem the prerequisite, rather than necessary disqualification, for a theory of revolutionary action.

The reclamation project which Los and his Sons perform upon the course of history emphasizes not the linear continuity of a homogenous temporality, but the constant punctuation of the historical timeline:

> [O]thers of the Sons of Los build Moments & Minutes & Hours
> And Days & Months & Years & Ages & Periods; wondrous buildings
> And every Moment has a Couch of gold for soft repose,
> . . .
> And between every two Moments stands a Daughter of Beulah
> To feed the Sleepers on their Couches with maternal care.

And every Minute has an azure Tent with silken Veils.
And every Hour has a bright golden Gate carved with skill.
And every Day & Night, has Walls of brass & Gates of adament,
Shining like precious stones & ornamented with appropriate signs:
And every Month, a silver paved Terrace builded high:
And every Year, invulnerable Barriers with high Towers.
And every Age is Moated deep with Bridges of silver & gold.
And every Seven Ages is Incircled with a Flaming Fire.

(*M*28:44–6, 48–57, E126–7)

Besides the continued spatialization of time, carried here to its logical extreme, one must note the necessary corollary of that spatialization: a discovery of the gaps within time. By taking the atomic view of time, reducing time to its smallest particle, Blake is discovering the nontemporal crisis between Moments themselves, the time which is "less than a pulsation of the artery" (itself a spatial measurement) in which "the Poets Work is Done: and all Great / Events of time start forth" (28:62, 29:1–2, E127). What else is Revolution but such a "Great Event," conceived in the timeless space between moments? Blake as well as Paine, then, rejects the linear vision of Burke and the theoreticians of progress for an alternative history, itself emanating from the crisis of counterrevolutionary England, which depicts time as a broad-loom fabric permeated by points of crisis, timeless gaps which escape the authority of the forward-directed line. As Paine wrote of the American and French Revolutions, "The progress of time and circumstances, which men assign to the accomplishment of great changes, is too mechanical to measure the force of mind, and the rapidity of reflection, by which revolutions are generated" (*Rights of Man*, 143). The "rapidity" of that revolutionary reflection, as well as the rapidity of poetic inspiration, is finally too swift for any temporal measure whatsoever. Paine's reference to "the force of the mind" clearly should remind us of the profound differences between his and Blake's theories of utopian revolution and those of Marx and the twentieth-century Marxists. S. Foster Damon's comment that "*Milton* is the most personal document which Blake has left us"[28] has set the tone for much of the commentary on the poem, encouraging critics to find intricate personal allegories in the "Bard's Song" of Satan and Palamabron. But *Milton* reveals its profound subjectivity not so much in any biographical detail it may or may not shadow forth as in Blake's firm conviction that consciousness, "the force of the mind," is the engine of revolutionary action. Blake's rejection of the "Daughters of Memory" for the "Daughters of Inspiration" is a redirection of utopian energy towards interior subjective states: "We do not want either Greek or Roman Models if we are but just & true to our own Imaginations, those Worlds of Eternity in which we shall live for ever; in Jesus our Lord" (1, E95). And although the invocation of Beulah at the beginning of the poem raises the questions which that sexual dreamscape always raises in the Blakean text, the final source of creative energy is situated more securely in "the Portals of my Brain, where by your [i.e., Beulah's] ministry / The Eternal Great Humanity Divine. planted his Paradise" (2:7–8, E96). Paine's own profound humanism issues in the statement that "Man" was the "high and only title" of earth's first inhabitant, and that "a higher title cannot be given him" (*Rights of Man*, 65). For Paine, the French Revolution, as we have noted above, was "no more than the consequence of a mental revolution priorily existing in France." The mind of man is thus singled out as the only engine swift enough to drive the instantaneous changes of revolution, the only possible site of revolutionary crisis, for which the world changes in an instant, a "pulsation of the artery."

It is precisely at this point, however, the point of the advancement of humanity and human consciousness as the vehicle for revolutionary change, that Marx and Althusser themselves "break" with Blake and Paine in their conception of crisis, of epistemological break. For Marx in *The German Ideology*, the "work of the break" consists in a break from consciousness, from the sublimated mentality of the Young Hegelians: "The production of ideas, of conceptions, of consciousness, is at first directly interwoven with the material activity and the material intercourse of men, the language of real life . . . Consciousness can never be anything else than conscious existence, and the existence of men is their actual life-process."[29] For the postideological Marx, Althusser claims an even more profound antihumanism, a break with man's "actual life-process" itself, which break forms the necessary prerequisite for revolutionary change: "[O]ne can and must speak openly of Marx's theoretical antihumanism, and see in this theoretical antihumanism the absolute . . . precondition of . . . knowledge of the human world itself, and of its practical transformation."[30] The possibility remains, in other words, that Blake and Paine's solution to the problem of the "break" which is revolution, the break which definitively separates ideology from utopia, is itself merely an imported species of the "German" ideology criticized by Marx. To posit a "mental revolution priorily existing in France," or a hitherto unknown ancient prophecy, as explanation for the material and political revolution is to *displace* the problem of revolution rather than to *solve* it: if it is impossible to think of political revolution as "a creation from a chaos," it must be equally impossible to conceive of an instantaneous mental revolution. For Blake also, the idea of instantaneous mental revolution falls subject to the Marxist critique: if "recollection" was the vehicle of Los's movement from despair to revolutionary zeal, the source of that serendipitous recollection has yet to be identified. Similarly, Milton's spontaneous decision to "go to Eternal Death" (14:14, E108) issues from a mind previously content with the stasis of Eden's Elect. We are compelled to ask, if mind is the source of change, what is the source of change of mind? Before we can understand how Milton's decision moves the fallen world towards its apocalypse, we must, in the words of Blake's Bard, "[s]ay first! what mov'd Milton" (2:16, E96). It is in this concern with movement, however, the movement of mankind towards revolution, the movement of an audience towards a desired end, that Blake most definitively anticipates the Marxist critique and advances his concept of crisis to its utopian status. Blake's idea of a "moving" poetry, then, must complete the concept of revolutionary crisis, mapping the utopian point at which a mind instantaneously moves from stasis in ideology to an active revolutionary consciousness.

III

Upon all subjects . . . there is often passing in the mind a train of ideas [Man] has not yet accustomed himself to encourage and communicate. Restrained by something that puts on the character of prudence, he acts the hypocrite upon himself as well as to others. It is, however, curious to observe how soon this spell can be dissolved. A single expression, boldly conceived and uttered, will sometimes put a whole company into their proper feelings; and whole nations are acted upon in the same manner. (*Rights of Man*, 236)

Given the forcefulness of Blake's rejection of issues of comprehensibility and clarity (as popularly conceived), it is not surprising that the pragmatic, the rhetorical, dimensions of his texts have, until relatively recently, gone unperceived. Charges of elitism, of quasi-aristocratic aloofness, have been leveled at the Blake who uttered such statements as, "That which can be made Explicit to the Idiot is not worth my care" (E702).[31] The evidence of the texts themselves, especially the late prophetic works, would seem to support such a criticism: what kind of poet could possibly expect his reader to decipher the complexities of the "Bard's Song" in *Milton* or, indeed, the majority of *Jerusalem*'s convoluted text? Yet, despite these charges, suggestions of an intense concern for his texts' reception abound in Blake's late prophecies, especially in the "work of the break," *Milton*. As W. J. T. Mitchell noted in his groundbreaking article on the subject, "*Milton* calls the reader, not to contemplation, but to action. It dramatizes the eternal perspective only to subvert its detachment from history and to force the reader to abandon his position of aesthetic disinterest."[32] At least the hint of a Brechtian distancing effect informs Blake's suggestion, immediately following his contemptuous dismissal of "the Idiot," that "[t]he wisest of the Ancients considered what is not too Explicit as the fittest for Instruction because it rouzes the faculties to act" (E702). In short, the obscurity of Blake's texts should not be understood as a device for limiting his audience, or for limiting his audience's comprehension of the text, but instead as a means of "moving" his readership to a new level of awareness. A contradiction still persists in this portrait of Blake's revolutionary rhetoric, however: if that which can be made explicit to the idiot is not worth saying, it naturally follows that whatever *is* worth saying cannot be made explicit to the idiot. Unless he means to abandon most of his readership (Blake certainly makes idiots of most of us), the question yet remains of how to make the idiot understand, how to "rouze the [idiot's] faculties to act." A revolution which dispenses with the services of "idiots" – that is to say, with the majority of a population – will surely suffer the fate of all revolutions from above. The problem of *Milton*, then, is the problem of moving the "Idiot" from ignorance to knowledge by means of a crisis of revelation.

The model for this crisis of revelation is the vortex through which Milton, "moved" by the Bard's Song, descends on his track to Generation:

> The nature of infinity is this: That every thing has its
> Own Vortex; and when once a traveller thro Eternity.
> Has passd that Vortex, he perceives it roll backward behind
> His path, into a globe itself infolding; like a sun:

> Or like a moon, or like a universe of starry majesty,
> While he keeps onwards in his wondrous journey on the earth
> Or like a human form, a friend with whom he livd benevolent.
>
> (15:21–7, E109)

Considered as a description of the reading process, or the experience of listening to prophecy, this passage sheds light on Blake's idea of the "movement" that is possible within a single point of view. Passage through the vortex is itself the crisis which unconditionally separates pre-vortical perception from postvortical perception: the process of reading, or listening to, the vortex really does, then, make a difference. The "traveller thro Eternity" maintains a consistent "Identity," but in the formulation of *Milton* 32:23 – "States Change: but Individual Identities never change nor cease" – his "State" has changed entirely, and with it, his way of seeing the world. But even within this normative view of prophetic reception theory, Blake allows for a distinction between "human" readings and readings which might more properly be called "Idiotic." The vortex of prophetic reception spells a meaningful difference only for those who are able to see what they have passed as "a human form, a friend with whom [they] livd benevolent." For the Idiot, the new world will appear only "a sun . . . a moon, or a universe of starry majesty," astronomical images which in Blake's text usually indicate fallenness. Blake is tough-minded, then, in acknowledging that the simple reception of prophecy does not always achieve meaningful change, dividing his audience into "Classes" whose perception of the vortex indicates their receptivity to revolutionary prophecy.

This "class" division is not foreign to the prophetic tradition on which Blake draws, and it is useful to compare Blake's idea of audience to that of the biblical prophets. A most relevant parallel is to be found in the Lord's directive to Isaiah to actively enforce a deafening of his audience, to cause them to misunderstand his message lest they be converted:

Make the heart of this people fat, and make their ears heavy, and shut their eyes; lest they see with their eyes, and hear with their ears, and understand with their heart, and convert, and be healed.[33]

The intent here seems to be explicitly to deny the moment of crisis, of conversion, to a section of the population, to "Separat[e] . . . What has been mixed" (25:28, E122) in Los's words, or to insure that the Idiotic reader remain Idiotic. Blake's seemingly democratic epigraph for *Milton* – "Would to God that all the Lord's people were Prophets" (1, E96) – also admits of a more exclusionary interpretation. The context of this quotation pits Moses against the more orthodox Joshua, who suggests that his master forbid two freelance prophets from infringing on his franchise. Moses replies with a variant of Blake's citation: "Enviest thou for my sake? would God that all the Lord's people were prophets, and that the Lord would put his spirit upon them!"³⁴ Moses's instincts are certainly more democratic than Joshua's, but it is important to realize that he does not intend a universal prophetic franchise: even if all "the Lord's people" were prophets, there would yet remain the fact that not all the people are the "Lord's people." Blake's citation of this scripture replicates the ambiguity of its original. On the same prefatorial plate where the epigraph appears, he warns the "Young Men of the New Age" against the "Class of Men whose whole delight is in Destroying" (1, E95), and one cannot but imagine that this class of destroyers will not be welcomed to the prophetic fold: they are not among the "Lord's people."

The idea of "Classes" to which I have been referring constitutes, of course, one of *Milton*'s major contributions to the heterogeneous doctrine that Blake seems gradually to be constructing over the last thirty years of his life. The fullest statement of this idea occurs in the context of Los's advice to the Labourers of the Vintage, at the time of the Last Harvest:

> [Y]ou must bind the Sheaves not by Nations or Families
> You shall bind them in Three Classes; according to their Classes
> . . .
>   The Elect is one Class: You
> Shall bind them separate: they cannot Believe in Eternal Life
> Except by Miracle & a New Birth. The other two Classes;
> The Reprobate who never cease to Believe, and the Redeemd
> Who live in doubts & fears perpetually tormented by the Elect
> These you shall bind in a twin-bundle for the Consummation.
>
> (25:26–7, 32–7, E122)

Although Blake seems here to hold out hope that the Elect might eventually believe by the agency of a "Miracle & a New Birth," elsewhere he says that "the Elect cannot be Redeemd, but Created continually" (5:11, E98). Discounting this "outside chance" for the Elect to achieve redemption, we might note that only one of the three Classes is subject to the kind of "movement" undergone by

Milton as he listens to the Bard's Song. The Reprobate have always already passed the moment of crisis and the Elect never shall "[e]xcept by Miracle & a New Birth": only the Redeemed are subject to the movement from "doubts & fears" to full belief in the message of prophecy. Although Blake has purposely inverted the biblical schema of Paul's epistle to the Ephesians – "[God] hath chosen us in him before the foundation of the world, that we should be holy and without blame before him in love"[35] – he yet retains the notion of a "chosen people" for whom the crisis of conversion in the fallen world is never at issue. This biblical notion is then supplemented by the idea of a people "chosen" for damnation, eternally consigned to idiotic noncomprehension of the prophetic text, and the idea, from the prophecies, of a "remnant," for whom the question of salvation or damnation has yet to be decided. Blake's "class" theory thus reinforces the rigidity of scriptural notions of who can hear prophecy and who cannot.

The scene of prophetic and poetic reception, as W. J. T. Mitchell has noted, is recreated within the text in the varied reactions elicited in Eden by the rehearsal of the Bard's Song:

> The Bard ceas'd. All consider'd and a loud resounding murmur
> Continu'd round the Halls; and much they question'd the immortal
> Loud voicd Bard. and many condemn'd the high tone'd Song
> Saying Pity and Love are too venerable for the imputation
> Of Guilt. Others said. If it is true! if the acts have been perform'd
> Let the Bard himself witness. Where hadst thou this terrible Song.
>
> (13:45–50, E107)

For a "prophet" who had himself known considerable disappointment in his own poetry's reception, Blake is remarkably candid in this portrait of the reception of the Bard's Song in Eden. The audience is already beginning to split along class lines: for those Elect who condemn the Song, on the grounds that "Pity and Love are too venerable for the imputation of Guilt" (an essentialist argument), movement towards complete understanding would seem impossible short of a "Miracle & a New Birth"; for the Redeemed, who only require to know "[i]f it is true" (they are literary realists), some hope for change would seem warranted. The Bard himself, who, when asked to reveal his source, says only "I am Inspired! I know it is Truth! for I Sing / According to the inspiration of the Poetic Genius" (13:51–14:1, E107–8), would seem to be among

Blake's Reprobate, "who never cease to Believe." Not only does his belief know no ending, it also seems to have had no beginning, for nowhere are we presented with the picture of a Bard who himself needed convincing to "move" him to the point of "moving" Milton: in his version of the biblical class system, Blake would seem to have "elected" the Bard to the status of unmoved mover, for whom the question of a crisis of conscience is never at issue. At this point in the poem, then, Blake would seem to be committed to a rigid class analysis in his appraisal of his audience and of their potential for revolutionary change.

This rigidity begins to break down, however, and the space for redemptive change begins to open up, when one realizes that Blake's class categories are not only intended as intersubjective markers, separating the sheep from the goats, but also intrasubjective components of a single mind. This accounts for Blake's sometimes confusing and radically innovative device of splitting Milton's persona into three parts. The Redeemed Milton, revealed most clearly in his susceptibility to "movement," is that figure whose response to the Bard's Song differs so completely from that of the Eternals. After the Bard has taken refuge in his bosom, that is, after Milton has received prophecy's true message, he manifests his revolution in consciousness by a "movement" which disrupts the placidity of Eden: "Then Milton rose up from the heavens of Albion arduous!" (14:7, E108). With no prior indication of restiveness in Eden – "he obey'd, he murmur'd not. he was silent" (2:18, E96) – Milton has undergone a crisis of thought, triggered by, although not entirely reducible to, the forceful rhetoric of the Bard's Song. Milton has been "moved," not only because the Bard's Song was "moving," but also because he was of the Redeemed, and thus always capable of movement. The Reprobate Milton, for his part, is that "real Human," largely without effect in the poem, who "walkd above in power and majesty" (20:13, E114) attended by the "Seven Angels of the Presence." Without a speaking part in the poem, the Reprobate Milton seems oddly like a *doppelgänger*: unlike his Elect portion, "frozen in the rock of Horeb" (20:11, E114), the "real Human" can move, can walk "in power and majesty," but he, like the Bard, seems himself largely "unmoved" by the course of events passing below. Although Blake has attempted to displace the sterile serenity of the Heavenly perspective in *Paradise Lost* by his rewriting of the Miltonic text, it reenters precisely at the point of Blake's "election" of the dehumanized Reprobate Milton, for whom the crisis is always already passed. It is as though the discontent which had initially inspired Milton's move from Eternity, "[u]nhappy tho in heav'n" (2:18, E96), had been surgically excised in Blake's attempt to portray a postvortical, a postcrisis, Milton.

It is from the perspective of the Elect, however, that portion of the populace that "cannot Believe in Eternal Life Except by Miracle & a New Birth," that Blake enacts his most thorough revision of the rigid class analysis of biblical prophecy. The beginnings of this revision are to be found in two subtle descriptions of fallen consciousness, one from the perspective of the Elect Milton, the other from that of the Elect Blake, himself a character in the poem from its opening. In a casually expressed simile, already highlighted in the text by virtue of Blake's rare deployment of classical figures of speech, the poet attempts to portray the nature of what we might call "Idiotic" consciousness: "As when a man dreams, he reflects not that his body sleeps, / Else he would wake; so seem'd [Milton] entering his Shadow" (15:1–2, E109). The second moment occurs shortly after the descending Milton has entered Blake's left foot, as a generalization about Blake's still "unknowing" consciousness:

> I knew not that it was Milton, for man cannot know
> What passes in his members till periods of Space & Time
> Reveal the secrets of Eternity: for more extensive
> Than any other earthly things, are Mans earthly lineaments.
>
> (21:8–11, E115)

These two passages have several things in common: (1) They depict a moment of ignorance, of idiocy, in which the denial of a single piece of information – that man sleeps, that "it was Milton" – is the only obstacle separating the Elect from redemption, from wakefulness and saving knowledge. (2) But the point from which this ignorance is portrayed is always the utopian point of knowledge. Blake can only portray the sleeping Milton from the perspective of wakefulness: his difficulty with this portrayal is indicated by his having pushed this moment out of the poem proper, into a rare simile, abstracted from the "consciousness" of the poem as a generically consistent, and vehemently nonclassical, biblical prophecy. Similarly, the statement, "I knew not that it was Milton," can only be uttered from the perspective of someone who *did* know that it was Milton. To employ the terms of French semiotics, there is a

sharp disjunction here between the subject of the *énoncé* and the
subject of the *énonciation*: the subject of the *énoncé* is the Elect Blake,
idiotically unaware of his own body; the subject of the *énonciation* is
the Reprobate Blake, for whom the crisis of knowledge has passed.[36]
The Reprobate here, however, evinces a new-found interest in the
mentality of the fallen, perhaps by virtue of the symbiotic relationship of the two perspectives within a single sentence.

(3) Perhaps most importantly, these passages anticipate and even
predict, prophesy, from the prevortical point of ignorance, a moment
of knowledge, when the crisis of prophetic reception will have been
passed and understood. To say that a man "dreams" or "sleeps" is
merely a proleptic way of saying that he wakes and thinks waking
thoughts. (This metaphor will be of increasing importance in
Jerusalem.) To say that "I knew not" is merely a proleptic way of
saying "I know now," and Blake informs his reader that "periods of
Space & Time" will "[r]eveal the secrets of Eternity," carrying
prophecy's receiver past the moment of crisis into true realization.
We might say, then, while acknowledging that Blake explicitly rejects
"the Stolen and Perverted Writings" of classical precedent, that the
fundamental rhetorical stance of *Milton* is itself the classical figure of
prolepsis. The purpose of *Milton*'s prophetic poetics, in the words of
the late Song of Experience, "To Tirzah," is to "chang[e] Death
into Sleep" (6, E30), to convert terminal figures into anticipatory
figures. Prolepsis thus allows Blake to combine in one image the
disparate perspectives of the past and the future, the Elect and the
Reprobate, the ideological and the utopian. In short, these odd
passages in the text of *Milton* hold out hope that the Idiot's faculties
will ultimately be roused, that the "Miracle" and "New Birth"
which had seemed so unlikely for the Elect can in fact be achieved.
In the spirit of Christ's own class analysis – "It is easier for a camel
to go through the eye of a needle, than for a rich man to enter into
the kingdom of God"[37] – Blake has seemed to limit the salvability of
the Elect. But Blake leaves open the same door that Christ does in
the little quoted sequel: "With men this is impossible; but with God
all things are possible."[38] Both Blake's and Christ's theories of class
formation have more gaps, more space for salutary crisis, than first
appears.

As will already have become evident from my metaphorical,
perhaps unauthorized, use of the word, I have been powerfully
tempted to read Blake's theory of classes in terms of Marxist and

neo-Marxist theories of class formation, both to suggest ties of sympathy between Blake's project and those of the Marxists and perhaps to force Blake's own text to a crisis of revelation in the light of this seemingly inappropriate parallel. I wish particularly to reintroduce the work of Althusser at two points where his own sometimes rigid theory of classes allows gaps, crises, in which consciousness breaks down the strictly drawn lines of class solidarity. The first crisis occurs in the context of Althusser's distinction between "class instinct" and "class position," in *Lenin and Philosophy*:

> Proletarians have a "class instinct" which helps them on the way to proletarian "class positions." Intellectuals, on the contrary, have a petty-bourgeois class instinct which fiercely resists this transition. A proletarian *class position* is more than a mere proletarian "class instinct." It is the consciousness and practice which conform with the *objective* reality of the proletarian class struggle. Class instinct is subjective and spontaneous. Class position is objective and rational. To arrive at proletarian class positions, the class instinct of proletarians only needs to be *educated*; the class instinct of the petty bourgeoisie, and hence of intellectuals, has, on the contrary, to be *revolutionized*. This education and this revolution are, in the last analysis, determined by proletarian class struggle conducted on the basis of principles of Marxist–Leninist *theory*. As the *Communist Manifesto* says, knowledge of this *theory* can help *certain* intellectuals to go over to working-class positions.[39]

Althusser's salvational scheme is still fairly restrictive: the difference in force required to bring over a proletarian and a petty bourgeois is the difference between "education" and "revolution," and even at that, Althusser will still only allow that *"certain* intellectuals" (a chosen remnant) can adopt working-class positions. But even though the odds are steep, the chance of a "Miracle & a New Birth" is better than no chance at all. By splitting the already divisive categories of class difference into "class instinct" and "class position," Althusser has opened the same intrasubjective crisis that Blake had opened by dividing Milton's consciousness into Elect, Redeemed, and Reprobate portions. He has also reintroduced the categories of consciousness and humanism which had before stood as the single most ideological character of the Blakean and Painite models of revolutionary crisis as seen from the perspective of Marxist "theory." To be sure, he still draws a line between the "subjective and spontaneous" class instinct which is always ideological and the "objective and rational" class position which is truly "scientific." But the work of effecting the transition from "instinct" to "position," the work of passing the vortical crisis from idiocy to knowledge, is now placed in the realm of "education" (for the proletariat) and revolutionary "knowledge of [Marxist-Leninist] theory" (for the petty bourgeoisie). By all indications, passage through the "eye of the needle," the critical point of revolutionary knowledge, will be difficult for the intellectual bourgeoisie, but, fortunately, "with [Marxist science] all things are possible."[40]

The second crisis in Althusser's text occurs in the essay on "Ideology and Ideological State Apparatuses" (also in *Lenin and Philosophy*) and explicitly addresses the issue of prolepsis in the conversion from an ideological to a "scientific"/utopian position:

[T]hose who are in ideology believe themselves by definition outside ideology: one of the effects of ideology is the practical *denegation* of the ideological character of ideology by ideology: ideology never says, "I am ideological." It is necessary to be outside ideology, i.e. in scientific knowledge, to be able to say: I am in ideology (a quite exceptional case) or (the general case): I was in ideology. As is well known, the accusation of being in ideology only applies to others, never to oneself . . . Which amounts to saying that ideology *has no outside* (for itself), but at the same time *that it is nothing but outside* (for science and reality).[41]

Althusser's formulation includes many of the elements we have seen at work in Blake's text. (1) It includes a description of idiotic consciousness, for which ideology is universal, "has no outside." (2) It includes a description of utopian consciousness, the Reprobate perspective "nowhere" to be found in ideology, for which ideology is "nothing but outside." (3) Finally, it includes a statement very much like Blake's "I knew not that it was Milton" – "I am ideological" – which can only be spoken from the utopian position. It is at this critical point, in this off-hand addition to his most complete formulation of a theory of ideology,[42] that Althusser most usefully complicates his notion of Marx's scientific break with ideology. No longer is the break between ideology and utopia figured as a unique and definitive event, the "work of the break" which necessarily occurs only once in Marx's career. Instead it is conceived of as a proleptic form, a fusion of precrisis and postcrisis consciousness, in which only when one is outside of ideology can one say "I am in ideology." Like that mysterious event that "passes in [Man's] members" without his knowledge, "till periods of Space & Time reveal the secrets of Eternity," or, in Paine's words (from the epigraph), until "a single expression . . . put[s] a whole company into their proper feelings," Althusser's break with ideology always occurs before it is recognized, and can never be definitively periodized. Instead of the single point of break – *the* "work of the break," "The *German Ideology*" – Althusser here circulates the proleptic form of crisis until it is a "Moment in each day."

I invoke these seemingly inappropriate comparisons also to suggest some ways of reading the second book of *Milton* and its culminating moment of reunion, in which the group figure of Blake–Los–Milton–Ololon–Seven Angels–Jesus–Satan seems to break down all class distinctions whatsoever. For all its rigid classifications, itself instituting the doctrine of classes, the Bard's Song already had contained a prediction of future unity: "The Elect shall meet the Redeem'd on Albion's rocks they shall meet" (13:30, E107). It is only in the second book, however, with the descent of Ololon after Milton, that this reunion is actually achieved. It frequently has been noted that the reunion of Ololon with Milton in many ways signifies the reunion of Milton with his fallen text, with *Paradise Lost* as received in the fallen world of 1667 and thereafter.[43] However, it also signifies, I would claim, the more general scene of reunion between a poet and an audience, now initiated into the secrets of prophecy, past the revolutionary moment of realization. Early in the second book, in a trilingual marginal note, Blake had noted that the Seven Angels attending the Reprobate Milton are to be understood "as multitudes, רבים, Vox Populi" (E131).[44] Ololon also, given the expansive terms in which she is described, would seem to represent more than just Milton's three daughters and three wives: "[M]ighty were the multitudes of Ololon, vast the extent / Of their great sway reaching from Ulro to Eternity" (35:37–8, E135). The masses which Ololon represents expand the narrow vortex by which the prophetic message was previously received into "a wide road" (35:35, E135), finding the "Moment in each Day that Satan cannot find" and "multiply[ing]" it, as Blake said was possible (35:42–6, E136). Ololon understands prophecy from the perspective of a second reading, as her descent is a "second reading" of Milton's passage through the vortex in the first book. She thus reads prophecy from that point which Barthes identifies as necessary for a critical understanding of the text: "Rereading . . . alone saves the text from repetition (those who fail to reread are obliged to read the same story everywhere), and multiplies it in its variety and its plurality:

rereading draws the text out of its internal chronology ('this happens *before* or *after* that') and recaptures a mythic time (without *before* or *after*)."[45] Like those proleptic statements which are divided between *énoncé* and *énonciation*, and like the proleptic form of Althusser's statement "I am in ideology," the perspective from which Ololon reads the vortex for the "first" time is already a "knowing" one. In short, the reunion of Milton and Ololon figures forth the revolutionary hope that the *vox populi* will follow the *vox individualis*, that the Idiot and the Prophet can be united in the educative and revolutionary reading of the prophetic text.

Finally, the moment of crisis in which Milton, Ololon, and Blake are united in Satan's bosom realizes the potential of Milton's earlier statement of radical nonidentification with a particular class: "I in my Selfhood am that Satan: I am that Evil One!" (14:30, E108). By uttering this statement, Milton is identifying himself as one of the Redeemed, one who is capable of coming to the point of crisis, of being "in doubts & fears" about one's own position. He is also acknowledging the Elect Milton within him, who can come to crisis only by means of a "Miracle & a New Birth." Finally he is revealing that he is also among the Reprobate, for whom the point of crisis is always already passed: by realizing that "I in my Selfhood am that Satan," Milton has already passed the vortex without need of subsequent descent, is already reading the "I" of the *énoncé* from the perspective of the "I" of the *énonciation*. Milton's class instinct, the instinct of the Elect, to remain in heaven, though unhappy, obeying, murmuring not, is educated and revolutionized by his ability to identify across classes as they exist both outside and inside himself, to adopt a new "class position." The seeming chaos of intersubjective and intrasubjective cross-identifications which make *Milton* such a formidable text for the novice reader are the signs of crisis within Blake's apparently rigid system of classes. These textual obscurities, however, will become clearer on a second reading. The revolutionary hope of *Milton* is its continuing faith that the Idiot within us all can be brought to that crisis of knowledge, to the moment of alteration in class position, by the vehicle of a prophetic education, in such a way that, once we have gotten there, it will seem as if we had been there all along.

The effect of the second book of *Milton* is thus to expand to a fully social scope what had seemed at the beginning of the poem to be an individual, personal moment: the crisis of consciousness, of Milton "unhappy tho' in heaven" and of the unhappy Blake, in Hayley's oppressive "heaven." The job that remains for the epic that was to occupy Blake for much of the remainder of his life, *Jerusalem,* is the fully social expression of the revolutionary moment of realization. The problems of Blake's most difficult poem are, as we shall see, the problems which affect any social utopia, those of intercommunication, the organization of individual and cultural differences, the avoidance of rigidity and stultification. As such, the best analogue for Blake's efforts in this work is the man who dedicated himself most single-mindedly to the utopian organization of social systems, Robert Owen.

CHAPTER 6

The utopian city and the public sphere in Robert Owen and Jerusalem

I

If, as I have hoped to show, a utopian energy is at work throughout Blake's career in various forms and according to various strategies, it is only with the composition of *Jerusalem* that he undertakes a determinate utopian subgenre – the poem of the city. From its roots in the *Republic* and the *Laws* of Plato to its Renaissance revival in works such as Tommaso Campanella's *City of the Sun*, from the constructivist designs of early Soviet Russia to the modern urban planning of architects such as Le Corbusier, utopian thinking has taken the city as a primary locus of enactment. Indeed, Lewis Mumford, an acknowledged authority on both utopian thought and the idea of the city, claims that "the first utopia was the city itself,"[1] predating Plato by many centuries. For Mumford, utopian thought emerges definitively only with the heralding of forces and creative breadth afforded by the ancient city builders. Only city building could inspire the single-mindedness and unity of purpose central to the utopian endeavor, bringing together that constellation of factors characteristic of both utopianism's grand designs and the urban dreams of the early city builders: "a mobilization of manpower, a command over long distance transportation, an intensification of communication over long distances in space and time, an outburst of invention."[2] However, as Mumford well realized and as the urban experience of the last 200 years clearly reveals, the utopian aspirations of the urban planners also bring with them a host of problems, a spectrous reflection (as Blake might have called it) which darkly shadows the hopes of the city builders: "[i]solation, stratification, fixation, regimentation, standardization, militarization" ("Utopia" 9). It is to the double-faced city, then, so well formulated in Blake's poem by the opposition between Jerusalem and Babylon, between

Golgonooza, "the spiritual fourfold London" ($M$20:40, E114), and the dirty, impoverished London of Blake's day, that we turn for an examination of Blake's most positive utopian vision in his last poem, *Jerusalem.*

I have chosen Robert Owen as a figure parallel to Blake[3] for three primary reasons, one of which will appear obvious, the other two perhaps less so. First, and most obviously, is their relative contemporaneity: Owen's "great experiment,"[4] the alternative community at New Lanark, occupied him from 1800 until 1829; Blake, from the best evidence available, worked on *Jerusalem* from around 1804 (the date on the title page) until 1820, when the first complete etching appears to have been finished.[5] Their utopian ideals seem thus to have sprouted in the same climate, if not from precisely equivalent soils: Owen grew up in Montgomeryshire, Wales; Blake in what is now known as the Soho district of London. (Their divergent emphases on the rural and the urban might thus be explained by their divergent origins, although the reliance on industrialism is common to both.) Secondly, and perhaps less obviously, they share a concern with the miserable conditions of the working poor under the new industrial system and propose, in their plans for new communities, methods to relieve this misery, to change the system by creating a new one ("Striving with Systems to deliver Individuals from those Systems" ($J$11:5, E154)). From this shared social purpose, I would argue, springs their common conception of ideology as a formidable force in modern society, a concept which, as we shall see, is almost as highly developed in Owen as it is in Blake. Third, and perhaps least obvious of all, is the fact that their utopian thinking is characterized by its realization in the actual world. For Owen this perhaps goes without saying: his experimental community provided the strongest response to the anti-utopian critique – "Utopianism is only wishful thinking" – by virtue of its mere existence. Owen might have responded to the charge of vain utopianism by pointing to New Lanark and saying, "*There* is my nowhere," and, indeed, he rejected the "utopian" label by insisting that his "principles have been carried most successfully into practice."[6] The "actuality" of Blake's urban utopia, although less immediately obvious, will be the object of the remainder of this chapter.

Perhaps the most convincing evidence of the "actuality" of Owen's utopianism is the fact that his peculiar genius reaches us not so much in his writings – which, although frequently interesting, are burdened by the dominant utilitarianism of the day – but in the records and remains of his "actual" utopian communities, New Lanark (in Scotland) and New Harmony (in Indiana, USA). Owen came to New Lanark in 1800, having recently married the daughter of the owner of the New Lanark Twist Company, David Dale. Bought from Dale by Owen and his partners for £60,000, New Lanark's evolution over the next thirty years figures forth in architectural form the evolution in Owen's thought. From paternalistic philanthropy and rational entrepreneurship to landless communism and utopian communitarianism, New Lanark's financial and social arrangements reflect the changes in the thought of Robert Owen and that circle of like-minded individuals who called themselves "Owenites." But New Lanark, like New Harmony and the numerous American Owenite communities, eventually met with commercial and philosophical failure. As critics of Owen from Friedrich Engels to the present have not neglected to point out, the story of Owenism in England and the United States is in many ways the story of repeated and invariable failure. The victim of both outside commercial pressures and inside dissensions, New Lanark's dissolution, and the rapid dissolution of the many American experiments, has provided the most convincing support for the anti-utopian position – that human beings, by their very nature, cannot unite in an effort which simultaneously respects both inevitable individual differences and recognized communal interests. The critique, in other words, follows the pattern that we have already seen several times before: that utopia, despite its pretensions to extra-ideological existence, will eventually sink into the dominant ideology, into, in New Lanark's case, the rapacious and atomistic system of industrial capitalism and its ideology of individualistic competition.

Blake's utopian city, a city built entirely on the "stubborn structure of . . . Language" (*J*36:59, E183), has also been subject to accusations of failure, accusations based particularly on the seeming inefficacy and obscurity of its communicative means. As Jon Mee has recently and convincingly reminded us, the central question for a critique interested in the politics of Blake's text is the question of its audiences and how it imagines reaching those audiences with its paralyzingly difficult language.[7] The context of language and its intelligibility is no less crucial for the utopian city than it is for politics in general, for communication is, as Blake well realized, the necessary preliminary to any efforts at a general renovation of society. The move from *Milton* to *Jerusalem* is precisely the move from an individualistic psychological mode to a social communicative mode for the depiction of utopian change. But how are we to deal with a poem which so consciously addresses itself to its audiences – "To the Public," as the note preceding the first chapter is headed – but which makes that address in a language which has driven away all but the most persistent readers? If Blake's notion of a redeemed world is indeed, as the last plates of *Jerusalem* suggest, that of an eternal conversation, "in Visionary forms dramatic" (*J*98:28, E257), then how are we to square this with a medium which seems to reject conversational, "ordinary," language so decisively? Like Owen's splintering communities, Blake's utopian language would seem to disintegrate into a chaos of mutually unintelligible ideolects, as incapable of serving as the foundation for a new utopian city as the babble of tongues with which Jehovah halted an earlier construction project.

However compelling these critiques might seem, the following pages suggest a new way to assess the enormous "failure" of the Owenite communities and a new way to view what has frequently been seen as the comparably vast poetic "failure" of Blake's formidable *Jerusalem*. As Blake's metaphor for his elusive mental structure might suggest, the breakdown of the Owenite communities should not be interpreted primarily as the failure of Owen's utopian aspirations, but merely as a cycle in that urban labor, "continually building & continually decaying" (*J*53:19, E203), which rebuilds the structures of the utopian future from the ruins of the ideological past. Blake's difficult formulations in *Jerusalem* will thus call upon us to rethink the nature of ruins, of failure and of success. Similarly, there is much to suggest that Blake's address to the various publics of *Jerusalem* cannot be judged by a simply conceived standard of immediate intelligibility. It is the stubbornness, indeed, of the stubborn structure of language that its communicative function is always mediated by matters of class, history, nationality, and other factors of social positioning. But the strength of Blake's last poem is the way in which it takes up the issue of language's stubbornness, concerns itself explicitly with those features of language which prevent it from being an ideally communicative medium, and thus suggests, by means of critique, what such a utopian language might look like. I will suggest, in the third section of this chapter, that Blake's address "to the public" should thus not simply be cited as evidence of a colossal disproportion between intention and execution, but should instead be taken as part of a more general reflection on the notion of a communicative "public sphere," a notion I hope to clarify by reference to the major theorist of the public sphere, Jürgen Habermas. Prior to that, the second section deals with Owen's and Blake's notions of the relation between ideology and utopia, especially the idea of a provisional separatism whereby a community might be isolated from pervasive ideological influences. Throughout, I hope to open up *Jerusalem* to the present day, to construct a gate whereby to enter the poem, if not to open the western gate which has been closed, that we may be seen to live in at least the outer suburbs of what Morton Paley, following Paul, has wisely called the "continuing city."[8]

II

Mr. Owen is a man remarkable for one idea. It is that of himself and the Lanark cotton-mills. He carries this idea backwards and forwards with him from Glasgow to London, without allowing any thing for attrition, and expects to find it in the same state of purity and perfection in the latter place as at the former. (William Hazlitt "On People with One Idea"[9])

In many ways, Robert Owen's "one idea," the idea "of himself and the Lanark cotton-mills," was ideology itself. Although neither he nor Hazlitt would ever have phrased it as such, the dominant note in Owen's theory of character formation, the note which so troubled proponents of a Christian free will, was a nascent theory of ideology. Owen's "doctrine of circumstances," repeated so frequently in his writings as to completely justify Hazlitt's frustration, amounts to nothing less than a general statement on the suprapersonal origins of the seemingly most inward of subjective states:

[E]very day will make it more evident *that the character of man is, without a single exception, always formed for him; and that it may be, and is, chiefly created by his predecessors; that they give him, or may give him, his ideas and habits, which are the powers that govern and direct his conduct. Man, therefore, never did, nor is it possible that he ever can, form his own character.*[10]

As J. F. C. Harrison has noted, in relation to others of the many versions of the "doctrine of circumstances," "[t]he concept of ideology (in the sense of the total idea structure considered as a function of social background and life experience) is implicit in much Owenite thought."[11] In particular, what we have earlier described as a "universal" concept of ideology is implicit in Owen's doctrine of circumstances. Note, for example, the tone of absolutism in the above quotation: "without a single exception," "always," "never," "nor is it possible." The repeated emphasis on absolute constructions indicates Owen's desire to portray a completely pervasive system, which, like Blake's concept of ideology, begins with the very creation of man, before the emergence of even a single thought. To perversely paraphrase a modern proponent of the doctrine of free will, we might say that, for Owen, ideology precedes the idea.

Yet even within the text of Owen's "one idea" it is possible to detect signs of tension, rhetorical and logical stresses which might indicate gaps within the universal theory of ideology. Twice within this brief passage Owen juxtaposes positive and conditional constructions: "[the character of man] *may be, and is*, chiefly created by his predecessors . . . they *give* him, *or may give him*, his ideas and habits." The order of the positive and the conditional is reversed in these two examples, but the impression remains of an ambiguity between universal and partial senses of the ideology which Owen proposes. In the light of this discontinuity in Owen's tone, the absolutism of the rest of the passage begins to assume new significance. Why would Owen need to stress and restress the universality of his doctrine of circumstances – "Man, therefore, *never did, nor is it possible that he ever can*, form his own character" – unless there remained a possibility that his theory was less than universal, that man perhaps could, under very special circumstances, form his own character or at least the characters of others? The final gap within the passage is, of course, that opened by the paradox of ideology-critique itself: Owen's "one idea" proposes the subordination of ideas – man's "ideas and habits" – to ideology, the "predecessors" who create them. To the precise extent that Owen is successful in enforcing his "one idea," he will therefore most definitively undermine it. Without a utopian point from which to regard ideology, Owen, like Mannheim after him, finds himself staring at the back of his own head.

In thus examining the ambiguities of Owen's language, we are not, as it might first seem, attempting to uncover deep-seated anxieties in his character, nor are we engaging in that recently popular pastime of abyss hunting, whose final satisfaction is to be found in the declaration that the text is unreadable. Rather, we are attempting to describe the ambiguity at the heart of ideology itself, an ambiguity which Owen consciously and intentionally exploited in his plans for utopian communities. The corollary of the doctrine of circumstances – that man's character is created for him by external circumstances – is that man's (and woman's) character may always be created anew. Owen says as much in the opening of his retrospective *Life*, published in 1857. Having restated his "one idea" in a theological formulation – "the made receives all its qualities from its maker" – he goes on to enumerate the many benefits of his "greatest discovery," in a catalog whose entries each begin with the phrase "It is the greatest discovery, because . . ." Among the items listed Owen includes many which stress the transformative nature of the ideological thesis: "It is the greatest discovery, – because it will terminate all anger, ill-will, contests, and wars, among men and nations, and will make the art of war to be no longer taught, and to cease for ever."[12] In a manner reminiscent of Blake's doctrine that evil must be fully revealed in order to be overcome, Owen formulates the two-sided doctrine of circumstances, in its ideological and utopian dimensions: "It is the greatest discovery, – because it . . . discloses the origin of evil among men, and the means by which to remove the evil for ever" (*Life*, xxxv). The ambiguity of Owen's seemingly universal theory of ideology is thus not at all arbitrary or coincidental, but is the result of a fundamental duplicity at the heart of the doctrine of circumstances itself. The fact that man's character is created for him and not by him reveals both the source of mankind's misery in the present day (a botched creation) and the ultimate solution to that misery (a recreation). The ideological thesis thus facilitates the utopian project, ideology standing as the mirror image of utopia's transformative aspirations.

The two-sidedness of Owen's doctrine of circumstances can equally be traced in the prehistory of New Lanark itself, a prehistory which includes the ideological forms of many structures reflected in their utopian fullness only in the mirror of Owen's ideal community. Harrison, the leading "archaeologist" of New Lanark and the other Owenite communities, outlines a thorough and convincing pedigree for Owen's social and economic structures, establishing New Lanark's ties to many institutions which those sympathetic to Owen would no doubt rather overlook. One must first of all bear in mind that New Lanark was initially intended to be merely a profitable enterprise and that it was to the model factory that Owen originally turned for inspiration. The model factory, influenced by new utilitarian notions of rationality in labor management, aspired to a standard of absolute efficiency. As a consequence, women and children were encouraged to work beside the men, the children often working twelve-hour days on every day but Sunday. Any religious or secular education within these industrial communities existed, for the most part, merely to extend the workmaster's zone of influence, to discipline the minds as well as the bodies of potentially unruly workers. Owen, although he later became a leading advocate for child-labor laws, began his "great experiment" with the example of the model factory very much in mind: by 1816, as Harrison reports, New Lanark was "the largest cotton undertaking, measured by numbers employed, in Britain,"[13] with a large percentage accounted for by women and children ages ten and up. At least on this point, it would seem, Owen had no trouble in defending himself against the charge of dreamy utopianism. In addition to the new standard of efficiency, however, Owen also had recourse to an ancient feudal ideal of benevolent paternalism. Owen was often the "father" to his communities of "children," and his relationship to his workers cannot help but remind the cynical observer of the pastoral squir- earchy so beloved of the eighteenth century. Indeed, Owen's example frequently serves to warn of the rapidity with which well- meaning egalitarian social engineers can come to sound like con- descending aristocrats. Owen, with one foot in the individualistic ideology of his own times and one foot in the feudal ideology of the eighteenth century, had most dubious building materials for a project such as New Lanark.

We must not, however, confuse an institution's origins with its ultimate purposes. As Harrison notes, neither of Owen's experimen- tal communities, New Lanark and New Harmony, was "started from scratch": "In each case he bought from a pioneer founder a going concern and adapted it to his own ends" (*Quest for the New Moral World*, 154). As Blake was to discover independently in his plans for the construction of Jerusalem and Golgonooza, the building of the utopian city cannot wait for its proper materials: the stones of Golgonooza must be formed of "pity," the curtains of "woven tears & sighs" (*J*12:30, 39, E155), or they will not be formed at all. Similarly, Owen's communities are "New" only to the extent that they refurbish old materials, materials which show the marks of other uses until they are effectively reconstituted. What shall interest us most in our comparison of Owen's and Blake's strategies of utopian construction, then, will be their ingenuity in reshaping their flawed materials, their skill in exploiting the double-faced doctrine of circumstances, its ideological and utopian dimensions. Both Owen's and Blake's utopian cities are constructed on the principle that the ideological content of the fallen world can be reflected in a different way, in the mirror of a community arranged along the lines of utopian thought. Just as Marx was influentially to formulate the concept of ideology as the inversion of man's actual life processes, Blake's and Owen's utopian strategies are the inversion of that inversion, the righting of mankind's ideological existence in the mirror of the utopian community. Although Blake was to employ more explicitly the technique of "mirror writing" in several plates of *Jerusalem* (plates 37 (see figure 10), 72, and 81), Owen's physical and mental labors can also be thought of as a variety of "mirror writing" in their reversals of the ideological thesis, their "righting" of the structures of the ideological world. Blake had long realized that his backwards etching in copper plates was perversely seen as "normal" in the ideological world,[14] so his plans for utopian fulfillment naturally appear backwards in the text of *Jerusalem*, or, to characterize the other qualities of what has been seen as a perverse backwardness in Blake's last poem, they seem needlessly obscure, convoluted, curiously hidden in the darkness of an almost opaque textual surface. It is to Blake's backwardness, then, that we shall turn next in our assessment of his and Owen's utopian strategies.

Blake, much in the manner of Owen, includes in *Jerusalem* a characterization of the ideological world which initially seems absolute, universal in its inclusion of every experience of a fallen mankind:

> What seems to Be: Is: To those to whom
> It seems to Be, & is productive of the most dreadful
> Consequences to those to whom it seems to Be: even of
> Torments, Despair, Eternal Death.   (32:51–4, E179)

The effect of this passage, spoken by "those in Great Eternity" (32:50), is to equate appearance and reality, the "seems to Be" and the "Is," or, in the terms of Blake's inherited epistemology, the *esse* and the *percipi*. And since the senses of Blake's fallen world are, as described in the plates immediately preceding this passage, "bended

10 Plate 41 of *Jerusalem: The Emanation of the Giant Albion*.

. . . down to Earth" (30:47, E177), there would seem to be no chance
of a saving perception of the world beyond the fall. "If the Perceptive
Organs close," as Blake pessimistically puts it, "their Objects seem
to close also" (30:56, E177), and it is to the closed circuit of fallen
perception – represented equally by the senses of men bent to earth,
the circular caves of the eyes (30:53) and the seemingly circular dome
of the sky called by Blake the "Mundane Shell" – that Blake's
ideological thesis seems to doom us. The consequences of the
equation of appearance and reality are clearly delineated: "Tor-
ments, Despair, [and] Eternal Death." But within this seemingly
universal description of mankind's fallen perceptions, as within
Owen's seemingly universal doctrine of circumstances, there persist
spaces for difference, moments of utopian surplus. Reminiscent as it
is of Owen's juxtaposition of the conditional and the absolute,
Blake's juxtaposition of the "seems to Be" and the "Is" also
foreshadows Los's triumphant challenge to his Sons during the
culmination of chapter 4: "Will you suffer this Satan this Body of
Doubt that *Seems but is Not* / to occupy the very threshold of Eternal
Life?" (93:20–1, E253; emphasis added). The "Is" – that which
"Eternally Exists. Really & Unchangeably" (*VLJ*, E554), as Blake
had described the proper object of art in his notebook at this time –
is no longer equated with the "seems to Be," but rather stands as its
mirror image, the utopian inversion of perverse appearance. Los
does not reject the tragedy of fallen perception, but instead cele-
brates it as the harbinger of its own overcoming: "[I]f Bacon,
Newton, Locke, / Deny a Conscience in Man & the Communion of
Saints & Angels," Los proposes, echoing Blake's formula for the
dominant ideology of his day, "[i]s it not that Signal of the Morning
which was told us in the Beginning?" (93:21–2, 26, E253–4). The
seeds of this utopian surplus are also present in the earlier passage,
for after the Eternal's equation of appearance and reality they
include an "escape clause" of salvational potential: "but the Divine
Mercy / Steps beyond and Redeems Man in the Body of Jesus
Amen" (32:54–5, E179). Central to an understanding of the role of
Jesus in *Jerusalem*, which has been interpreted as Blake's return to
religious orthodoxy, is a conception of Christ as the utopian surplus
which exceeds the ideological formulation and a notion of the
relation between Christ and Antichrist. A key to the operations of
Jerusalem is Blake's depiction of the close mirroring of Christ and
Antichrist – a mirroring indicated even in the similarity of their

names – by which that which is most fallen can paradoxically become a "Signal of the Morning" of Christ's return.

The mirroring of the fallen and the redeemed, of the ideological and the utopian, is revealed most clearly in that scene at the center of the last chapter where "the Antichrist" is first introduced, "a Human Dragon terrible / And bright, stretched over Europe & Asia gorgeous" (89:10, 11–12, E248). Blake's description of this "Covering Cherub" does much to further our understanding of the central dynamic of *Jerusalem*, that "inversion of an inversion" which constitutes the utopian city:

> His head dark, deadly, in its Brain incloses *a reflexion*
> *Of Eden all perverted*; Eden on the Gihon many tongued
> And many mouthed: Ethiopia, Lybia, the Sea of Rephaim
> Minute Particulars in slavery I behold among the brick-kilns
> Disorganizd, & there is a Pharoh in his iron Court:
> And the Dragon of the River & the Furnaces of iron.
> Outwoven from Thames & Tweed & Severn awful streams
> Twelve ridges of Stone frown over all the Earth in tyrant pride
> Frown over each River stupendous Works of Albions Druid Sons.
>
> (89:14–22, E248; my emphasis)

Northrop Frye,[15] whose groundbreaking discussion of Blake's concept of "Divine Analogy" represents the most enduring legacy of *Fearful Symmetry*, was the first to highlight the place of inversion in Blake's system. But it is yet necessary to point out the relation between Blake's idea of the fallen world – "a reflexion of Eden all perverted" – and the budding thesis of ideology, as formulated in the works of thinkers such as Robert Owen. Blake's "perverted Eden," like Owen's, is composed of the modern city and its system of industrialism, "brick-kilns / Disorganizd . . . the Furnaces of iron. / Outwoven from Thames & Tweed & Severn awful streams."[16] By extended analogy with ancient Egypt, Blake portrays an ideological world which expresses itself most clearly in its depraved architectural schemes and its exploitation of slave (and wage-slave) labor, resulting in inhuman dwelling places, "Twelve ridges of Stone."[17] But Blake's solution to the miserable conditions of the industrial city, like Owen's, does not involve a renunciation of the industrial method, nor an abandonment of the hopes of the city builders, but rather their refinement within the limits of a truly utopian architecture. The proper response to "a reflexion of Eden all perverted," as Blake had learned in his experiments with mirror writing, is its reinversion in the mirror of utopian art and architecture. As much is implied in an earlier description of Los's architectural designs, which stand throughout *Jerusalem* as the utopian obverse of the perverse Urizenic city: "And the Four Gates of Los surround the Universe Within and / Without; & whatever is visible in the Vegetable Earth, the same / Is visible in the Mundane Shell; *reversd* in mountain & vale" (72:45–7, E227; my emphasis). Los does not abandon the fallen materials of the "Mundane Shell" or the "Vegetable Earth," but inverts them in such a way as to reveal their utopian potential. Blake's and Los's labors, which have astutely been characterized as a kind of "urban renewal,"[18] might even more precisely be called an "urban reversal," in the way they invert the potentials of the ideological city for utopian purposes.

The formula which Los includes in his plan for a utopian city, its existence both "Within and Without" the fallen universe, comprises, in its very unimaginability, another feature of the "backwardness" which equally characterizes Blake and Owen. Blake had employed this formula earlier in the poem, immediately preceding his most complete architectural plan, the design for Golgonooza in plates 12 and 13: "God is within, & without! he is even in the depths of Hell!" (12:15, E155). Does this formulation merely echo medieval paradoxical descriptions of the Divine Being, the circle whose center is everywhere and whose circumference is nowhere? In terms of the plan for a utopian city, how would one build a gate with supports both "within and without" the fallen universe? In short, the obscurity, the "backwardness," of Blake's language, at the very point where he most explicitly outlines his plans for the utopian city, threatens to render his city-building aspirations unrealizable, "utopian" in the pejorative sense of being unable to imagine. There remains, however, the possibility of putting a different construction on these obscure words, seemingly perverse in their resistance to ordinary sense. Owen's own cities, which, as we have said, represent the most compelling refutation of the charge of "vain utopianism" by their very existence, themselves lie both within and without the fallen world of English ideology. They are "within" in the sense that we have already indicated, in that they use the flawed resources of the ideological world – its industrial system, its benevolent paternalism – for utopian ends. The "withoutness" of the Owenite communities is best indicated, however, by their isolation from society at large, by Owen's propensity to remove his communities from undue ideological influences and from the miserable conditions of the established manufacturing communities. The centerpiece of Owen's theory of ideological transformation, his educational system, is itself founded on the principle that children are the most fertile ground for the seeds of utopian communitarianism, in that they are the individuals most "without" the dominant ideology of their times, not so inured to systems of capitalistic control as their beleaguered parents. The success of Owen's utopianism thus depends on a simultaneous "withinness" and "withoutness," a separatism from society at large in communities which themselves employ the ideological materials of the fallen world for utopian purposes. Owen's experiment thus stands as an historical gloss on Althusser's statement (noted earlier) that ideology simultaneously "has no outside" and "is nothing but outside."

The simultaneity of "withinness" and "withoutness" in Blake's utopian city occurs in a series of images and statements. Standing as something of a motto to *Jerusalem* on the frontispiece, Blake's repetition of a phrase uttered by Ololon in *Milton* (41:37–42:1, E143) summarizes neatly and intriguingly the double location of the utopian city: "There is a Void, outside of Existence, which if enterd into / Englobes itself & becomes a Womb" (1:1–2, E144). The peculiarity of this brief passage, apparent on close examination, is its combination of images of the most sublime "withoutness" – "a Void, outside of Existence" – and the most insulated "withinness" – an "englob[ing] . . . Womb." To the Urizenic mind, which fears both extremes of vastness and of constriction, the uncanny "Womb outside of Existence" must inspire an oddly simultaneous agora- and claustrophobia, each synergistically augmented by being fused with its opposite in a single figure. Despite this figure's unpicturability, however, despite its capacity to frustrate the expectations of the innocent reader by its obscurity and seeming "backwardness," it can reasonably stand (as Blake's positioning of it in the frontispiece would indicate)[19] as an emblem for the work as a whole, much as it could stand as an emblem for the simultaneous "withinness" and "withoutness" of Owen's utopian project. Blake, like Owen, employs a provisional separatism, isolating his audience from pervasive ideological influences, from the standards of meaning of the Urizenic world, while at the same time working with the materials of that world to transform them from within. The success of Blake's cunning utopianism, as we shall see, depends upon its well-timed oscillations between these two contraries, avoiding the pitfalls both of otherworldliness (naive withoutness) and ideological complicity (naive withinness). Blake's oft-quoted program in *Jerusalem* – "Striving with Systems to deliver Individuals from those Systems" (11:5, E154) – must thus be seen as both a "Striving with[in]" and a "Striving with[out]" the very Systems he seeks to escape.

It is not surprising, then, that one of the prime building blocks in Blake's utopian architecture is the gate, marking as it does the boundary between the within and the without. Los's Gate, as described in the second chapter, is the only saving portal to the world outside the fall, but is only to be found, paradoxically, within the heart of ideological London:

> There is in Albion a Gate of precious stones and gold
> Seen only by Emanations, by vegetations viewless,
> Bending across the road of Oxford Street; it from Hyde Park
> To Tyburns deathful shades, admits the wandering souls
> Of multitudes who die from Earth: this Gate cannot be found
> By Satans Watch-fiends tho' they search numbering every grain
> Of sand on Earth every night, they never find this Gate.
> It is the Gate of Los.   (34:55–35:3, E181)

By locating Los's Gate near "Tyburn's deathful shades" – that is, near the site of the numerous executions orchestrated by the repressive British government – Blake is stressing how far "within" the ideological system the Gate "without" truly lies. On one level, of course, the Gate merely represents the loosing of the souls of those whose bodies have been claimed by Tyburn Gallows. But it also represents the release to the outside hidden in the most unlikely of places. The entrance is hidden, invisible to the authorities of Blake's ideological world, to "Satans Watch-fiends," who search for it in vain. The Gate, like Blake's poem, is thus curiously "backward," obscure, unable to be deciphered by the mass of potential searchers. But Los's Gate, like every gate, can be approached from two directions, a fact which Albion discovers too late when he flees from Eternity through the Gate to the world of fallen London, crying "I die! I go to Eternal Death!" (35:16). Like almost every other image in *Jerusalem*, the image of the gate is fundamentally duplicitous, possessing an ideological and a utopian form. In its ideological guise the gate is the Druidic trilithon, representative of the unforgiving law of vengeance and the stony limits of fallen perception, as pictured in the illumination for plate 70 (figure 11). To see the gate in its utopian

11 Plate 70 of *Jerusalem: The Emanation of the Giant Albion*.

dimension, as the Gate of Los, will require the cunning to appreciate the "backwardness" of Blake's text, to reinvert the perverse trilithon which appears to be the only gate of this world. The path "without" thus appears only to the reader willing to get "within" the symbol, to transform the ideological image into its utopian reflection. Blake suggests such a reading strategy, although in terms of the medium of painting, in describing the most useful way of looking at the images in his *A Vision of the Last Judgment*:

> If the Spectator could Enter into these Images in his Imagination approaching them on the Fiery Chariot of his Contemplative Thought if he could Enter into Noahs Rainbow or into his bosom or could make a Friend & Companion of one of these Images of wonder which always intreats him to leave mortal things as he must know then would he arise from his Grave then would he meet the Lord in the Air & then he would be happy. (*VLJ*, E560)

In painting as in poetry, the way out in the late Blake, the path to utopian salvation, lies paradoxically inward, toward the gates of the text or image, rewarding the reader willing to labor at entering the ideological forms of the work of art.

A similar "hiddenness," a cunning backwardness, characterizes Blake's relationship to his audience in *Jerusalem*, curiously circumspect and even duplicitous after the bold rhetoric of *Milton*. Much of this can be explained autobiographically, for *Jerusalem* was composed, at least in its initial stages, under the pressure of Blake's confrontation with John Schofield (a recurrent villain in the poem), and with the painful memory of the subsequent sedition trial. As Erdman reports in his account of the trial, Blake was compelled by legitimate self-interest to keep silent while his defender, Samuel Rose, attributed to him a sacred respect for the English monarch.[20] However much these sentiments must have rankled the man who, in his description of the apocalypse, had included a bloody portrait of righteous regicide (*FZ*119:1–13, E388), Blake cunningly kept his feelings hidden. In an annotation to the works of Sir Joshua Reynolds, written during the composition of *Jerusalem*, Blake suggests another reason for his circumspection, one more relevant to his "backwardness" with the readers of his most obscure poem:

> Having spent the Vigour of my Youth & Genius under the Oppression of Sr Joshua & his Gang of Cunning Hired Knaves Without Employment & as much as could possibly be Without Bread, The Reader must Expect to Read in all my Remarks on these Books Nothing but Indignation &

Resentment . . . Reynolds & Gainsborough . . . Divided all the English
World between them Fuseli Indignant <almost> hid himself – I [*was*]
<am> hid. (E636)

Erdman's editorial italics indicate the deletion of the word "was"
and its replacement with "am," a sign of Blake's own willingness to
continue his deceit in the present, to remain "hid" behind the walls
of obscure and little-read books. Although Blake accuses Reynolds
and "his Gang" of base "Cunning" in a manner entirely consistent
with his normal use of that word, he reserves to himself his own
peculiar brand of cunning in protecting himself from the prying eyes
of "Satans Watch-fiends" and their representatives in the artistic
world. In the fallen world of ideology, of vicious accusers and
neglectful readers, Erin's glum diagnosis at the end of chapter 2 –
that "deep dissimulation is the only defence an honest man has left"
(49:23, E198) – seems entirely justified.

But more than autobiography is needed to explain Blake's new
"hiddenness" in *Jerusalem*. In the famous letter to Butts of 6 July,
1803, in the course of a description of the recently completed *Milton*,
Blake includes a definition of "Sublime Allegory" which does much
to explain his cunning strategy in *Jerusalem*: "Allegory addressed to
the Intellectual powers while it is *altogether hidden* from the Corporeal
Understanding is My Definition of the Most Sublime Poetry" (E730;
emphasis added). Blake's "doubling" of the organ which his poetry
addresses – both the "Intellectual Powers" and the "Corporeal
Understanding" – suggests a meaning for the duplicity of his deal-
ings with the audience of his last poem. The doubleness of his
language, its existence in both utopian and ideological senses, seeks a
similar doubleness in his audience. To those who can understand his
prophetic message, Blake's poem appears an open gate, the gate
which formerly was hid amidst a chaos of obscure reference and
"backward" syntax; to those deaf to his message, however, *Jerusalem*
will remain a forbidding wall, unassailable in its solid opacity.[21] One
is reminded of Christ's own ministry to the cities in Matthew,
perhaps a model for Blake in its inclusion of a prayer of thanksgiving
for duplicity: "I thank thee, O Father, Lord of heaven and earth,
because thou hast hid these things from the wise and prudent, and
hast revealed them unto babes" (11.25). Christ's prayer, like Blake's
definition of "Sublime Allegory," distinguishes between the two
audiences for a single text, one which can gain access to the

message, one which cannot. Christ's message to the cities, like Blake's message to the Babylon called London, builds a salutary wall between its two audiences, separating one from the other, so that a poem or a prophecy might appear either "within" or "without" a given hearer's comprehension depending on his point of view. The passage to that other city, the heavenly city promised by both Christ and Blake, depends upon one's relation to the text, whether it is seen as a hidden gate or an unscalable wall.[22]

One need only examine the preface to chapter 1 of *Jerusalem*, addressed blithely "To the Public," to begin to understand the operation of Blake's utopian cunning, simultaneously "within" and "without" the ideological world. There, on a plate headed by the carefully segregated words "Sheep" and "Goats," Blake cunningly impersonates the amiable author of the eighteenth-century preface:

> After my three years slumber on the banks of the Ocean, I again display my Giant forms to the Public: My former Giants & Fairies having reciev'd the highest reward possible: the [*love*] and [*friendship*] of those with whom to be connected, is to be [*blessed*]: I cannot doubt that this more consolidated & extended Work, will be as kindly recieved. (3, E145)

To an unsuspecting reader, this amicable opening might seem the prelude to a production as innocuous as Hayley's *The Triumphs of Temper*. But this unassuming passage hides depths apparent only to the Blakean initiate, hidden as thoroughly as the ambivalent "love" and "friendship" which Blake obscured in later revision. The knowing reader must then initially bristle at Blake's reference to his titanic characters as "Giants & Fairies," as if they were equivalent to the characters of some contemporary children's tale.[23] The reader familiar with Blake's corpus summons his "Intellectual powers" to remember the parodic introduction to *Europe*, where Blake describes how a "tipsie" Fairy dictated that prophecy to him: there, as here, Blake invokes English popular legend ironically, contemptuous of its frilly visions. It is, of course, possible that Blake truly appreciated the enthusiasm of his small circle of readers, that he considered the recognition of an audience "fit, though few" to be "the highest reward possible." But his erasure of the "love" and "friendship" with which these readers presumably showered him, and of the "blessed[ness]" which he felt under their influence, indicates unacknowledged depths hidden beneath this bland exterior. Only by the most imaginative standard could Blake's previous work be described as "kindly received," only by a standard that would not normally occur to any reader not "in" the know. The first paragraph of this first preface, although it is addressed inclusively to "the Public," thus enforces the preliminary separatism between two groups of readers – between the "Sheep" and the "Goats" – which will allow *Jerusalem* to construct its utopian city on sounder principles. Like Owen's New Lanark, "hidden" in the lowlands of Scotland, Blake's New Jerusalem is removed from the prying eyes of the uninitiate: while both are "within" the ideological system of their time, and use the flawed materials of that system, they are "without" to the extent that they remove themselves from its immediate control, to a "Void, outside of Existence."

In acknowledging Blake's cunning relation to his audience, we are doing nothing less than acknowledging the basic constructive principles of *Jerusalem*, too often overlooked for more arcane formulae.[24] Blake's poem, although it may reveal many different formal rhythms, is primarily constructed on the four-square foundation of strict numerology: four chapters, 100 plates, each chapter ending on an even twenty-five. While Morton Paley's suggestion of a dialectic between the poem's "organization" (its strict, four-chapter structure) and its "form" (its variable interior rhythms) contains many fruitful hints for the reader, we must insist that *Jerusalem*'s primary form is more than just a "container" for a more loosely constructed content.[25] Blake's separation of the "Sheep" and the "Goats," like his separation of his four audiences – "the Public," "the Jews," "the Deists," "the Christians," none of which we can automatically assume to be interinclusive – and his precise separation of his four chapters, indicates the extension of his artistic theory of the "bounding line" (E550) to the construction of *Jerusalem*. In this case, the "line" is that which cunningly separates the "within" from the "without," the initiate from the uninitiate, in such a way as to preserve the integrity of Blake's utopian city. Although Blake had included in earlier poems descriptions of his city of art, Golgonooza (whose etymology Bloom has intriguingly traced to the Hebrew for "hidden hub"),[26] the reader must acknowledge that *Jerusalem* is peculiar for its precise architecture, its finely constructed walls and its well-balanced gates. This precision, I would argue, in its difference from the asymmetrical design of *Milton* and the other prophecies, indicates Blake's different relationship with his audience in *Jerusalem*, his desire to separate them with well-designed and well-constructed walls of verse and description. But these questions involve only the approach to Blake's utopian city, whether it appears as a forbidding wall or a welcoming gate. The city itself, a city built on eternal conversation, will require a reconstituted idea of communication, a language which can reach across the segregated spheres of separate ideological discourses to a properly "public" sphere of mutual exchange.

III

In an 1810 supplement to his descriptive catalog of pictures, in the document now commonly referred to as *A Vision of the Last Judgment*, Blake specifies the manner in which his individual images should be regarded and, in the course of this recommendation, formulates an unusually powerful description of the "Public" to which his paintings and poems were directed:

> [I]t ought to be understood that the Persons Moses & Abraham are not here meant but the States Signified by those Names the Individuals being representatives or Visions of those States as they were reveald to Mortal Man in the Series of Divine Revelations. as they are written in the Bible these various States I have seen in my Imagination when distant they appear as One Man but as you approach they appear Multitudes of Nations. (E556–7)

Blake's "One Man," like the "public" so frequently invoked by pollsters, politicians, advertisers, and others, possesses a crucial dual existence.[27] It must be the representative of vast quantities, of the "many," of "Multitudes of Nations," in order to bear the weight of significance granted it; but it must also act and appear as a unitary form, speaking with one voice, in order for it to be coherent and for it to have meaning in the contexts in which it is invoked. In grammatical terms, it must be a collective noun, extending singularity of action to a concept which still retains some of its sense of plurality. In the context of *A Vision*, the notion of the corporate "One Man" has not yet reached the point of universality, in that Blake is here imagining a "State of Moses" to be distinguished from a "State of Abraham" and so on, but it is not very far from this idea of competing unitary states to the all-embracing "One Man, Albion" whose reawakening at the end of *Jerusalem* signals the beginnings of humanity's regeneration: "[T]hey walked / To & fro in Eternity as One Man reflecting each in each & clearly seen / And seeing:

according to fitness & order" (*J*98:38–40, E258). If the city of Jerusalem is the architectural form of Blake's utopian vision, the "Emanation of The Giant Albion" as the poem's full title has it, then this "One Man," Albion himself, is the utopian social form, Blake's most fully realized notion of a redeemed humanity.

However, as my reference to the realms of polling and politicking might already have indicated, the positing of a unitary public is by no means unproblematic. For one thing, the invocation of the public, or of "public opinion," is never neutral, but always occurs in the context of some ideological expression of power. In fact, it is precisely because "public opinion" possesses the appearance of neutrality – standing as a mere measurement or survey of what is on "the public mind" – that it carries such enormous importance in its strategic positioning by those in power. One might go so far as to identify the role of "the public" as the ideal and necessary replacement for older universal theories (religious and philosophical) in the maintenance of an unequal distribution of power: if the Church and traditional codes of a natural order of things no longer possess the capacity to justify asymmetrical relations of power (and were beginning to lose this capacity in Blake's day), then the seemingly neutral voice of "the public" serves to fill the gap nicely, providing an apparently nonideological justification for clearly ideological social and political arrangements. Of course, as we all know, the public can be invoked in support of widely various causes and often speaks with seemingly inconsistent voices. The "One Man" can sometimes seem to be alarmingly of two (or more) minds. These inconsistencies merely stand as direct evidence for a second problem with the invocation of the public, corollary to the first, that it often (if not always) fails to do justice to the variety of the individual voices of which it is presumably composed. Teased out by purposefully framed questions or ventriloquized by a self-designated "man of the people," the public is usually compelled to speak with a coherent unified voice which obscures the cacophany that remains just out of earshot. However, as is frequently the case with such uses of the public, if we look closely at the face of power that professes to invoke the public voice, we should not be at all surprised to see the lips move.

How, then, are we to understand the reappearance of the "One Man," now in a universal formulation, at the end of *Jerusalem*, in a context which clearly suggests his emergence as a triumphant

conclusion to fallen history? Besides the immediate exclusion in-
scribed in Blake's use of the word *Man* to refer to the entire human
community, we might well wonder whether this image of the utopian
society – arranged, in Blake's words, "according to fitness & order"
(98:40) – involves exclusions of other kinds, of differences in belief,
custom, and class. Blake declares, at the head of plate 99, that in the
Edenic state "All Human Forms [are] identified" (99:1, E258), but
we must yet question whether this identification occurs only at the
cost of the suppression of difference, only with the subjugation of
humankind to the "One Law" which Blake had earlier in his career
called "oppression." Indeed, a survey of Blake's evolving idea of the
"One," beginning with this formula that "One Law for the Lion &
Ox is Opression" (appearing in *The Marriage of Heaven and Hell* [24,
E44] and repeated in an ironic context in *Visions of the Daughters of
Albion* [4:22, E48]), would itself suggest an immanent critique of the
"One Man" with which his poetic career uncharacteristically ends.
A significant entry in this survey would be Urizen's recitation from
"the Book / Of eternal brass" (*BU*4:32–3, E72) in *The Book of Urizen*:

> Let each chuse one habitation:
> His ancient infinite mansion:
> One command, one joy, one desire,
> One curse, one weight, one measure
> One King, one God, one Law.   (4:36–40, E72)

In the world of the Lambeth prophecies, Urizen is clearly the model
of a tyrant, extending the "stonifying" power of the "One" to every
aspect of mankind's fallen world. Urizen's single-mindedness extends
even to the emotional and physical dimensions of the onefold world,
in his insistence on "a joy without pain" and "a solid without
fluctuation" (4:10–11, E71). It is only against the background of
Urizen's "one Law," then, that the "One Man" of Blake's consummate utopian vision in *Jerusalem* can be fully understood. We would
seem compelled to choose between two equally distressing alternatives: either Blake's development of the "One" in *The Book of Urizen*
is incomplete or the "One Man" of *Jerusalem* is a sign of Blake's
slipping into the ideology of unitary order which he had earlier
rejected.

The choice need not be so stark, however, if we are able to
imagine, and trace Blake's development of, a different model of the
public, one which might allow for a unity not directed from above,

or invoked for purely ideological reasons, but arrived at through an exchange of differing and freely expressed views. Students of the eighteenth century and of recent developments in sociological thought will recognize this terrain – that of an alternatively conceived model of public discourse, capable of arriving at nuanced and equitable decisions – as the special demesne of the German sociologist Jürgen Habermas, and, in particular, as the subject of his first book, *The Structural Transformation of the Public Sphere*. In that book (first published in German in 1962 and translated into English in 1989) Habermas traces the emergence in eighteenth-century Europe (England, France, and Germany, in particular) of a substantially new model of public deliberation, the bourgeois public sphere. According to Habermas, the bourgeois public sphere differed from earlier publics in its ability to entertain various points of view: whereas the notion of "public" interests had formerly (under feudal regimes) been identified with the concerns of the lord and king, the sole embodiment of general welfare, the bourgeois public sphere distinguished itself from the state apparatus in its ability to oppose, question, challenge, or (alternatively) to endorse actions of the state.[28] Habermas is thus as concerned with the imagery of the body as a figure for public power as Blake is: the difference between a feudal and a bourgeois public sphere as he describes them is the difference between a notion of the "One Man" which weights the priority of the unitary (regal) body perceived at a distance and one which emphasizes the "Multitudes of Nations" which appear on closer inspection. But where the feudal eye can see only the king, seeing the king even in his individual subjects, the bourgeois eye possesses the double vision implied by Blake's description, capable of distinguishing individual competing points of view while also acknowledging the existence of a general and distinct public sphere. In the public coffeehouses, in salons, in the emergent popular press, and in the consumption and discussion of cultural objects newly addressed to a "public at large," the bourgeois created itself as the class capable of critiquing the state and society, open to the variety of views within its own ranks, as well as those of the residual aristocracy and the emergent working classes.[29]

Such, in very broad outline, is the substance of Habermas's historical argument. But to assess the relevance of this model for Blake's "One Man," and to fill out the details and complexities of the bourgeois public sphere, we might do well to consider some of the leading criticisms of Habermas's ideas. It is fitting, indeed, that a theory of open debate be developed in its confrontation both with the criticism of others and with Habermas's own rethinking and realignment of certain elements of his early thought, via an "intellectual war" (*FZ*139:10, E407) which lies at the heart of Blake's utopian vision also. Along these lines, one criticism of Habermas's historic model registers a preliminary exclusion in the very constitution of the public sphere *as public*. Nancy Fraser, for instance, rightly notes that the logical opposition between the public and the private is not fixed for all time, but has shifted from one historical period to another and in ways which unfairly benefit some groups at the expense of others:

For example, until quite recently, feminists were in the minority in thinking that domestic violence against women was a matter of common concern and thus a legitimate topic of public discourse. The great majority of people considered this issue to be a private matter . . . Then feminists formed a subaltern counterpublic from which we disseminated a view of domestic violence as a widespread systemic feature of male-dominated societies. Eventually, after sustained discursive contestation, we succeeded in *making* it a common concern.[30]

In this way, the very act of drawing a line between public and private, of tracing the bounding line by which the One Man's form is made clear or by which a sphere's inside is distinguished from its outside, is itself an ideological act expressive of unequal relations of power. Fraser's example well illustrates the ways in which a strategic definition of matters of "public" concern can have real consequences for the group whose interests are thus ruled out of bounds. And, as Fraser well knows, this distinction is of no small concern for Habermas, underpinning as it does his notion that participants in the public sphere were capable of rising above their various private interests in order to unite as a group in the discussion of issues of common concern. But, as Fraser's example indicates, no such private/public distinction can be assumed prior to deliberation in the public sphere; it is, rather, the outcome of (explicit or implicit) negotiation, the product of a "making," as Fraser says, which makes different distinctions at different times. As a challenge to the public sphere and, by extension, to Blake's "One Man," this first criticism suggests that even before the "Multitudes of Nations" have begun their eternal conversation, the terms of the debate have been set.

    In framing an answer to this criticism, we must bear in mind the nuanced relationship between the public and the private in Habermas's work, in particular, the fact that for Habermas as well as for his critics the passage from the private to the public is indeed *a passage*, requiring discursive labor and negotiation. In Habermas's concise formulation, the bourgeois public is precisely "the sphere of private people come together as a public" (*Structural Transformation*, 27). Thus, a particularly crucial locus for the development of the bourgeois public sphere as he describes it is the private bourgeois family, especially for its creation of a new kind of subjectivity: "[B]efore the public sphere explicitly assumed political functions in the tension-charged field of state–society relations, the subjectivity originating in the intimate sphere of the conjugal family created, so to speak, its own public" (*Structural Transformation*, 29). The passage from private to public is implicit in this formulation and bears further explication. The importance of the private domestic sphere for the development of a properly bourgeois public sphere lies in the critical power of the rich subjectivity, the "saturated and free interiority" (*Structural Transformation*, 28), idealized and to some extent actually created in the domestic sphere. No longer simply an economic unit in a household economy, the domestic sphere in the eighteenth century took on a role consciously opposed to the impersonal mechanistic imperatives of the marketplace, and thus assumed a public function in the very act of producing a new form of "private" subjectivity. One should be very quick to note that Habermas is not denying the very real ways in which the domestic sphere, far from nurturing free subjectivity, actually served to preclude it, by reproducing the patriarchal family structure of the past, by fulfilling its function in the reproduction of the capitalist economic system, and so on. But neither does he ignore the critical function of the domestic sphere's idea of itself, and the role that idea plays in the development of a substantially new and socially critical public sphere. Indeed, in proposing a realm where human relations were predicated on mutual love and respect among cultivated free individuals, rather than on the economic calculation of wage, price and profit, the domestic sphere, in Habermas's words, "raised bourgeois ideology above ideology itself" (*Structural Transformation*, 48). Only in the context of this preliminary development in the "private" sphere of the family, a privacy already oriented to a public, can the transition to a reconstituted public sphere, newly awake to its critical function, be adequately imagined.

Blake also, in tracing the passage from ideological Babylon to the "spiritual fourfold London" and the redeemed One Man, carefully balances the demands of the private and the public or, in his terms, the Particular and the General. These terms become particularly important in the third chapter, addressed "To the Deists," as Blake cautiously distinguishes his own utopian ideas from the abstract benificence of Enlightenment reformers who claim to act in the common interest while never understanding that interests are rarely if ever held in "common." In a context which emphasizes the importance of the real experience of private individuals and the need for attention to particulars in the creation of a just society, Blake records "the voices of the Living Creatures" (55:55, E205) in Eden:

> Let all Indefinites be thrown into Demonstrations
> To be pounded to dust & melted in the Furnaces of Affliction:
> He who would do good to another must do it in Minute Particulars
> General Good is the plea of the scoundrel hypocrite & flatterer.

> (55:58–61)

We should be careful to note that even while he expresses a keen distrust of claims for a "General Good," Blake is not, through the "Living Creatures," abandoning such goals in favor of some alternatively conceived "local politics." On this same plate which casts such a suspicious eye on "General Good," and from the same perspective of Eternity, the "Living Creatures" can still confidently affirm that "Every one knows, we are One Family! One Man blessed for ever" (55:46). The distinction that Blake is drawing through the Eternals, a distinction drawn from the perspective of a clear understanding of the workings of ideology, is between those whose "plea" is "General Good" and those who actually effect good by "do[ing] it in Minute Particulars." The ironic truth of our inverted world is that those who plead General Good are usually the last ones to bring it about. The only way to adjudicate these various claims or to distinguish between the particular and the general themselves, is to submit them to debate. Just as Fraser notes that the claim to speak for a public always represents the outcome of an explicit or implied negotiation and a debatable setting of boundaries between private and public, so do the Living Creatures call for all "Indefinites [to] be thrown into Demonstrations," into "the Furnaces of Affliction." While not abandoning the need to constitute society as "One Man," Blake does seem to acknowledge here the need for contestation in the establishment of "General Good," and fluidity in the distinction between the public and the private, the general and the particular. The "General Good," the public, must never be shut off from the influence of particular concerns, but instead must issue from the free expression of those concerns.[31]

A second criticism of Habermas's public sphere, related to this first one, takes as its target not the establishment of the sphere itself, the distinction between the public and the private, but instead the body of rules and protocols which obtain once public debate has begun. A great deal of recent sociological thought might be cited here, thought which has been directed towards, among other things, a critique of the assumptions of the liberal democratic state and its "open society."[32] Pierre Bourdieu, for example, has suggested that many of the institutions of the liberal democratic state, institutions whose legitimacy depends on a presumption of their neutrality and openness to all views, actually employ a subtly weighted language and system of behavior. The educational system, the legal system, as well as other organs of state and social power, implicitly reward participants who have mastered a culturally dominant way of speaking and way of acting (Bourdieu's *habitus*), necessarily penalizing, if not silencing, those who lack the approved cultural behaviors.[33] Along these lines, Jane Mansbridge, in an article also cited by Fraser, has suggested that formally egalitarian social systems (characterized by universal adult suffrage, among other things) can obscure inequalities which lie at the more "molecular" level of differences in speech and self-presentation:

Even the language people use as they reason together usually favors one way of seeing things and discourages others. Subordinate groups sometimes cannot find the right voice or words to express their thoughts, and when they do, they discover they are not heard.[34]

In the court of the public sphere, to borrow metaphorically from one of the most prominent of public institutions, some evidence cannot be given, is ruled out of bounds simply because it does not meet the requirements of a "proper" statement. In terms of our assessment of various criticisms of the public sphere, and by extension of Blake's "One Man," this critique would seem to have moved beyond merely suggesting problems with the boundaries of the One Man's body, and into the realm of "internal medicine," identifying crucial flaws in the inner workings of public debate itself.

It is important in answering this criticism not to deny its partial validity. The path to preserving a potentially liberative public sphere from the charge that public discourse *always* reproduces conditions of inequality does not lie, it seems to me, in asserting that it *never* does. Instead, one must develop a social analysis which can describe both the conditions under which public institutions rigidly close themselves to varied debate and the alternative conditions which allow for a more egalitarian kind of participation. Habermas provides the basis for such a fluid model of institutional analysis in some of the works which follow *Structural Transformation*, particularly in the magisterial text which is perhaps the key to his mature thought, *The Theory of Communicative Action* (first published in German in 1981). There, in the course of a reassessment of Max Weber's concept of the historical rationalization of society, Habermas derives a crucial distinction between two types of social organization which he calls "system" and "life-world." "System" refers to that portion of society which is organized according to the principles of instrumental reason, which calculates and makes decisions via a noncommunicative medium (such as money or power), including most prominently the economic system and the bureaucratic state apparatus. The (instrumental) rationalization proper to this sector of society is reflected most clearly in the complexity and pervasiveness of the modern democratic state and its economy, as they have developed over the last two centuries. "Life-world," on the other hand, refers to the traditional, nonofficial sectors of society – the family, the cultural spheres of art and entertainment, grass-roots political affiliations, and so on – whose functioning depends upon the communicative means of linguistic exchange. It is in this latter sector, with its dependence on language and interpretation, that something like equal participation can occur, free from the uneven distribution of economic and bureaucratic power. The key to preserving the utopian potential latent in social structures thus lies, as it did for Owen's utopian communities and Blake's imagined cities, in a preliminary segregation, although this time a segregation dividing system from life-world.[35]

Such a division remains subject, of course, to the same criticism as the earlier distinction between the public and the private, even though Habermas has here resituated his realm of communicative interaction in a sphere which embraces both the "private" family and the "public" culture. It might be noted, for instance, that the institutions of the life-world, far from being independent of the economic system, actually serve that system by providing properly trained workers and consumers. By the same token, some might object that depending on traditional structures such as the family and representational culture for liberative debate is not at all satisfactory. These criticisms might be fatal for the concept of the life-world if it were not for Habermas's notion of a rationalization different from that which organizes economic and state systems: instead of being subject solely to a mechanical instrumental reason, the life-world, according to Habermas, undergoes a process of rationalization intimately tied to its foundation in communicative exchange. Its reliance on communication, on linguistic exchange, means that the life-world is subject to a host of self-critical processes – confrontation between unlike points of view, the potential for challenges to the validity of any statement uttered by any speaker or contained in any text – which truly distinguish it from the more abstract rationalizations of societal systems. The problem with critiques such as Mansbridge's, despite their accuracy in pointing out the actual power differentials among participants in any public debate, is that they treat the communicative medium of language as if it were precisely the same as the noncommunicative media of money and power. Language is not owned by any of its users in the same way that we might speak of owning money or power: it is always "between" its users, held in "common," and thus subject to challenges from all participants in the speech situation. Of course, this distinction between system and life-world, and their respective resources of money/power and language, does not imply that the two are utterly distinct in their historical functioning, nor free of each other's influence. But it does identify a different process at work in those public spheres which rely upon language for their operation, a process which inevitably includes a critique of the very principles upon which such spheres have been traditionally grounded. The initial segregation of system and life-world thus opens a space for a mode of social interaction which really can lead to egalitarian communicative exchange, the result of harsh contention among the participants in such a discursive space.

It would be too simple at this point to imagine a Habermasian Blake claiming, to invert the famous phrase, that he must "Create a [Life-world], or be enslav'd by another Mans [System]" (*J*10:20, E153) or even that his meaning was precisely parallel in describing

Los's labors as "Striving with Systems to deliver Individuals from those Systems" (*J*11:5, E154). But something of a connection between the two thinkers can be traced in Blake's own descriptions of repressive monolithic social structures which limit free exchange, in particular, in his descriptions of the "One Male" who so closely resembles the utopian "One Man":

> Then all the Males combined into One Male & every one
> Became a ravening eating Cancer growing in the Female
> A Polypus of Roots of Reasoning Doubt Despair & Death.
> Going forth & returning from Albions Rocks to Canaan:
> Devouring Jerusalem from every Nation of the Earth.
>
> Envying stood the enormous Form at variance with Itself
> In all its Members: in eternal torment of love & jealousy.
>
> (69:1–7, E223)

As we approach the utopian climax of the poem, on plate 99, the ironic counterpoint of this earlier plate returns in refigured form in the last description of the "One Man":

> All Human Forms identified even Tree Metal Earth & Stone. all
> Human Forms identified, living going forth & returning wearied
> Into the Planetary lives of Years Months Days & Hours reposing
> And then Awaking into his Bosom in the Life of Immortality.
>
> (99:1–4, E258)

The similarities between these two passages are suggestive: each describes a corporate form, uniting aspects of the "One" and the many, and each includes a notion of action, the "Going forth & returning" which verbally links the two descriptions. It seems odd that Blake would use such similar formulations to describe his visions of both the "one-dimensional" Male of enforced conformity and the "One Man" of Eternal Conversation, until one reflects on the crucial differences that he is here suggesting between his own "System" and "Life-World." Putting aside the highly colored but perhaps conceptually impoverished imagery of "Cancer" in the One Male, we can note the way in which the former description preserves invidious distinctions between "Male" and "Female," as well as between nations, the One Male's "Going forth & returning" figured as a sort of British imperial domination of "every Nation of the Earth."[36] These distinctions, which indicate the One Male's continuing dependence on an unequal distribution of power, find their meaning in the very different word which introduces each passage's description of its characteristic activity: for the One Male, "Going forth & returning" is the activity of a "Polypus" of "Despair & *Death*"; for the One Man, the same activity is introduced, not with the substantive "Death," but the carefully chosen verbal "living." The debate of the One Male, if one can even characterize it as debate, is not the "living" process of the life-world, but instead a static exchange of reified tokens, rightly conceived of as an "eternal torment of love and jealousy" since it never goes beyond the problematic of ownership and the "variance" of proper selves, each "envying" the other for his or her intellectual property.

In distinction to this unproductive internal variance, the One Man's public body is composed of a process of "identification" fruitfully ambiguous in its very roots. In the One Man, "All Human Forms [are] identified," but in what does this identification consist? It could be that each form is recognized in its quiddity, its essential "whatness," in the sense that one identifies a biological or geological specimen. We have, after all, been told earlier that one of Los's tasks in building the utopian city of Golgonooza is to preserve "all that has existed in the space of six thousand years: / Permanent, & not lost not lost nor vanishd, & every little act, / Word, work, & wish, that has existed" (*J*13:59–61, E157–8). It could be, on the other hand, that the Human Forms are identified *one with the other*, as we speak of identical twins or, even better, of the process of identification whereby a theatrical viewer puts himself or herself in the place of a dramatic character. The process of "identification" preserves the same tension as the balance between the General and the Particular, but goes even further in characterizing the communicative resources of the life-world. For language is precisely that medium which, not owned by any of its users, creates individual identities only while at the same time "identifying" or bringing together the various members of the group.[37] Identification in the One Man is an active process, a "living going forth & returning," in which to identify is the (provisional) outcome of communicative interaction, never solidified into an unchanging self but always subject to further modification and revision, in the temporality of "Years Months Days & Hours." In defense of such a process, Los warns against its contrary in a passage which implicitly describes the "One Male" while clearing ground for the One Man:

No Individual ought to appropriate to Himself
Or to his Emanation, any of the Universal Characteristics
Of David or of Eve, of the Woman, or of the Lord.
Of Reuben or of Benjamin, of Joseph or Judah or Levi
Those who dare appropriate to themselves Universal Attributes
Are the Blasphemous Selfhoods & must be broken asunder.

$(\mathcal{J}90{:}28{-}33, E250)$

Once again, what the One Male and the One Man have in common is their combination of the general and the particular, but in the case of the degenerate One Male the relationship between "Selfhood" and "Universal Characteristics" is precisely one of ownership, of the "appropriation" of Universality by the individual. In a manner reminiscent of one of the central definitions of ideology, which claims universal significance for the experience of a single class or group, Selfhood is here revealed as a deviant attempt to make Universality one's own. The fluid concept of identification, on the other hand, allows for the coming together of particulars in various forms of contestation and consolidation.

These considerations aside, the last and most devastating critique of utopias, whether they be Owen's experiments in communal living, or Blake's and Habermas's historico-theoretical formulations, is the claim that they cannot be realized. As noted above, Owen and Blake have each been subject to this critique, Owen for the repeated and relatively rapid failure of his various social experiments, Blake for the obscurity of his poem addressed "To the Public." Habermas also has been criticized on this ground. An oft-repeated charge of his critics, voiced particularly in reference to his description of the eighteenth-century bourgeois public sphere, justly points out that the promise of openness and egalitarianism which constitutes this sphere's uniqueness was never actually redeemed in its actual historical functioning.[38] In this view, a wide gap divides the sphere's theory of itself from its realization (or lack thereof) in historical institutions. Put in this context, Habermas's shift of emphasis from the historical thesis of *Structural Transformation* to the more theoretical formulation of *The Theory of Communicative Action* seems particularly significant. Habermas himself acknowledges that the utopian potential of the bourgeois public sphere was never fully realized, but by moving to the theoretical formulations of his later work he implies that a more fruitful ground for true communicative exchange is to be found in ordinary experiences which characterize all historical periods, including the present. Seen in retrospect, the exercise of sifting the ruins of Owen's utopias or surveying the shortcomings of the eighteenth-century public sphere in order to save what is useful from what is not, seems a fool's game. Much better is to seek out the building blocks of a communicative utopia in the world at hand and in the features of everyday conversation. Looking at the past for realized utopias, or lamenting their failures, comes to seem the profitless office of the "Daughters of Memory" (*M*1, E95). In much the same way, although this time with reference to the future, Blake would distinguish himself from those eternally patient waiters on the apocalypse by claiming that "whenever any Individual Rejects Error & Embraces Truth a Last Judgment passes upon that Individual" (*VLJ*, E562). In each case, the response to those who would say that "the time is [or was] at hand" is to declare that the time for utopia is now.

But the trajectory of Habermas's work after *Structural Transformation* is not only towards the ordinary but also towards the theoretical, and it is in this latter regard that he might still be criticized as "unrealistic." The same might of course be said of the author of the theoretical *Jerusalem*, and for this reason we would do well to consider the similarities between these two authors' most theoretical formulations. I wish in particular to suggest similarities between Blake's notion of Eternal Conversation and Habermas's description of an ideal speech situation. References to the theme of conversation are sprinkled throughout chapter 4 of *Jerusalem*, with increasing frequency towards the end of the chapter, but I turn for my example to a particularly apt formulation uttered by Los before the One Man has risen:

> When in Eternity Man converses with Man they enter
> Into each others Bosom (which are Universes of delight)
> In mutual interchange. and first their Emanations meet
> Surrounded by their Children. if they embrace & comingle
> The Human Four-fold Forms mingle also in thunders of Intellect
> But if the Emanations mingle not; with storms & agitations
> Of earthquakes & consuming fires they roll apart in fear
> For Man cannot unite with Man but by their Emanations.
>
> (*J*88:3–10, E246)

In an almost equally visionary frame of mind, Habermas imagines what he calls the "ideal speech situation," which is characterized for him by total intersubjectivity and "a symmetrical distribution of chances to choose and apply speech-acts."[39] The ideal speech situation is, in a very real sense, the definitive response to all criticisms of the concept of the public sphere, both those I have mentioned here and others that might be raised, and one's opinion of the public sphere is thus quite likely to be intimately related to one's opinion of the ideal speech situation. Where Habermas's critics challenge the validity of the very basis of the public/private distinction and deny that the rules in a public exchange can ever be completely egalitarian, the ideal speech situation imagines a communicative setting in which all constraints have been superseded and ideology itself no longer stands as a systematic distortion of communication.

The quickest and easiest response to this formulation, as to Owen's utopias and Blake's ideal constructions, is, of course, to dismiss them all as unrealizable, as naive pipe-dreams or abstract mental experiments. It is in this regard that Habermas's notion of the status of the "ideal" becomes particularly important. To call the conditions of pure subjectivity and the symmetrical distribution of speech opportunities "ideal" is indeed to suggest that they do not possess the same kind of reality as, for instance, capitalist relations of production, but it is not to deny any function whatsoever for them:

[T]he ideal speech situation is neither an empirical phenomenon nor simply a construct, but a reciprocal supposition unavoidable in discourse. This supposition can, but need not be, contrafactual; but even when contrafactual it is a fiction which is operatively effective in communication. I would therefore prefer to speak of an anticipation of an ideal speech situation . . . This anticipation alone is the warrant which permits us to join to an actually attained consensus the claim of a rational consensus. At the same time it is a critical standard against which every actually realized consensus can be called into question and checked.[40]

Rather than being "idealized" to the point of complete inconsequentiality, the principles of the ideal speech situation are present in *every* speech situation, not as an established and self-evident procedural model, but as the very foundation of the attempt to communicate. The characteristics of the ideal speech situation are, in fact, an apt illustration of the ways in which the standards of utopia are a "nowhere" which is always "here": communication begins only by being directed towards the (perhaps unrealizable) goal of complete intersubjective understanding. Without the anticipation of this ideal state, speech itself would lack a rationale for appealing to its hearer and that hearer would have no motivation for response. And, as Habermas makes clear, the rationale for critique also emerges from the belief both that communicative understanding can be achieved and that the current speech situation falls short of the ideal against which it "can be called into question and checked." For this reason, we might identify as the best evidence for the indirect functioning of an ideal speech situation the vigor and cogency of Habermas's own critics: they have, in the course of a protracted debate on the public sphere, created a public sphere of their own, open to further contributions and implicitly anticipatory of an ideal speech situation.

It is necessary, of course, to preserve this critical gap between the ideal speech situation and its mere "anticipation" in the actual speech situations of the ordinary world. This gap characterizes Los's anticipation of the conversation he describes in the passage quoted above and gives new meaning to the opening, "When in Eternity . . ." The temporality of this passage is both precise and ambiguous: the initial "When" separates Los from the ideal speech situation of complete intersubjectivity, Men "enter[ing] / Into each others Bosom," but the present tense used throughout grounds Los's vision in both his own present and that of the reader. The passage stands, indeed, as a gloss on every actual reading or speaking situation in much the same way as does Habermas's formulation of the ideal speech situation: the claim of achieved intersubjectivity can be either "factual" or contrafactual, depending on whether the Emanations (utterances?) "embrace & comingle" or "mingle not." The ideality of achieved communication is operative in both situations, either as a visionary confirmation of the ultimate meaning of conversation or (negatively) as a critical standard against which to evaluate failed or incomplete communication. Every utterance, however, actual or imagined, must be brought to the court of the ideal speech situation, to test whether or not a moment of Eternal Conversation has broken out in the "ruins of time" (E705). The doubleness of Los's description, divided between a statement of achieved intersubjectivity and a statement of its failure, also makes sense in the context in which it appears, since Los speaks at a time prior to Albion's resurrection, but even in the visionary moments at the end of the poem, Blake preserves a critical ambiguity in his description of the Edenic speech situation. As described on plate 98, the language of Eternal Conversation never settles into rigid forms:

[E]very Word & Every Character
Was Human according to the Expansion or Contraction, the Translucence
or
Opakeness of Nervous fibres such was the variation of Time & Space
Which vary according as the Organs of Perception vary.

(34–37, E258)

Just as the conditions of the ideal speech situation can never be empirically verified, the communicative means of the Eternal Conversation are always subject to twin perspectives, one expansively imagining the realization of full intersubjectivity while the other contracts to consider if all the conditions for equality and symmetry of opportunity have been met.

It is difficult indeed to imagine a utopian city, to imagine the means by which the inhabitants of a utopia would communicate with one another, without having one's vision collapse into either mere dreaminess or, conversely, frightening uniformity. The social schemes of Owen, the speech pragmatics of Habermas, and the grand visions of Blake's last poem have all been subject to these criticisms. But, contrary to those who see in *Jerusalem* a rejection of temporal concerns and issues of social justice, it can actually be read as Blake's definitive turn toward that resource which is always closest at hand for human beings, the resource of language. *Jerusalem* is indeed built on the "stubborn structure of Language," which, as Blake says in the coda to that memorable phrase, "act[ed] against / Albions melancholy, who must else have been a Dumb despair" (*J*36:59–60, E183). One should never underestimate the stubbornness of that structure, those blocks to understanding and persistent features of asymmetry which frustrate the desire for active debate – Blake's "Intellectual War" – and for equity of participation. But the realization of the late Blake seems to be that there is no other reliable ground for change, no other structure which can so effectively help us to see beyond the limitations of our Selfhood to our existence in a thoroughly social universe. The ideal speech situation, the intersubjectivity of the "One Man," when interlocutors can enter into each other's bosoms, is both nowhere and everywhere, unrealized in any established institutional context, but nevertheless underpinning even the seemingly most trivial of verbal exchanges. What begins as a mere alternative to "Dumb despair" ends as the means for entering the western gate, which, as Blake the corporeal architect tells us, is the Gate of the Tongue.

CHAPTER 7

Conclusion: the function of utopianism at the present time

A common gesture in assessments of utopianism is the lamentation (or celebration, depending on the point of view) of a general decline in utopian thought at the present time, reflected both in the relative dearth of recent literary utopias and in the less palpable but still pervasive enervation of an ill-defined utopian "energy" in practical life. Karl Mannheim, in his highly influential *Ideology and Utopia* (1929), perhaps inaugurates this species of historical reflection in concluding that the last of his four utopian mentalities, the socialist–communist, tolls the death knell of utopianism in its very success at social transformation:

> Thus, after a long tortuous, but heroic development, just at the highest stage of awareness, when history is ceasing to be blind fate, and is becoming more and more man's own creation, with the relinquishment of utopias, man would lose his will to shape history and therewith his ability to understand it.[1]

A student of methodologies might note that the seeds of this conclusion are contained in Mannheim's initial definitions of both ideology and utopia, characterized, respectively, in terms of their propensity either to uphold or to transform the existing order of things. History is thus canted towards its own self-transformative visions, until the moment when it institutes the formation which itself embodies transformation, the socialist–communist "transformed" society. Through some combination of the Hegelian Absolute and the Peter Principle, utopia is thus discarded at the moment of its greatest success, a ladder pushed aside when social conglomerates have achieved the heights of an organization in which "the order of things" is precisely equal to the will-to-transformation.

Mannheim's diagnosis, itself half lament and half celebration, must, however, drive us back to a consideration of utopianism for a number of reasons. Disbelievers in the theoretical Absolute as well as their more practical counterparts, the disbelievers in the achieved utopia of the modern socialist state, can unite in rejecting Mannheim's analysis for reasons that could roughly be termed "antiutopian" in their very formulation.[2] This constellation of opinion can generally be identified as, on the one hand, a distrust of totalizing ideas and theoretical constructs in general, and, on the other, a fear of political movements whose aim is radical transformation, all of them tarred with the ominous label of "social engineering." Karl Popper is perhaps the best representative of this position, but we might turn also to the ideas of Daniel Bell, whose notion of an "end of ideology" (in the sense of a totalizing belief system organizing political action) also necessarily entails an "end of utopia."[3] The nonutopian world these thinkers endorse then takes the form of either a liberal democratic "open society" (which bears an uncanny resemblance to postwar Western democracy) or a "postindustrial," "postscarcity" technocracy where political conflicts have blissfully evaporated, largely, it seems, due to the availability of an expanded range of consumer goods and cable channels.[4] These postutopias would then actually seem to agree, to all practical effects, with Mannheim's collapsing of the gap between utopia and the present moment, with the difference that it is the mediatized world of "the West" which they celebrate and, rather than simply kicking away the ladder of historical progress, they choose to kick away history itself, in the conviction that we have always, at least potentially, been here in the plush present. Rather than a Mannheimian sublation, the "end of utopia" celebrated from this perspective is the end of something that never really existed anyway, a big dream which merely served to obscure the myriad little gratifications which were always there for the taking.

However, if Bell and Popper represent the way to reject everything utopian in Mannheim, accepting only those elements of his thought which promise an end of utopia, there remains the possibility of qualifying Mannheim's analysis with the express purpose of preserving a functional concept of utopia. What Mannheim and the liberal-democratic anti-utopians have in common is a thematization of the present moment, whether in terms of socialism's historical break with the past or along the lines of a transhistorical democratic present latent in all historical periods. But what might cause us some initial doubts about this thematized present is the fact that Mannheim, Popper, and Bell each refer to very different "presents," incapable of providing a standardized "end" to utopia. One historical datum which suggests this difficulty is that these various historical "ends" – Mannheim's interwar Soviet Union, Popper's and Bell's postwar "American century" – are each followed by bursts of utopian energy, Mannheim's by the nightmare utopian dreams of Nazi Germany, the liberal democrats' by the widespread transformative visions of the 1960s, including the Third World independence movements. What these inconsistencies suggest is that there is something in the concept of "the present" itself, *regardless of its particular content*, which militates against utopian consciousness. From the point of view of *the* present (a perspective which already contains its limitation in an erroneous emphasis on singularity, a blindness to the possibility of other presents), utopia will always appear to be at an end. Such closure names the structure of the present. But beside this structured present, serving as its shadow or ghost, stands what Ernst Bloch, in qualification of the seeming "fulfillment" of modern times, has called "a residue," a sense of lack of incompleteness, of wishes unmet and happiness unachieved.[5]

Where does this leave us in the current manifestation of the present? Interestingly enough, the years since Bell's prediction of an "end of ideology" have not produced that unanimity under the sign of technology which his conservative vision seemed to promise for the West, but rather a proliferation of opposing points of view, organized around race, gender, class (this not so often), sexualities, and other variously conceived "subject positions." Even if one does not regard this emergent pluralism as a rebirth of ideology, in the sense of a limited class-based perspective passing itself off as a universal truth, we can at least note that the technologization of decision-making, the blithe transference of discursive and political power from a sated mass consumer society to a body of credentialed "experts" has failed to materialize. But what does this destabilization of knowledge, this splintering of class and group allegiances, this breakdown of singular standards in aesthetics and ethics alike – all part of a broad movement usually characterized as "postmodernism" – what does this mean for the concept of utopia? Is the postmodern present any better a breeding ground for utopian thought than the different modern presents whose foundations rested on a variously characterized "end of utopia"? By way of reflecting on this question and as a last historical thought experiment, I turn to a work which has been glancingly referred to throughout but has received no sustained treatment, a work which, as much as postmodernism, claims that "a new heaven is begun" (E34) and takes its place as an active participant in the new order. *The Marriage of Heaven and Hell* (1793), with its generic instability among prophecy, philosophical pamphlet, satire, fiction anthology, proverb book, and so on, best approximates in Blake's *œuvre* that kind of postmodern work which Jean-François Lyotard has identified as "that which denies itself the solace of good forms."[6] By considering the role of utopianism in this fractured piece of proto-postmodernism, we may perhaps find the way to a consideration of the fate of utopia in postmodernism proper (if such an oxymoronic construction can be momentarily allowed).[7]

I wish in particular to consider one of those interpolated fictions, amusing or quizzical by turns, which Blake included in the *Marriage* under the name of "Memorable Fancies," ironically transmuting Emanual Swedenborg's "memorable relations." The fourth Memorable Fancy, occupying all or part of plates 17 through 20, seems designed to illustrate a proposition established immediately prior to its telling, that the "two classes of men [the Prolific and the Devouring] are always upon earth, & they should be enemies; whoever tries to reconcile them seeks to destroy existence" (E40). For the Fancy also tells of two characters – a first-person narrator whom tradition has identified with Blake and an oppressively orthodox "Angel" – whose chance of mutual reconciliation seems dim indeed. The Angel has described to Blake (adopting the traditional designation) a hellish future being prepared for his evil ways, and Blake, in the puckish spirit which characterizes this work, proposes that each show the other his future fate to "see whether your lot or mine is most desirable" (E41). The Angel goes first in acting as cosmic tour guide, taking Blake on a psychedelic journey through a church and a mill and finally to an unimaginably enormous underground vault whose infernal scene of "vast spiders" and a "monstrous serpent" with "the head of Leviathan" reveals the Angel as a creator solidly in the tradition of the biblical and Miltonic sublime. When the Angel leaves the scene, however, the scene comically deflates to a pastoral setting of a river and a harper who sings that "[t]he man who never alters his opinion is like standing water, & breeds reptiles of the mind" (E42). Blake then returns the favor by showing the Angel his own future, this time in the rudely satirical rather than the sublime mode:

[S]oon we saw seven houses of brick, one we entered; in it were a number of monkeys, baboons, & all of that species chained by the middle, grinning and snatching at one another, but witheld by the shortness of their chains: however I saw that they sometimes grew numerous, and then the weak were caught by the strong and with a grinning aspect, first coupled with & then devoured. (E42)

One would like to think that even if Blake had not given himself the advantage of going last in this game of competing damnations, his comical imagination of the Angel's future state would still bear the greatest weight in a work which consistently refuses the sanctimonious certainty of the Angel's contrastingly serious and fearsome picture of Blake's doom.

More important for our limited purposes of assessing the place of utopia in the postmodern are the conclusions drawn by the two participants about the validity of these competing visions of the future. Perhaps predictably, the Angel comes to the myopic conclusion that "thy fantasy has imposed upon me & thou oughtest to be ashamed." But Blake, instead of responding with the banal obverse, concludes that "we impose on one another, & it is but lost time to converse with you whose works are only Analytics" (E42). In the gap between these two conclusions, we in a sense trace the movement from a preideological to a properly ideological view of social relations. The Angel, speaking from a stable orthodoxy which cannot question the grounds of its own beliefs, can interpret deviance from that orthodoxy only as imposition, an imposition which should shame the perpetrator because he necessarily carries within himself the knowledge of this violation of the "self-evident" eternal standard. Blake's response is in a different intellectual register altogether, admitting a form of the ideological thesis in the notion that *both* proposed visions are impositions, the necessary outcome of their respective cultural backgrounds and limited experiences. Blake had already hinted at such a conclusion when he had earlier witnessed the degeneration of the Angel's sublime vision to the pastoral scene of the harper. At this point, he explains to the Angel: "All that we saw was owing to your metaphysics: for when you ran away, I found myself on a bank by moonlight hearing a harper" (E42). The immediate debunking of the Angel's vision casts

Blake in a role quite familiar to followers of the recent literary-critical scene, especially during the ascendancy of deconstruction: the role of underminer and exploder of metaphysical pretension, "unreader" of the orthodox text. This preliminary gesture also changes the status of what is to follow – Blake's vision of monkey hell – short-circuiting the representational pretensions of his own description, creating that uniquely postmodern form of a representation which refuses to present or, in Lyotard's terms, the "unpresentable."[8]

Beyond its implications for the status of representation, this diagnosis of the encounter – "we impose on one another" – also has implications for the nature and possibilities of social interaction. More than just a commentary on the ideological nature of both participants' opinions, Blake's characterization of the visionary contest also effectively brings their conversation to an end. After he has stated his final verdict, that "it is but lost time to converse with you," nothing more can be said, and the Memorable Fancy breaks off with only the motto at the bottom of the page, that "Opposition is true Friendship" (E42). But in what sense has this episode depicted either "Opposition" or "Friendship?" As suggested above, it would seem to be an illustration of the eternal enmity of the Prolific and the Devouring, but even those two "classes of men" found some more substantive mode of interaction: "the Prolific would cease to be Prolific unless the Devourer as a sea received the excess of his delights" (E40). The encounter between Blake and the Angel, on the other hand, reflects neither Intellectual War without quarter, nor the "Oppositional Friendship" of the concluding motto, but rather an anticlimactic "agreement to disagree," a silent parting of the ways. If it is "lost time" to converse with the Angel, one wonders where and at what pursuit Blake will choose to spend his time as he wanders off the margins of the page: perhaps he will enroll in a course at his local community college or take to assembling model airplanes. Whatever the case, we must register the way in which the combative tension of this encounter, which begins with a desire of one party to convert the other, with the Angel's direct address to Blake – "O pitiable foolish young man! O horrible! O dreadful state!" – ends by undercutting the concept of conversion, of the persuasive transformation of one by another, altogether.

The breakdown of communication along lines conceived of as ideological or otherwise represents, in a related manner, postmodernism's most profound challenge to utopian thought. Fredric Jameson, in his powerful assessment of postmodernism in its economic and cultural determinations, has identified an "ideology of difference," commonly referred to as "pluralism," as the key to developments in social formation over the last thirty years:

> Everyone today is, if not organized, then at least organizable: and the ideological category that slowly moves into place to cover the results of such organization is the concept of the "group" . . . What someone once said about Washington, D.C., that you only apparently met individuals there, who all eventually turned out to be lobbies in the end, is now true of the social life of advanced capitalism generally, except that everyone "represents" several groups all at once.[9]

Along with this positive formative principle goes a corollary critique of utopianism, now criticized for its aspirations to totality, to an analysis which attempts to transcend the limits of local knowledge and organization. Along these lines, Lyotard's celebration of localized "language games" as a constitutive element of the "postmodern condition" is accompanied by a complementary analysis of the obsolescence of metanarratives, those totalizing world-views (Hegelian Idealism, Marxian Economic Determinism, etc.) which have served as universal keys in earlier periods.[10] We are now perhaps in a position to trace the fates of both concepts, ideology, and utopia, in their passage from the postwar liberal democrats to postmodernism. Ideology, first of all, would seem not to have ended at all, as Bell predicted, but certainly to have transmuted: no longer part of a systemic critique, as it was in its most powerful Marxist formulation, ideology now serves a mere marker of difference, the final linkage of mentality with group adherence. Utopia, on the other hand, retains all of the threatening connotations it carried with Popper and Bell, with the fascinating extension that now Popper's and Bell's liberal-democratic state is itself classed among the very utopias they sought to avoid. Any attempt to posit an optimum state, any presumption to show people their "eternal lot," as Blake called it, is regarded as a phantasm, and potentially a very dangerous one, the only adequate response to which is that "we impose on one another."

This picture of social organization (or micro-organization, as it might be called) should perhaps be allowed to stand, even by those with a nostalgia for broader social coalitions, if only for its tang of bracing realism: like it or not, the "ideology of difference" does seem to account for many features of postmodern life. But just as we were led to wonder where Blake and the Angel go when their dialogue abruptly ends, we might also wonder about the destinations of the various groups on the postmodern scene. Do they actually constitute discreet enclaves, self-referring and self-subsisting, or does this appearance of "localism," particularity, conceal the workings of an underlying system? We might indeed say that one of the classical elements of ideology has been overcome, in that the self-legitimizing statements of many of the new groups forgo that universalization of particular class interest which has heretofore marked every historically dominant group. (Even this new "localized" formative principle remains subject to further analysis, however, to the degree that every statement, regardless of its explicit testimony, possesses a vocation for universality.) But beneath this rejection of universalism, beyond the celebration of localism and the "ideology of difference," we should not be surprised to discover the power of a centralized media formation and its operative system, the marketplace. Indeed, as Jameson notes, in a world which has dethroned government and traditional culture as sources of authority, the media and the market are the only exceptions to the rule, the only spheres of activity which seem "somehow universal" in a sea of particularity.[11] In turning away from forms of consensus or even of active contestation, as Blake and the Angel silently part in the *Marriage*, the new groups risk being interpellated as new entries in the political/aesthetic equivalent of "niche marketing." The charge and countercharge that "we impose on one another," although it seems the prelude to a salutary disillusionment, might thus come to be merely the pretext of a more pervasive imposition at a higher level.

This conclusion, the reading of imposition not only at the level of individual visions but at the more general level of the *response* to the nonequivalence of visions, leads us back to Blake's text and to further consideration of its relation to a postmodern ideology of difference. For there are aspects of the fourth Memorable Fancy which suggest that the reading provided above is still incomplete and which direct our attention to other portions of the *Marriage* and beyond. Not the least of these incongruities is the transformed version of the Angel's original orthodox hell, that scene of the harper beside the river singing that "[t]he man who never alters his opinion is like standing water, & breeds reptiles of the mind." As discussed above, this alternation provides the ground for the radically destabilizing conclusion, suggesting as it does that no version of reality possesses more inherent validity than another. But in passing from these merely formal considerations – the juxtaposition of unlike visions – to the content of Blake's revised perspective, we begin to find further meanings in the "difference" of world-views. The differences between Angel and Blake are not reducible to a simple clash of cultures, but instead represent the difference between an orthodox vision which will brook no challenges and a more flexible, creative version of reality. From the perspective of Blake's vision, the moral of the story would seem to be that perspective can change at any time: he has occupied the "same" reality in two very different ways. From the perspective of the angel, if he could imagine himself in the vault with Blake or with the hindsight provided by Blake's satirical vision, any change from the original orthodoxy represents a degradation of the sacred. With this complication, we might suspect that the vision of the harper is, in one very real sense, not utterly distinct from the Angel's vision, not possessing only local signifi-cance: rather than a discreet alternative, the harper and his song clearly represent a *response* to the Angel's orthodoxy, a fluidity and flexibility consciously, if subtly, addressing itself to the rigid harshness of the Angel's perspective. In this pastoral scene which "alters" the previous landscape, the Angel is addressed *in absentia* as "the man who never alters his opinions," the "standing water" which has bred the reptilian Leviathan but which has also produced, as its contrary, the flowing river under a changeable moon.

The Angel's and Blake's visions are thus related to each other as "forms of worship" to "poetic tales," to borrow the terms of the poem's earlier thumbnail sketch of religious history: "[T]hus began Priesthood. Choosing forms of worship from poetic tales" (plate 11, E38). They are in active relation to each other, each thematizing the same fundamental content of the existence of humanity in the natural world, but their manner of thematization varies between static orthodoxy (or orthodoxy that would at least wish to be static) and poetic polymorphism. This relationship, which can better be described as opposition than as mutual imposition, might lead us to reconsider another aspect of the Memorable Fancy, its motto that "Opposition is true Friendship." In particular, we might need to rethink the ways in which statements can be mottoes "to" poems or stories: does the motto invariably mirror the content of the main text or might it also be possible that a tag line qualifies, resists, undercuts the main text? What is at stake is whether the motto must be a "friend" to the text, or whether it might also "oppose" the text, or, as a third alternative, whether its best gesture of friendship might be to oppose.[12] In the gap between the speaker's final verdict – "we impose on one another" – and the motto, a space of some five centimeters in Blake's original, there is room for many possible interrelationships of the two, among them the critical appraisal of text by motto on the grounds that the mutual imposition of Angel and speaker (perhaps not Blake?) and their resultant parting of the ways is *not* "true Friendship" but that "Opposition *is*."[13] Perhaps the speaker as much as the Angel, by the end of the plate, is revealed as a "man who never alters his opinion" and thus a breeder of mental reptiles.

Such mutability of terms, such dynamic interplay of parts, is further supported by the fact that the fourth Memorable Fancy seems to find its own opponent, and thus perhaps its own true friend, in the last narrative section of the text, another story of opposed viewpoints. But if the earlier encounter initially encouraged us to read the motto with the emphasis on "opposition" – reading the tale perhaps too quickly as an illustration of the virtues of nonagreement – the fifth and last Memorable Fancy will, by its end, lay the stress on "Friendship." The cast of characters has been complicated in the transition to the latter story: the bipolar opposition of "Blake" and the Angel is now refigured as a debate between Angel and Devil, with a first-person narrator (again commonly identified with Blake) looking on as witness and recorder. The topic, rather than a matter of "eternal lots," is now the true worship of God, which the Devil says is "Honouring his gifts in other men each according to his genius. and loving the greatest men best" (E43), but which the Angel claims resides in obedience to the Ten Commandments and to the only good man, Jesus Christ. The debate, if it can even be called debate, is foreshortened in this narrative, with the Angel getting only one speech before he is definitively answered by the Devil: "I tell you, no virtue can exist without breaking these ten commandments: Jesus was all virtue and acted from impulse: not from rules" (E43). In one sense, of course, such verbal sparring is much closer to debate than the visionary contest of the fourth Memorable Fancy, in that it represents an actual exchange, counter-referencing between the two opponents as they quarrel over the meaning of "true worship," Christ and the Ten Commandments. But in another sense, the Angel seems too precariously perched on his position of orthodoxy, always ready to fall into the Devil's perspective. Hard on the Devil's refutation, the conversion of the Angel is complete:

When he had so spoken: I beheld the Angel who stretched out his arms embracing the flame of fire & he was consumed and arose as Elijah. Note. This Angel, who is now become a Devil, is my particular friend: we often read the Bible together in its infernal or diabolical sense which the world shall have if they behave well. (E43–44)

Where the fourth Memorable Fancy ended with opposition taken to the point of noncommunication, this final Fancy brings friendship to the point of almost complete identification, Angel become Devil, the triad closed with the collapsing of narrator and Angel/Devil in the person of a "we" whose reading procedures are undifferentiated.

From the postmodern perspective, such unanimity seems precisely the kind of totalizing conformity which is dreaded under the heading of "utopianism." Oddly enough, the motto to this last fancy, occupying the same terminal position on plate 24 that the earlier motto held on plate 20, can support just this postmodern reading: "One Law for the Lion & Ox is Oppression" (E44). A reading which, conversely, would "befriend" text and motto might cite the Angel's preconversion stance – "Thou Idolater, is not God One?" – as evidence that the motto recommends the new friendship of Angel/Devil, Devil and narrator, in that all have escaped the "One Law" of the Angel's earlier position. But paradoxically, in this work which encourages constant mental shuttling between and among alternatives, the victory over the "One Law," if it is conceived as such, takes the form of an unsettling singleness. Much as this final Fancy seems to provide a triumphant close for the work as a whole, and much as it seems the antidote to the previous Fancy's endless disputations, it can be critiqued from the postmodern perspective along two complimentary lines: (1) it lacks psychological verisimilitude in its hasty conversion of Angel to Devil's point of view, and (2) it denies difference in the name of this dubiously achieved consensus. These objections coincide with the postmodern rejection of utopia for, respectively, its unreality and its authoritarianism. Between the excessive disputatiousness of the earlier Fancy, a disputation which eventually destroys all communication whatsoever, and the facile conversion to unanimity in the last Fancy, there thus seems little to choose.

It is just at this point, however, the point where the instability of Blake's text would seem to frustrate all interpretative efforts, that the category of the postmodern reenters, not in its doctrinal form of a rejection of utopianism, but in the aesthetic formulation, already mentioned, of a work whose leading characteristic is a fidelity to the unpresentable. The unpresentable, even though one of the banners of a movement whose stated ideology could roughly be termed "anti-utopian," works in the same negative register as the utopian: the "not here" of the postmodern work of art nicely echoes the "nowhere" of utopian configurations. For the most part, to be sure, it is the purely critical function of unpresentability that has been emphasized in postmodernism's accounts of itself, its capacity to (in Lyotard's terms) "impart no knowledge about reality. . . prevent the free union of the faculties which gives rise to the sentiment of the beautiful; and . . . prevent the formation and stabilization of taste."[14] But within this general project of denial, denying the suspect pleasures of the past, there is also a positive, if nearly indefinable, vocation: "to impart a stronger sense of the unpresentable . . . [to] be witnesses of the unpresentable" ("What is Postmodernism?," 81–2). The inadequacy of either of the Memorable Fancies which end the *Marriage*, of either the conclusion that "we impose on one another" or that conversion and consensus are easily won, points not to an empty destruction of all meaning whatsoever, but rather to an as yet unrealized configuration where these opposed perspectives could be "true friends" without being equated. The contrariness, the opposition, not only of these two opposed units, but also of the components of each taken separately (motto and main text), creates a text which never "presents" its meaning (in the verbal representational sense) and never puts its meaning entirely in a "present" which, as we have seen, too often spells an "end of utopia."

The failure of the two Fancies, considered independently, finally bears on the failure of the concepts of ideology and utopia themselves, when taken in isolation one from the other. To the extent that each presents a static picture, the pictures of "eternal lots" or the picture of an harmonious scene of reading, they fail to do justice to the unpresentable destiny which, taken together, they ineffably indicate. To imagine a place in which Opposition really is true Friendship, in which the most detailed location of thought in its social, sexual, ethnic, and historical setting really is the necessary prelude to significant interchange among constructed individualities, that is the challenge of the reader of the *Marriage* and of anyone who would think ideology and utopia simultaneously. The dynamic quality of Blake's philosophical vitalism – "Energy is the only life and is from the Body and Reason is the bound or outward circumference of Energy" (E34) – is also an aesthetics of unpresentability, in which any provisional presentations always look to their own overcoming in the next "bound" form. By means of this transhistorical exchange, Blake's text conversing with a postmodern aesthetics, postmodernism comes to exceed its status as merely an end of history, the hypostasization of the present as an unsurpassable limit, and to reveal the utopian valency of its method of unpresentability. On their own, the visions of ideology and utopia degenerate into, on the one hand, simplistic univocal "stances," sharply drawn "world-views," and, on the other, dreamy wish fulfillments. Established as such they cannot avoid collapsing into one another, ideology coming to seem the dream of individual coherence and stasis, utopia's visions unveiling themselves as the narrowest ideological programs. But if opposed in a mutually defining, though not mutually imposing, aesthetics of unpresentability, they, like the sheaves of wheat bound "in a twin bundle for the Consummation" (*M*25:31, E122), revive the utopian dynamics at the heart of even our most resistant present moment.

Notes

PREFACE

1 Northrop Frye, *Fearful Symmetry: A Study of William Blake* (Princeton, New Jersey: Princeton University Press, 1947), 420.
2 David V. Erdman, *Blake: Prophet Against Empire*, revised edition (Princeton, New Jersey: Princeton University Press, 1970), xi.
3 William Blake, *Milton: A Poem in 2 Books*, plate 1, in *The Complete Poetry and Prose of William Blake*, newly revised edition, ed. David Erdman with commentary by Harold Bloom (Garden City, New York: Doubleday Press, 1982), 95. All subsequent references to Blake's works will be to this edition and will be given in parentheses in the text. Following the conventions of Blake citation, described in my "note on the text," I will give new titles of Blake's works, followed by plate and line number (where appropriate) and then page number in the Erdman edition (designated by the letter *E*).
4 Morton D. Paley, *Energy and the Imagination: A Study of the Development of Blake's Thought* (Oxford: Clarendon Press, 1970); E. D. Hirsch, *Innocence and Experience: An Introduction to Blake* (New Haven, Connecticut: Yale University Press, 1964).
5 Leopold Damrosch, Jr., *Symbol and Truth in Blake's Myth* (Princeton, New Jersey: Princeton University Press, 1980).
6 Walter Benjamin's fullest explication of his notion of "correspondences" between different authors and events of a particular historical period appears in his *Charles Baudelaire: A Lyric Poet in the Era of High Capitalism*, trans. Harry Zohn (London: New Left Books, 1973).

I. BLAKE, IDEOLOGY AND UTOPIA: STRATEGIES FOR CHANGE

1 The participants in this exchange were Stuart Peterfreund (review of *Blake in Context* by Stewart Crehan, *Blake: An Illustrated Quarterly* 19:3 [winter 1985–6], 113–16; "Reply to Stewart Crehan," *Blake: An Illustrated Quarterly* 20:3 [winter 1986–7], 108–9) and Stewart Crehan ("Blake, Context and Ideology," *Blake: An Illustrated Quarterly* 20:3 [winter 1986–7], 104–7), the "aesthetic" and the "social" critic respectively.

2 Terry Eagleton's *The Ideology of the Aesthetic* (Oxford and Cambridge, Massachusetts: Basil Blackwell, 1990) takes up the general issue of the political/class status of the aesthetic worldview; Jerome McGann's *The Romantic Ideology: A Critical Investigation* (Chicago and London: University of Chicago Press, 1983) considers the particular developments of aesthetic ideology during the Romantic period, developments which most often stress an artistic transcendence of the social and the historical. I will be stressing throughout that such a description does not tell the entire story for Blake, who remains particularly interested in a liberative description of his society and refuses the consolations of a simply defined aestheticism.

3 Prominent among considerations of Blake in his sociohistorical context are Michael Ferber's *The Social Vision of William Blake* (Princeton, New Jersey: Princeton University Press, 1985), Stewart Crehan's *Blake in Context* (London: Gill and Macmillan, 1984), Jon Mee's *Dangerous Enthusiasm: William Blake and the Culture of Radicalism in the 1790s* (Oxford: Clarendon Press, 1992) and E. P. Thompson's *Witness Against the Beast* (New York: New Press, 1993).

4 Karl Mannheim, *Ideology and Utopia: An Introduction to the Sociology of Knowledge*, trans. Louis Wirth and Edward Shils (New York: Harcourt Brace and World, 1936), 211–47.

5 The problem, indeed, with much literary historical analysis, not only of Blake but of other figures also, is its use of critical frameworks which might make sense in the critic's present, but make little sense in the world of the writer being considered. Such is the case with an overhasty distinction between religion and politics, a distinction which has been invoked in many narratives of Blake's career (political in his youth, religious in age), but which ignores the imbrication of the two concepts in the 1790s (and in other periods as well). In this regard, Jon Mee's description of Blake's connection to religious radicalism, and its own struggles with the rational radicalism of Paine and others, is immensely useful (*Dangerous Enthusiasm*, see especially 20–74).

6 For this survey of the history of the concept, I have employed, although by no means strictly adhered to, Raymond Williams's *Marxism and Literature* (Oxford and New York: Oxford University Press, 1977) and, for a non-Marxist perspective on ideology, Paul Ricoeur's *Lectures on Ideology and Utopia*, ed. George H. Taylor (New York: Columbia University Press, 1986).

7 Karl Marx, *A Contribution to the Critique of Political Economy*, trans. N. I. Stone (Chicago: Charles H. Kerr, 1904).

8 Karl Marx, *Critique of Hegel's "Philosophy of Right,"* trans. Joseph O'Malley and Annette Jolin (Cambridge: Cambridge University Press, 1970), 137; Karl Marx, *The Economic and Philosophical Manuscripts of 1844*, trans. Dirk J. Struik (New York: International Publishers, 1964).

9 Karl Marx, *Capital*, trans. Ben Fowkes, 3 vols. (New York: Vintage Books, 1977), vol. I, 103.

10 Karl Marx and Frederick Engels, *The German Ideology*, trans. and ed. C. J. Arthur (New York: International Publishers, 1970), 47.

11 See Ricoeur's *Lectures on Ideology and Utopia*, 78, for a discussion of the inadequacy of Marx's metaphor, in particular, the fact that images as presented to consciousness *never* appear inverted, but always reinverted.

12 Karl Marx, "Theses on Feuerbach" in *The German Ideology*, 123.

13 Althusser's theory of ideology is, of course, the subject of much dispute. Someone could certainly cite his statement on aesthetics – "I do not rank real art among the ideologies" (*Lenin and Philosophy and Other Essays*, trans. Ben Brewster [New York and London: Monthly Review Press, 1971], 221) – as evidence that his concept of ideology is not universal. More central to our concern here, however, is the following: "Only an ideological outlook could have imagined societies *without ideology* and accepted the utopian idea of a world in which ideology (not just one of its historical forms) would disappear without a trace" (*For Marx*, trans. Ben Brewster [New York: Pantheon Books, 1969], 232). Althusser thus universalizes ideology and dismisses utopia in a single stroke.

14 Williams, *Marxism and Literature*, 84.

15 We might also refer here, as Williams himself does, to the work of V. N. Volosinov in *Marxism and the Philosophy of Language*, trans. Ladislav Matejka and I. R. Titunik (New York: Seminar Press, 1973). Volosinov revises the narrow base/superstructure model by reintroducing real material production and social experience into the sphere of human usage, thus evading a linguistic determinism every bit as limiting as economic determinism. Williams, by his own admission, borrows much of his revised sense of "determinism" from Volosinov's analysis of practical language usage.

16 See Raymond Williams's *Keywords: A Vocabulary of Culture and Society*, revised edition (Oxford and New York: Oxford University Press, 1983), 60–9, for a detailed description of the history of the word *class*.

17 Georg Lukács, *History and Class Consciousness: Studies in Marxist Dialectics*, trans. Rodney Livingstone (Cambridge, Massachusetts: MIT Press, 1971), 105.

18 See the essay "Repressive Tolerance" in *A Critique of Pure Tolerance* by Herbert Marcuse, R. H. Wolff and Barrington Moore, Jr. (Boston: Beacon Press, 1965). Also see Marcuse's analyses in *One-Dimensional Man: Studies in the Ideology of Advanced Industrial Society* (Boston: Beacon Press, 1964) and *Eros and Civilization: A Philosophical Inquiry into Freud* (Boston: Beacon Press, 1955), the latter for Marcuse's view of the erotics of capitalism and "repressive desublimation."

19 David Punter has convincingly discussed the "sinister and intricately connected system" (9) underlying "London" in his "Blake and the Shapes of London" (*Criticism* 23:1 [Winter 1981], 1–23). Heather Glen

has anticipated me in my identification of the speaker with the very
system he indicts in an insightful reading of the poem included in her
"Blake's Criticism of Moral Thinking in *Songs of Innocence and Experience*,"
Interpreting Blake, ed. Michael Phillips (Cambridge: Cambridge University Press, 1978), 32–69.

20 Quoted in Marcuse, *One-Dimensional Man*, 120.

21 The treatment of utopia within a Marxist framework or in conjunction
with a concept of ideology is still fairly limited: in addition to Ricoeur's
Lectures on Ideology and Utopia, which is central to this investigation, the
reader is referred to Ernst Bloch's groundbreaking works, *Geist der Utopie*
(Munich, 1918), *The Principle of Hope*, 3 vols., trans. Neville Plaice,
Stephen Plaice, and Paul Knight (Cambridge, Massachusetts: MIT
Press, 1986), and the essays collected in *The Utopian Function of Art and
Literature*, trans. Jack Zipes and Frank Mecklenburg (Cambridge, Massachusetts: MIT Press, 1988); Mannheim's *Ideology and Utopia*; Walter
Benjamin's essay "Paris, Capital of the Nineteenth Century" (first
published 1955) in *Reflections*, trans. Edmund Jephcott (New York:
Schocken Books, 1986); Marcuse's chapter on "Phantasy and Utopia"
in *Eros and Civilization*; and Fredric Jameson's concluding chapter to *The
Political Unconscious* (Ithaca, New York: Cornell University Press, 1981),
as well as his essay in *Minnesota Review* 6 (1976), "Introduction/
Prospectus: To Reconsider the Relationship of Marxism to Utopian
Thought," and his book-length treatment of the subject, *The Seeds of
Time* (New York: Columbia University Press, 1994). For a more general
survey of the topic see Vincent Geoghehan's *Utopianism and Marxism*
(London and New York: Methuen, 1987). This of course is only a partial
list of what hopefully will be a continuing project within Marxist
criticism. Also useful, for both an explication of Bloch's thought and its
connection to Romantic radicalism, is Ruth Levitas's "Marxism, Romanticism and Utopia: Ernst Bloch and William Morris," *Radical
Philosophy* 51 (spring 1989), 27–36. For the connection of utopia to Blake
in particular, see John Brenkman's well-conceived chapter in *Culture and
Domination*, "The Concrete Utopia of Poetry" (Ithaca and London:
Cornell University Press, 1987), 102–38, and Eileen Sanzo's comparative approach – "Blake, Teilhard, and the Idea of the Future of
Man" – in *William Blake and the Moderns*, ed. Robert J. Bertholf and
Annette S. Levitt (New York: New York University Press, 1978).

22 Frederick Engels, *Socialism: Utopian and Scientific*, trans. Edward Aveling
(Chicago: Charles H. Kerr, 1908), 74–5.

23 By "regressive analysis," Ricoeur refers to his typical philosophical
method of beginning with the most usual sense of a concept – as, for
instance, the sense of ideology as "distortion" – and then proceeding to
deeper and less accessible meanings of the term (*Lectures on Ideology and
Utopia*, 311). I hope to have conveyed some of the value of a regressive
analysis in my own inventory of the senses in which "ideology" can be

used, which owes a debt of method, if not always of content, to Ricoeur's technique.

24 William Morris, *New from Nowhere or An Epoch of Rest being Some Chapters from a Utopian Romance*, ed. James Redmond (London, Boston and Henley: Routledge and Kegan Paul, 1970) and Thomas More, *Utopia*, trans. H. V. S. Ogden (Arlington Heights, Illinois: Harlan Davidson, 1949).

25 Bloch, *Principle of Hope*, 158.

26 Wordsworth's "spots of time" appear in book 12 of the 1850 edition of *The Prelude or, Growth of a Poet's Mind*, lines 208–18, in *Selected Poems and Prefaces*, ed. Jack Stillinger (Boston: Houghton Mifflin, 1965).

2. THE IDEOLOGY OF INSTRUCTION IN *EMILE* AND *SONGS OF INNOCENCE AND OF EXPERIENCE*

1 Pierre Bourdieu, "Cultural Reproduction and Social Reproduction" in *Power and Ideology in Education*, ed. Jerome Karabel and A. H. Halsey (New York and Oxford: Oxford University Press, 1977), 494.

2 Placement of Blake's book (and, to a certain extent, its companion volume of Experience) in this instructional genre has long been acknowledged, if just from the large number of parallels proposed between individual songs and various prominent eighteenth-century examples of the genre, including works by Isaac Watts, Anna Barbauld, Charles Wesley, and others. For a general discussion of Blake's relation to the burgeoning market for children's literature, see the fine discussions in Zachary Leader's *Reading Blake's Songs* (Boston and London: Routledge, 1981), 1–36, and Heather Glen's indispensable *Vision and Disenchantment: Blake's "Songs" and Wordsworth's "Lyrical Ballads"* (Cambridge: Cambridge University Press, 1983), especially 8–32.

3 Destutt de Tracy, *Elements d'idéologie* (Paris: Chez Madame Levi Libraire, 1827). See Jorge Larrain's discussion of de Tracy in *The Concept of Ideology* (Athens: University of Georgia Press, 1979), 26–8.

4 Louis Althusser, "Ideology and Ideological State Apparatuses (Notes towards an Investigation" in *Lenin and Philosophy and Other Essays*, trans. Ben Brewster (New York and London: Monthly Review Press, 1971), 132.

5 Pierre Bourdieu and Jean-Claude Passeron, *Reproduction in Education, Society and Culture*, trans. Richard Nice (London and Beverly Hills: Sage Publications, 1977), 116.

6 See Richard Altick's still definitive description of this process in *The English Common Reader: A Social History of the Mass Reading Public, 1800–1900* (Chicago: University of Chicago Press, 1957), 30–66.

7 See Guillory's reading of Thomas Gray's "Elegy written in a Country Churchyard" in *Cultural Capital: The Problem of Literary Canon Formation* (Chicago: University of Chicago Press, 1993), especially 93–107.

8 See Bernard de Mandeville's *Essay on Charity and Charity Schools* (1723) and Isaac Watts's reply, *An Essay towards the Encouragement of Charity Schools* (1728), for a single instance of the debate on the social function of education for the poor.

9 See Glen, *Vision and Disenchantment*, 10 and note 7, 349.

10 See Murray Cohen's *Sensible Words: Linguistic Practice in England, 1640–1785* (Baltimore and London: Johns Hopkins University Press, 1977), especially chapter 3, "Theories of Language and the Grammar of Sentences, 1740–1785" (78–136).

11 For an analogy to the eighteenth-century contest for the schools, we might turn to the current debate over multiculturalism in secondary and higher education. See, for example, the work of the Critical Pedagogy movement and especially Henry Giroux's *Border Crossings: Cultural Workers and the Politics of Education* (New York and London: Routledge, 1992).

12 Quoted in Alan Richardson, *Literature, Education, and Romanticism* (Cambridge: Cambridge University Press, 1994), 65.

13 James Chandler, *Wordsworth's Second Nature: A Study of the Poetry and the Politics* (Chicago and London: University of Chicago Press, 1984), 98.

14 Jean-Jacques Rousseau, *Emile, or On Education*, trans. Barbara Foxley (London: Everyman, 1993), 5.

15 Andrew Lincoln suggests in his notes to the Princeton University Press edition of the *Songs* that one of the ropes appears to grow from the man's head, thus offering a parallel to the origin of the Tree of Mystery "in the Human Brain" (*The Illuminated Books*, 5 volumes, ed. Andrew Lincoln, vol. II [Princeton, New Jersey: Princeton University Press, 1991], 195), but from the illumination we could as easily conclude that the rope passes *behind* the man's head rather than through it.

16 See "A Letter on Art in Reply to André Daspre" in Althusser, *Lenin and Philosophy*, 222–4.

17 See Pierre Bourdieu, *Reproduction in Education, Society and Culture*, especially 71–106, "Cultural Capital and Pedagogic Communication."

18 For more on Rousseau's rejection of early literacy training, in connection to a theme of education as property, see Francis Ferguson's fine essay, "Reading Morals: Locke and Rousseau on Education and Inequality," *Representations* 6 (Spring 1984), 66–84.

19 Carol Blum, *Rousseau and the Republic of Virtue: The Language of Politics in the French Revolution* (Ithaca: Cornell University Press, 1986), 45–7.

20 One of the enduring debates about Rousseau concerns the extent to which his own abandonment of parental duties contributed towards his writing of *Emile*. The father of five illegitimate children by his mistress Therese Levasseur, Rousseau put all of them in the care of the state. Depending on your point of view, *Emile* is either a "reaction formation" whereby the author defends himself by projecting the image of himself as the father of all children or a bold vindication of the proposition that

children are best educated by those with no natural tie to them. See Carol Blum's summary of the debate joined by both Rousseau's contemporaries and by modern critics (ibid., 74–82).

21 Northrop Frye, "Varieties of Literary Utopias" in *The Stubborn Structure: Essays on Criticism and Society* (London: Methuen, 1970), 122.

22 See Mee, *Dangerous Enthusiasm*, especially 62–74.

23 W. J. T. Mitchell, in his "Visible Language: Blake's Wond'rous Art of Writing" in *Romanticism and Contemporary Criticism*, ed. Morris Eaves and Michael Fischer (Ithaca, New York: Cornell University Press, 1986) sketches some of this background of Blake's attitude towards writing and print. But, while mentioning the relation between writing and the Revolution controversy, he does not place Blake in the context of the everyday world of book production.

24 For an extended treatment of this permeable boundary between word and design, consult Nelson Hilton's *Literal Imagination: Blake's Vision of Words* (Berkeley: University of California Press, 1983), especially chapter 1, "In Words into the Worlds of Thought," 1–18.

25 I refer to Glen's *Vision and Disenchantment* (57–73) and Mitchell's "Visible Language" (55–6).

26 Richard Palmer, for instance, in his *Hermeneutics: Interpretation Theory in Schleiermacher, Dilthey, Heidegger, and Gadamer* (Evanston: Northwestern University Press, 1969), suggests that one fundamental way to conceptualize hermeneutics is as the "saying" of the text either orally or in the subvocal performance heard by an "inner ear" (14–20).

27 See Walter J. Ong's *Orality and Literacy: The Technologizing of the Word* (London: Methuen, 1982) for the persistence of features of orality in written texts (especially 115–16).

28 Harold Bloom, *Blake's Apocalypse: A Study in Poetic Argument* (Ithaca, New York: Cornell University Press, 1963).

29 Interesting in this context is the fact that even so strong and convincing an advocate for Innocence as Heather Glen frequently (perhaps unconsciously) invokes a notion of experience in her reading of the Innocence volume. Consider, for example, the following from her fine reading of "Infant Joy":

["Infant Joy"] presents a moment of what I have called "play." But perhaps even more clearly (because what is being dramatized here is neither ceremony nor dream, but the simple baby-talk of mother with child) it suggests that the "play" which *Songs of Innocence* present . . . was not to Blake an utopian fiction, but a real *experience* basic to any creative sense of being in the world at all. (*Vision and Disenchantment*, 132; emphasis added)

I would, of course, object that it is precisely the utopian which allows for the introduction of liberative play into the world of "real experience," rather than confining it to the realm of the "make-believe" or to the sublimated space of artistic production. This disagreement is more a matter of terminology than substance, however, emerging from Glen's rather degraded notion of "utopia," implying, as it does in her book, mere wishful thinking.

30 Alan Richardson imagines such a progressive scheme for the poem, in the boy's creative revision of the mother's lesson, in *Literature, Education, and Romanticism*, 157–66. My disagreements with his approach, revolving especially around the mother's lesson, are indicated below.

31 Myra Glazer, for instance, in "Blake's Little Black Boys: On the Dynamics of Blake's Composite Art" (*Colby Library Quarterly* 16 [winter 1980], 220–36). Glazer also considers the poem's punning on the notion of "bearing" (233), but reads the conclusion as redemptive.

32 Andrew Lincoln suggests Isaiah 45.6 and 56.19 as possible sources for the association of God with the rising sun (*The Illuminated Books*, vol. II, 150). Interesting for the context of my argument is the fact that these verses record the reported speech of a God who emphasizes his exclusivity (45.6) and fearsomeness (59.19), aspects of the divinity that are usually presented negatively in Blake.

33 Joseph Viscomi, *Blake and the Idea of the Book* (Princeton, New Jersey: Princeton University Press, 1993), especially chapter 18, "Difference," 163–76. Myra Glazer's reading of the second plate of "The Little Black Boy" comes in for particular criticism in this section, raising an issue that will be of continuing significance for future commentators on the text–design relationship.

3. THE DISCOURSE OF WOMEN´S LIBERATION IN *VINDICATION OF THE RIGHTS OF WOMAN, EUROPE*, AND *VISIONS OF THE DAUGHTERS OF ALBION*

1 For the most detailed account of Blake's fallen and redeemed bodies, see Thomas R. Frosch's very convincing *The Awakening of Albion: The Renovation of the Body in the Poetry of William Blake* (Ithaca and London: Cornell University Press, 1974).

2 Feminism's utopianism expresses itself through both literary and theoretical channels. Among feminist literary utopias one must include Ursula K. LeGuin's *The Left Hand of Darkness* (New York: Ace Books, 1969) and *The Dispossessed* (New York: Avon Books, 1975), Joanna Russ's *The Female Man* (Boston: Beacon Press, 1975), Marge Piercy's *Woman on the Edge of Time* (New York: Fawcett Crest, 1976) and Monique Wittig's *Les Guerilleres* (New York: Viking, 1971), to name only a few. A sampling of feminist theoretical utopias is provided by editors Ruby Rohrlich and Elaine Hoffman Baruch in *Women in Search of Utopia: Mavericks and Mythmakers* (New York: Schocken Books, 1984). One must also note the concluding section – "Utopias" – of Elaine Marks and Isabelle de Courtivron's influential anthology *New French Feminisms: An Anthology* (New York: Schocken Books, 1981), which contains a generous sampling of contemporary feminist thought.

3 Anne K. Mellor, "Blake's Portrayal of Women," *Blake: An Illustrated Quarterly* 16 (winter 1982/3), 148–55, 154.

4 Susan Fox, "The Female as Metaphor in William Blake's Poetry," *Critical Inquiry* 3 (1977), 515.

5 See, in particular, Alicia Ostriker's "Desire Gratified and Ungratified: William Blake and Sexuality" (*Blake: An Illustrated Quarterly* 16 [winter 1982/3], 164), and Fox's essay, "The Female as Metaphor," for this rhetorical gesture.

6 Recognition of Blake's debt to Wollstonecraft begins as early as S. Foster Damon's *William Blake: His Philosophy and Symbols* (Boulder, Colorado: Shambhala Publications, 1979), 100, 106; J. Middleton Murry's *William Blake*, (London and Toronto: Jonathan Cape, 1933), 109; and Mark Schorer's *William Blake: The Politics of Vision* (New York: Vintage Books, 1946), 186–9. Later comparisons between the two include David V. Erdman's *Blake: Prophet Against Empire*, revised edition (Princeton, New Jersey: Princeton University Press, 1970), p. 243, Henry H. Wasser's "Notes on the *Visions of the Daughters of Albion*," *Modern Language Quarterly* 9 (1948), and Michael Ackland's "The Embattled Sexes: Blake's Debt to Wollstonecraft in *The Four Zoas*" (*Blake: An Illustrated Quarterly* 16 [winter 1982/3]).

7 Mary Wollstonecraft's sustained critique of modesty as a feminine virtue occurs in chapter 7 of *Vindication of the Rights of Woman*, ed. Miriam Kramnick (Harmondsworth, England: Penguin, 1975), 227–39.

8 See Erdman, *Prophet*, 155–62, and Nelson Hilton's "An Original Story," in *Unnam'd Forms: Blake and Textuality*, ed. Nelson Hilton and Thomas A. Vogler (Berkeley, Los Angeles, London: University of California Press, 1986), 70–8.

9 The prior speculation dates back at least to the work of S. Foster Damon, *A Blake Dictionary: The Ideas and Symbols of William Blake* (Boulder, Colorado: Shambhala Publications, 1979), 101; the latter is to be found in Alicia Ostriker's review of Janet M. Todd's *A Wollstonecraft Anthology* in *Blake: An Illustrated Quarterly* 14 (1980), 130. For further speculation on the Wollstonecraft–Fuseli relationship, see Hilton, "Original Story," 70–8.

10 See Mary Poovey's assessment of these two books, *The Proper Lady and the Woman Writer: Ideology as Style in the Works of Mary Wollstonecraft, Mary Shelley, and Jane Austen* (Chicago and London: University of Chicago Press, 1984), 55.

11 For a similar account of Blake's Female Will as his identification of women's situation in society, see David Aers's "Blake, Sex, Society and Ideology" in *Romanticism and Ideology: Studies in English Writing, 1765–1830*, ed. David Aers, Jonathan Cook, and David Punter (London and Boston: Routledge and Kegan Paul, 1981). I differ most from Aers, as shall be seen in the last section of this chapter, by not devaluing utopianism as is usually done in the context of Marxist studies.

12 Michael Tolley, "*Europe*: 'to those ychain'd in sleep' " in *Blake's Visionary Forms Dramatic*, ed. David Erdman and John E. Grant (Princeton, New Jersey: Princeton University Press, 1970).

13 Both Northrop Frye, *Fearful Symmetry: A Study of William Blake* (Princeton, New Jersey: Princeton University Press, 1947), 262–3, and Bloom, commentary to *The Complete Poetry and Prose of William Blake*, newly revised edition, ed. David Erdman (Garden City, New York: Doubleday Press, 1982), 904, make this connection. My usual fear in reading Frye and Bloom is that they make far too many and far too facile connections across the course of Blake's career, but I hope to have struck the balance here between a completely synoptic perspective on Blake's corpus and a wholly disconnected one (the fault of many of Blake's more casual critics). My contention is that the idea of Female Will is an enduring one in Blake's career – at least from the time of *Europe*'s composition – although its form and function change somewhat.

14 See Ostriker's "Desire Gratified and Ungratified," 163–4, for her description of Blake's "shift" in his later career. Interestingly enough, two of Blake's other critics propose different models for understanding his career: Susan Fox, in "The Female as Metaphor" suggests that in *Milton* and *Jerusalem* Blake was trying "to correct the damage" (517) that his earlier metaphoric uses of the feminine had wrought; Diana Hume George, in the last chapter of *Blake and Freud* (Ithaca and London: Cornell University Press, 1980), "Is She Also the Divine Image? Values for the Feminine in Blake," theorizes that Blake struggled to revise his limited earlier vocabulary for the feminine in *Jerusalem*, but that his problems with fallen language were insurmountable.

15 See Erdman, *Prophet*, 212; for the identification of Rintrah with William Pitt.

16 For the identification of Enitharmon with Queen Charlotte, see Erdman, *Prophet*, 221–3.

17 See MacKinnon's talk to the Unit for Criticism and Interpretive Theory at the University of Illinois at Urbana-Champaign in 1983, "Desire and Power: A Feminist Perspective," collected in *Marxism and the Interpretation of Culture*, ed. Cary Nelson and Lawrence Grossberg (Urbana and Chicago: University of Illinois Press, 1988), 110. For Andrea Dworkin's connection of sexual intercourse and rape see her *Pornography: Men Possessing Women* (New York: Putnam's, 1979).

18 For useful surveys of the radical religious tradition, see A. L. Morton, *The Everlasting Gospel: A Study in the Sources of William Blake* (London: Lawrence and Wishart, 1958); Michael Ferber, *The Social Vision of William Blake* (Princeton, New Jersey: Princeton University Press, 1985); E. P. Thompson, *Witness Against the Beast* (New York: New Press, 1993); and Jon Mee, *Dangerous Enthusiasm: William Blake and the Culture of Radicalism in 1790s*, especially 20–74.

19 See, for example, Hilton, "An Original Story," 90–2.

20 Harold Bloom, *Blake's Apocalypse: A Study in Poetic Argument* (Ithaca, New York: Cornell University Press, 1963), 102.
21 Thomas A. Vogler, " 'in vain the Eloquent tongue': An Un-Reading of *Visions of the Daughters of Albion*" in *Critical Paths: Blake and the Argument of Method*, ed. Dan Miller, Mark Bracher, and Donald Ault (Durham and London: Duke University Press, 1987), 275.
22 David Aers, "Blake, Sex, Society and Ideology," 31; Aers's emphasis.
23 Michel Foucault, "Powers and Strategies" in *Power/Knowledge: Selected Interviews and Other Writings, 1972–1977*, trans. Colin Gordon (New York: Pantheon Books, 1980), 141–2.
24 Vogler, "An Un-Reading," 302. See also Hilton, "An Original Story," 97.

4. EDMUND BURKE AND MODELS OF HISTORY IN *AMERICA*, THE *SONG OF LOS*, AND *THE FOUR ZOAS*

1 Karl Marx and Frederick Engels, *The German Ideology*, trans. and ed. C. J. Arthur (New York: International Publishers, 1970), 47; my emphasis.
2 Karl Mannheim, *Ideology and Utopia: An Introduction to the Sociology of Knowledge*, trans. Louis Wirth and Edward Shils (New York; Harcourt Brace and World, 1936), 215.
3 However general the notion of Burke as "conservative" may be, the present analysis is not alone in qualifying it. As Conor Cruise O'Brien points out in the polemical introduction to his biography of Burke, *The Great Melody: A Thematic Biography and Commented Anthology of Edmund Burke* (Chicago: University of Chicago Press, 1992), Burke had long stood in the nineteenth century and into the twentieth as a hero of the Liberal Party, for his defense of colonial liberties during the American crisis and for his stands against British abuses in India (xxxii–xli). As this chapter hopes to make clear, Burke's reliance on a notion of "tradition," gradual and continuous, provides one model for change Blake might have drawn upon during the 1790s, however he might have differed with Burke in his opinion of the Revolution in France. Compelling evidence for Blake's having read the *Reflections on the Revolution in France* is contained in a notebook poem, "Let the Brothels of Paris be opened," with its parodic reference to Burke's sublime portrait of Marie Antoinette ("The Queen of France just touchd this Globe / And the Pestilence darted from her robe," 17–18, E500). Such lines, using the figure of pestilence which will be so important in *America*, clearly show Blake's contempt for Burke's feudal nostalgia, but they do not dispel deeper connections between the two in regard to their thoughts on history.
4 Edmund Burke, *Reflections on the Revolution in France*, ed. Thomas H. D. Mahoney (Indianapolis, Indiana: Library of Liberal Arts, 1955).
5 Dating *Milton*, of course, is an extremely difficult task, as is dating any

of Blake's illuminated works, because the poet continually revised his work. Additionally, Blake's dates might refer to date of original conception, date of composition, or date of engraving. Joseph Viscomi suggests in *Blake and the Idea of the Book* (Princeton, New Jersey: Princeton University Press, 1993) that *Milton* was not actually completed and printed before 1810 (315).

6 Whether one does well to read Marx's mode of production narrative as a normative model is debatable. Nevertheless, Marx's formulation in *The German Ideology*, where ideology is explicitly defined as "that which has no history," itself indicates a narrative of progress in which history is the vehicle for escape from ideology. Whether or not we are to read Marx in the way that Blake suggests we read the prophets – not as "[S]uch a thing will happen let you do what you will," but as, "If you go on So / the result is So" (E617) – the fact remains that both "prophets" posit historical utopias at some points in their careers.

7 Friederich Nietzsche develops the concept of "eternal recurrence" in *Thus Spake Zarathustra*, trans. R. J. Hollingdale (Harmondsworth, England: Penguin, 1961).

8 It is perhaps interesting to note that Louis Althusser also uses the word *eternal* in his discussion of this section of *The German Ideology*: "ideology is eternal." But by this Althusser means not that ideology is left behind in its historical moment, but that ideology is "omni-historical," present in identical form in every period of history ("Ideology and Ideological State Apparatuses" in *Lenin and Philosophy and Other Essays*, trans. Ben Brewster [New York: Pantheon Books, 1969], 161). The eternal function of ideology, of course, is the interpellation by ideology of the individual as a subject (ibid., 170–7).

9 Marx makes explicit his denial of Western philosophy's definition of man earlier in *The German Ideology*: "Men can be distinguished from animals by consciousness, by religion or anything else you like. They themselves begin to distinguish themselves from animals as soon as they begin to *produce* their means of subsistence, a step which is conditioned by their physical organization" (7). By calling material production man's "real existence" and identifying production as the defining human characteristic, Marx is already well on the way to the antihumanistic focus on the mode of production *as such* (not as a human form) of the later works.

10 Of particular interest in this connection is Walter Reed's analysis of the dialectical roles of "evolution" and "revolution" in a series of Romantic texts ("A Defense of History: The Language of Transformation in Romantic Narrative," *Bucknell Review* 23:2 [fall 1977], 33–56). Reed suggests an interdependence of the two modes similar to the interdependence of "transformation" and "reproduction" that I am suggesting for the doctrine of progress and offers an engaging consideration of the dialectical roles of narrative continuity and narra-

tive crisis directly relevant to my claims for the narrative and the lyric modes in Blake's historical poems.

11 From the preface to *The Phenomenology of Mind*. See especially Walter Kaufmann's translation with commentary: *Hegel: Texts and Commentary*, trans. and ed. Walter Kaufmann (Notre Dame, Indiana: University of Notre Dame Press, 1977), 94–6.

12 See Joseph Epstein, *Radical Expression: Political Language, Ritual, and Symbol in England, 1790–1850* (New York and Oxford: Oxford University Press, 1994), especially 3–28. The relevant sections in Jon Mee, *Dangerous Enthusiasm: William Blake and the Culture of Radicalism in the 1790s* (Oxford: Clarendon Press, 1992), are 75–120 and in Michael Ferber, *The Social Vision of William Blake* (Princeton: Princeton University Press, 1985), 49–52.

13 For Burke's importance in the tradition of constitutional thought, see J. G. A. Pocock's essay, "Burke and the Ancient Constitution: A Problem in the History of Ideas," in *Politics, Language, and Time* (Chicago and London: University of Chicago Press, 1989), 202–32.

14 For another attempt to narrativize the difference between the earlier Burke and the Burke of *Reflections*, see Tom Furniss's *Edmund Burke's Aesthetic Ideology: Language, Gender, and Political Economy in Revolution* (Cambridge, Cambridge University Press, 1993). Furniss dispels the "crisis" in Burke's career by suggesting that some of the same aesthetic considerations are at work in both the early *Philosophical Enquiry* and the late *Reflections*, although he also identifies ideological contradictions at the heart of both works. The present argument differs from his in trying to isolate a strain of innovative historical thought in Burke which is not completely compromised by his particular position on the French Revolution (and, indeed, to suggest that this historical thought ultimately exceeds his opinions on the Revolution).

15 Jorge Larrain, *The Concept of Ideology* (Athens: University of Georgia Press, 1979), 22.

16 In this regard, see Raymond Williams's discussion, in *Culture and Society: 1780–1950* (New York: Columbia University Press, 1958), of a way of looking at Burke which has to do "less with his position than with his manner of thinking" (4). The point of Williams's opening "contrasts" in *Culture and Society* (Burke and William Cobbett; Robert Southey and Robert Owen) is, of course, to interrogate the usual right–left, liberal–conservative dichotomies, a goal with which I am in sympathy here.

17 James Chandler, *Wordsworth's Second Nature*, 64–9.

18 Edmund Burke, *An Appeal from the New to the Old Whigs*, reprinted in *The Works and Correspondence of the Right Honourable Edmund Burke* (London: Francis and John Rivington, 1955), vol. IV, 466.

19 David Bromwich, *A Choice of Inheritance: Self and Community from Edmund Burke to Robert Frost* (Cambridge, Massachusetts and London: Harvard University Press, 1989), 47.

20 O'Brien uses Vico's notion of "fantasia" in the introduction to *The Great Melody* (lx). Bromwich notes, in the midst of a discussion of Burke, that "[t]he striking fact about history, too, remains how far it is shaped by acts of the imagination" (*A Choice of Inheritance*, 48).

21 In a note, Bromwich highlights the figurative nature of some of Burke's references to history in *Reflections*: "considering our liberties *in the light* of our inheritance"; "always acting *as if in the presence* of our canonized forefathers" (*A Choice of Inheritance*, 297; Bromwich's emphasis).

22 Antonio Gramsci, *Selections from the Prison Notebooks*, ed. and trans. Quinton Hoare and Geoffrey Nowell Smith (New York: International Publishers, 1971), 376.

23 Mee, *Dangerous Enthusiasm*, 20–74.

24 Robert Essick, in "William Blake, Thomas Paine, and Biblical Revolution" (*Studies in Romanticism* 30 [summer 1991], 189–212), discusses the ways in which Blake parts ways with the rational liberalism of the Joseph Johnson circle, in spite of earlier professional associations and his broad sympathy with their political goals. Articles like Essick's are particularly useful in that they display the full complexity of the political context of the 1790s and Blake's position in it: Blake's intellectual formulations are never simply a matter of choosing sides, but are instead the product of synthesis and negotiation.

25 For a fine discussion of Gramsci's notion of hegemony and its marking a theoretical crisis in classical Marxist analysis, see Ernesto Laclau's and Chantel Mouffe's *Hegemony and Socialist Strategy: Towards a Radical Democratic Politics* (London and New York: Verso, 1985), especially 65–71. Laclau and Mouffe's goal, in part, is to explain the dynamics of the new, nonclass-oriented social movements (feminism, environmentalism, minority liberation movements, etc.), which rely, no doubt unwittingly, on a quasi-Burkean notion of community tradition and "prejudice."

26 For the fullest discussion of Burke's "antitheoreticalism" and its relation to a modern "resistance to theory," see David Simpson's *Romanticism, Nationalism, and the Revolt against Theory* (Chicago: University of Chicago Press, 1993), especially 172–88. My conclusions clearly differ from his in not reading a necessary conservatism into the critique of theory.

27 The term "saving history" [*Heilsgeschichte*] was coined by the great Old Testament scholar Gerhard von Rad, in his *Old Testament Theology*, trans. D. M. G. Stalker (New York: Harper, 1962) to characterize the numerous recitals of tradition in the Hebrew Bible, what God has done for "the people of Abraham, Isaac, and Jacob." Blake's relation to this type of biblical writing is complex, partly constituted by his contempt for a God who repeatedly "sacrifices" his children in order to "save" them, but also, as I suggest here, reflecting a respect for the story of a liberation from bondage in Egypt, a story which has provided the model for escapes from allegorical Egypts throughout history. See Leslie

Tannenbaum's excellent *Biblical Tradition in Blake's Early Prophecies: The Great Code of Art* (Princeton, New Jersey: Princeton University Press, 1982) for a sustained treatment of this subject.

28 My opinion of Blake's intent in *America* concurs here with that of Minna Doskow in "William Blake's *America*: The Story of a Revolution Betrayed," *Blake Studies* 8 (1979), 167–86. Using mostly the evidence of the illustrations, Doskow concludes that "Blake saw the American revolution as limited" (169). Where I differ with Doskow is in the generality of my thesis: she assigns Blake's problems with the American Revolution to limitations in the American situation; I, on the other hand, focus on Blake's ambiguous relationship to the concept of revolution as such. In effect, I am suggesting that the construct which has come to be known as the *Orc cycle* (thanks to Northrop Frye's powerful interpretation) be assigned to an earlier point in Blake's career than is usual. In this I am also resisting David Erdman's reading of *America* ("*America*: New Expanses" in *Blake's Visionary Forms Dramatic*, ed. David Erdman and John E. Grant [Princeton, New Jersey: Princeton University Press, 1970]), which denies the existence of a general critique of revolution, an Orc cycle, before the composition of *Milton* (see especially "A Note on the 'Orc Cycle,'" 112–14). Interestingly enough, Doskow herself indicates the beginnings of a general critique of revolution in *America* by admitting that the "less than triumphant revolutionary *progress*" (her word) in the poem "provides some ominous forebodings about revolution in general" ("Blake's *America*," 185). The point, well-taken I believe, nevertheless contradicts the thrust of her article. David Bindman, in " 'My own mind is my own church': Blake, Paine and the French Revolution" in *Reflections of Revolution: Images of Romanticism*, ed. Alison Yarrington and Kelvin Everest (London and New York: Routledge, 1993), has also suggested that *America* might be read in the context of the Revolution Controversy and particularly the Burke–Paine debate. But Bindman's sense of the poem's relation to this context casts Burke in a more straightforwardly villainous role than the current discussion, identifying him with Albion's Angel.

29 It might be tempting, from a perspective which more diametrically contrasts the political views of Blake and Burke, to compare the speech of Albion's Angel on plate 9 to Burke's criticism of Richard Price, a sympathizer with the French Revolution whose speech in the Old Jewry provided the initial occasion for the *Reflections*: "Dr. Price seems rather to overvalue the great acquisitions of light which he has obtained and diffused in this age. The last century appears to me to have been quite as much enlightened . . . Dr. Price, when he talks as if he had made a discovery, only follows a precedent" (75). However, if both Burke and Albion's Angel seem to deny the "newness" of revolutionary belief, there remains the fact that Burke clearly acknowledged the potential for

events in France to change conditions both in that country and (his greatest fear) in England. Burke's characterization of this potential for change will be considered below.

30 Raymond Williams, *Keywords: A Vocabulary of Culture and Society*, revised edition (Oxford and New York: Oxford University Press, 1983), 270–4.

31 David Erdman, *Blake: Prophet Against Empire*, revised edition (Princeton, New Jersey: Princeton University Press, 1970), 24.

32 Erdman, textual note to *The Complete Poetry and Prose of William Blake*, E802.

33 Williams, *Culture and Society*, 10.

34 For Ritson, see Mee, *Dangerous Enthusiasm*, 113–20.

35 Edmund Burke, *The Speeches of the Right Honourable Edmund Burke, in the House of Commons, and in Westminster-Hall*, 4 vols. (London: Longman, Hurst, Rees, Orme, and Brown, 1816), vol. iii, 458.

36 Erdman, *Prophet Against Empire*, 56–9.

37 Mee, *Dangerous Enthusiasm*, 3.

38 The hegemonic struggle for the figure of fire is well indicated by the fact that Richard Price, Burke and Blake all use it to their own ends. Price's *Discourse on the Love of Our Country* in *Political Writings of the 1790s*, ed. Gregory Claeys, vol. iii, *Radicalism and Reform, 1790–1792* (London: Pickering and Chatto, 1995), addresses the "friends of freedom" in its concluding paragraphs: "Behold, the light you have struck out, after setting AMERICA free, reflected to FRANCE, and there kindled into a blaze that lays despotism in ashes, and warms and illuminates EUROPE!" (22). Price's language here suggests two things about Blake's later use of the same figure: that fire, as I suggest below, can be a figure for communication as much as for destruction; but that Orc's possession of only the heat, rather than also the light which Price here includes, indicates something about Blake's opinion of revolution falling short of its potential.

39 Erdman offers specific referents for these personages, but also indicates that they "are employed as types of humanity" (*Prophet Against Empire*, 57), a conclusion supported by the "all" of line 19.

40 I am deviating here from Erdman's identification of Boston's Angel as Samuel Adams, an identification he bases in a parallel with Joel Barlow's epic *Visions of Columbus* (*Prophet Against Empire*, 26).

41 From his use of the word in *America* – to subsume "a serpent in Canada . . . In Mexico an Eagle, and a Lion in Peru" under the general heading "my American plains" (*A*2:10, 12–13, E52) – Blake would seem to apply "America" equally to what we refer to as North and South America. Blake's "four-harp" song – "Africa," *America, Europe*, "Asia" – thus really does attempt to effect a global vision, touching on every known continent with the exception of Australia, whose penal colony had been established only quite recently (1788). We are within our rights, then, to label America a "colonial" continent (as the shackles

would indicate) because of the persistence of Spanish, Portuguese and (in Canada) English imperialism.

42 James Thomson, *Liberty, A Poem*, 5:2 in *Liberty, The Castle of Indolence and Other Poems*, ed. James Sambrook (Oxford: Clarendon Press, 1986).

43 Thomas Gray, "The Progress of Poesy" in *Thomas Gray and William Collins: Poetical Works*, ed. Roger Lonsdale (Oxford and New York: Oxford University Press, 1971), lines 59–62.

44 William Collins, "Ode to Liberty" in *Thomas Gray and William Collins: Poetical Works*, ed. Roger Lonsdale (Oxford and New York: Oxford University Press, 1971), line 88.

45 Although technically, of course, Mount Ararat is in Eastern Turkey and thus on the boundary between Europe and Asia, Blake creates a kind of generalized "Africa" by placing Ararat, the black "sunny African" (3:10) and even "Brama in the East" (3:11) within the same geographical sphere.

46 Paul Ricoeur, *Lectures on Ideology and Utopia*, ed. George H. Taylor (New York: Columbia University Press, 1986), 312.

47 Walter Benjamin, "Theses on the Philosophy of History" in *Illuminations*, ed. Hannah Arendt, trans. Harry Zohn (New York: Schocken Books, 1969), 258.

48 Northrop Frye, *Fearful Symmetry: A Study of William Blake* (Princeton, New Jersey: Princeton University Press, 1947), 219.

49 I would be remiss if I neglected to mention Morton Paley's discussion of the Seven Eyes of God within a problematic of "breaking the bound circle" (cf., chapter 5 of *Energy and the Imagination: A Study of the Development of Blake's Thought* [Oxford: Clarendon Press, 1970]). My analysis unavoidably bears many similarities to his perceptive reading, but I hope to have situated my discussion within the context of late eighteenth-century political thought and thereby to have contributed something significant to his insights.

50 Evidence for this concluding section of "Night the First" as a late addition can be found in Erdman's textual notes to *The Complete Poetry and Prose of William Blake*. On the preceding page (18) the words "End of the First Night" had been written twice – once after line 10 (and then erased) and once after line 15 – indicating that pages 19–22 had been added at a later date. In addition, pages 19–22 are the only pages in "Night the First" lacking numbering of any sort (see Erdman's notes, 817 and 827).

51 Sources for this extremely resonant passage are, of course, innumerable and its existence within Blake's text is, to adopt an equally resonant word, overdetermined. Before Revelations, we might point to the passage that John of Patmos is obviously invoking, from Zechariah, where the prophet is shown a candlestick with "seven lamps thereon," which are then revealed as "the eyes of the Lord, which run to and fro through the whole earth" (4:2, 10). This is Blake's primary source, but,

as Paley notes, sevenfold schemes of history or development characterize thinkers as various as Boehme, Paracelsus, Augustine, and Luther (138). Milton's reference to Uriel as "one of the sev'n . . . Eyes / that run through all the Heav'ns, or down to th' Earth" (*Complete Poetry and Major Prose*, ed. Merritt Y. Hughes, Indianapolis [Indiana: Bobbs-Merrill Educational Publishing, 1957], *PL*3:648, 50–1) suggests a source that Michael Ferber says can be taken "only in an infernal sense" (*The Social Vision of William Blake* [Princeton, New Jersey: Princeton University Press, 1985], 218), but a more proximate relation might be asserted between Blake's Seven Eyes and the roll call of devils in book 1: admittedly, Milton names more than seven demons, but the important inclusion of Molech (lines 392–405) and the quasi-historical outline of Milton's demonic "progress poem" suggest an intriguing connection to Blake's more abstract formulation. Whatever the source may be, however, what remains important to an historical understanding of Blake's poem is his placement within a tradition of *interpretation* of these sources: that is to say, while the Zechariah scripture cannot be ignored, the placement of Blake within a tradition of scriptural exegesis must take priority. This is to value reception history over source criticism and inevitably, in the case of seventeenth- and eighteenth-century biblical exegesis, to invoke the idea of progress.

52 See Ernest Tuveson, *Millenium and Utopia: A Study in the Background of the Idea of Progress* (New York, Evanston, and London: Harper and Row, 1964), 22–74. As early examples of cyclical historiography, Tuveson cites Jean Bodin and Loys Le Roy (56–70), as a seventeenth-century English example, George Hakewill (71–4). Tuveson characterizes the seventeenth century in terms of the triumph of the idea of cyclical progress over the idea of linear decline.

53 One might also attribute *Vala*'s transformation to the superimposition of Revelation as a progressive narrative on the generally antiprogressive narrative of the poem as first conceived. Although interpreted pessimistically in the Middle Ages, Revelation was later recognized as an apocalyptic retelling of the Exodus story in a heavenly setting. I owe this insight to Walter Reed.

54 Frye, *Fearful Symmetry*, 128–34.

55 Ricoeur, *Lectures on Ideology and Utopia*, 312.

56 Frye, *Fearful Symmetry*, 308–9.

5. THE UTOPIAN MOMENT IN *RIGHTS OF MAN* AND *MILTON*

1 Louis Althusser, *For Marx*, trans. Ben Brewster (London and New York: Pantheon Books, 1969), 33; Althusser's emphasis.

2 E. D. Hirsch, *Innocence and Experience: An Introduction to Blake* (New Haven, Connecticut: Yale University Press, 1964), 106–48.

3 Blake's "conquering" would seem to have been only provisional,

however. As long as two years later, Blake is again declaring (in a letter to Hayley of 4 December 1804), "I have indeed fought thro a Hell of terrors & horrors (which none could know but myself.) in a Divided Existence now no longer Divided. nor at war with myself" (E758). At least on the biographical level, then, Blake's crisis would seem to have occupied more time than just the "Pulsation of the Artery" in which the poet's work is done. But each time, from the perspective of an already changed man, the past is looked back upon as a moment already passed.

4 The phrase is Althusser's, *For Marx*, 34.

5 Althusser discusses Marx and Engel's statement from *The German Ideology* (47) in "Ideology and Ideological State Apparatuses," *Lenin and Philosophy and Other Essays*, trans. Ben Brewster (New York: Pantheon Books, 1969) 159–62.

6 For a related, although highly critical, commentary on Althusser's concept of the "epistemological break," see Paul Ricoeur, *Lectures on Ideology and Utopia*, ed. George H. Taylor (New York: Columbia University Press, 1986), 103–58. Ricoeur dismisses the notion of "epistemological break" as fundamentally unthinkable outside the category of subjectivity, which Althusser, of course, rejects as ideological. Ricoeur's critique is thus connected to his general project of reclaiming humanism and human consciousness in the theory of ideology, a project with which my study and, I would assert, Blake's thought, are entirely sympathetic.

7 Althusser, *Lenin and Philosophy*, 7–8; Althusser's emphasis.

8 The issue of Blake's rhetorical purpose in *Milton*, the idea that Blake could even have had a rhetorical purpose, has been raised most effectively by W. J. T. Mitchell in his article, "Blake's Radical Comedy: Dramatic Structure as Meaning in *Milton*" in *Blake's Sublime Allegory: Essays on "The Four Zoas," "Milton" and "Jerusalem,"* ed. Stuart Curran and Joseph Anthony Wittreich, Jr. (Madison: University of Wisconsin Press, 1973). As will be apparent in my third section, I have adopted Mitchell's suggestion that *Milton* must be read as a rhetorical text, "a force for inciting people to imaginative action" (282), as the foundation for my thoughts on Blake's conception of his audience.

9 Marx's entire analytic apparatus in *Capital*, of course, relies upon the figure of crisis: the continual contradiction in the development of capital, the internalized crisis of the alienated worker. These crises, however, are presented as mere premonitions, or, even worse, as deceptive masks, for the fuller crisis that occurs at the end of capitalistic prehistory. In Blake's terms, we might say that capitalism's sense of "crisis" is a Satanic parody of the true crisis which unconditionally divides capitalism from the achieved communist state. For a discussion of Marx's theory of crisis in the context of critical theory and utopian thought, see Seyla Benhabib's *Critique, Norm, and Utopia: A Study of the*

Foundations of Critical Theory (New York: Columbia University Press, 1986), especially chapter 4.

10 Romans 13.11; my emphasis. This and all subsequent references are from the King James Bible.

11 Karl Mannheim, *Ideology and Utopia: An Introduction to the Sociology of Knowledge*, trans. Louis Wirth and Edward Shils (New York; Harcourt Brace and World, 1936), 215.

12 Thomas Paine, "The Crisis" in *"Common Sense" and "The Crisis"* (Garden City, New York: Dolphin Books, 1960), 69.

13 Walter Benjamin, "Theses on the Philosophy of History," *Illuminations*, ed. Hannah Arendt, trans. Harry Zohn (New York: Schocken Books, 1969), 257.

14 Suggestions persist of a close friendship between the two men. Springing for the most part from Alexander Gilchrist's suggestion that Blake played a part in saving Paine's life in September 1792, these suppositions are considered by David V. Erdman in *Blake: Prophet Against Empire*, revised edition (Princeton, New Jersey: Princeton University Press, 1970), 154–7. Several fine considerations of the Blake–Paine relationship exist, including Robert Essick's "William Blake, Thomas Paine, and Biblical Revolution," *Studies in Romanticism* 30 (summer 1991), 189–212; David Bindman's " 'My own mind is my own church' ": Blake, Paine and the French Revolution" in *Reflections of Revolution: Images of Romanticism*, ed. Alison Yarrington and Kelvin Everest (London and New York: Routledge, 1993); and Bruce Woodcock's "Reason and Prophecy – Paine, Blake and the Dialectic of Revolution" in *Combative Styles: Romantic Writing and Ideology: Two Contrasting Interpretations*, ed. Bruce Woodcock and John Coates (Hull: University of Hull Press, 1995). Essick's essay is particularly useful in the way it shows the complex – neither wholly assimilative nor wholly rejecting – nature of the connection, but none of these treatments considers the longer-lasting effects of Paine's influence on Blake, into the period of the major prophecies.

15 See Louis James's *English Popular Literature, 1819–1851* (New York: Columbia University Press, 1976), 28–9, for an assessment of Paine's role in the "battle for the mind" being waged by new independent sources against the establishment press.

16 Thomas Paine, *Rights of Man* (Harmondsworth: Penguin, 1984), 93.

17 Althusser, "Ideology and Ideological State Apparatuses," 127.

18 Burke, *Reflections on the Revolution in France*, ed. Thomas H. D. Mahoney (Indianapolis, Indiana: Library for Liberal Arts, 1955), 24.

19 Benjamin, "Theses on the Philosophy of History," 256.

20 Nancy M. Goslee, " 'In Englands Green & Pleasant Land': The Building of Vision in Blake's Stanzas from *Milton*," *Studies in Romanticism* 13 (1974), 109.

21 See, for example, Harold Bloom's claim that book 1 is dedicated to the

representation of Generation (the world of time and space), book 2 to the redemption of Beulah ("the passive, receptive life") (*Blake's Apocalypse: A Study in Poetic Argument* [Ithaca, New York: Cornell University Press, 1963], 341).

22 William Wordsworth, "Ode: Intimations of Immortality from Recollections of Early Childhood," line 23, *Selected Poems and Prefaces*, ed. Jack Stillinger.

23 For parallels between *Milton* and Isaiah, see Donna Rix's "*Milton*: Blake's Reading of Second Isaiah" in *Poetic Prophecy in Western Literature*, ed. Jan Wojcik and Raymond-Jean Frontain (Rutherford, Madison, Teaneck: Fairleigh Dickinson University Press, 1984).

24 Leslie Brisman, *Milton's Poetry of Choice and its Romantic Heirs* (Ithaca and London: Cornell University Press, 1973), 196.

25 Roland Barthes, *S/Z: An Essay*, trans. Richard Miller (New York: Hill and Wang, 1974), 75; Barthes's emphasis.

26 Susan Fox seems to intend something like this when she claims that *Milton* "details the preparation and completion of a single event, a single instant" ("The Structure of a Moment: Parallelism in the Two Books of Blake's *Milton*," *Blake Studies* 2 [1969], 21). See also Fox's book-length expansion of this article, *Poetic Form in Blake's "Milton"* (Princeton, New Jersey: Princeton University Press, 1976).

27 Benjamin, "Theses on the Philosophy of History," 256.

28 S. Foster Damon, *William Blake: His Philosophy and Symbols* (Boston: Houghton Mifflin, 1924), 182.

29 Marx and Engels, *The German Ideology*, 13–14.

30 Althusser, *For Marx*, 229–30.

31 See, for example, Jerome McGann's criticism that Blake's radical "critical devices" work to reveal "fundamental truth in a way which sets the poet apart from other men" (*The Romantic Ideology: A Critical Investigation* [Chicago and London: University of Chicago Press, 1983], 70). McGann's doubts are shared by most critics who reject the prophetic books for the simplicities of the "Innocent" early Blake.

32 Mitchell, "Blake's Radical Comedy," 283.

33 Isaiah 6.10.

34 Numbers 11.29.

35 Ephesians 1.4.

36 See Emile Benveniste, *Problems in General Linguistics*, trans. Mary Elizabeth Meek (Coral Gables, Florida: University of Miami Press, 1971), 223–30, for the distinction between the *énoncé* and the *énonciation*.

37 Matthew 19.24.

38 Matthew 19.26.

39 Althusser, *Lenin and Philosophy*, 12–13; Althusser's emphasis.

40 It is perhaps proper at this point to introduce another utopian reading of the Althusserian and traditional Marxian notion of class: Fredric Jameson's concluding chapter to *The Political Unconscious* (Ithaca, New

York: Cornell University Press, 1981), "The Dialectic of Utopia and Ideology" (281–99). Jameson uses class to ground his notion of the utopianism manifested in every literary and cultural text whatsoever. He thus avoids the pitfall of utopian theory that we have been labeling "wishful thinking." For Jameson, class consciousness (of any variety, not merely proletarian) is a proleptic form (although Jameson does not use precisely those words) of the classless unity of the achieved communist state. Jameson is thus able to preserve the contrary relation between utopia and ideology, simultaneously distinct and interrelated: "*All* class consciousness – or, in other words, all ideology in the strongest sense, including the most exclusive forms of ruling-class consciousness just as much as that of the oppositional or oppressed classes – is in its very nature Utopian" (289; Jameson's emphasis). This formulation, of course, is in agreement with the rereading of Althusser's notion of class that I am suggesting here.

41 Althusser, "Ideology and Ideological State Apparatuses," 175, Althusser's emphasis.

42 This passage occurs near the end of Althusser's classic essay, in a paragraph beginning "I might add . . . " (ibid., 175). One is tempted to see in this odd revision of his prior formulations a Derridean "supplement" (Jacques Derrida, *Of Grammatology*, trans. Gayatri Chakravorty Spivak [Baltimore and London: Johns Hopkins University Press, 1976], 141–64) to the rigid class analysis and ideological theory of this and prior essays.

43 See Harold Bloom's note that Ololon represents Milton's "marriages and family, but also his poems and their prophecy" (*Blake's Apocalypse*, 308).

44 The changing signification of the Seven Angels, the Seven Eyes of God, from historic periods (*FZ*115:42–50, E381) to corporate entities, representations of the "Vox Populi" (*M*:32:10–21, E131–2), reinforces the general outline of the differences I am suggesting exist between the liberal progressivism of *The Four Zoas* and the chiliasm of the later *Milton*.

45 Barthes, *S/Z*, 16; Barthes's emphasis.

6. THE UTOPIAN CITY AND THE PUBLIC SPHERE IN ROBERT OWEN AND *JERUSALEM*

1 Lewis Mumford, "Utopia, The City and The Machine" in *Utopias and Utopian Thought*, ed. Frank E. Manuel (Boston: Houghton Mifflin, 1965), 3.

2 Lewis Mumford, *The City in History: Its Origins, Its Transformations and Its Prospects* (New York: Harcourt Brace and World, 1961), 30.

3 This connection has at least been hinted at in the works of A. L. Morton, who has written extensively on both Blake and Owen: cf. *The*

Everlasting Gospel (59), *The English Utopia* (London: Lawrence and Wishart, 1952), especially chapter 5, "Reason in Revolt." I hope to make more explicit the connection between the two and between their respective concepts of ideology and utopia, but Morton's work represents an early and acute appraisal of the mental and political undercurrents of the time.

4 Robert Owen, *The Life of Robert Owen* (London: Charles Knight and Company, 1971), 59.

5 For the dating of *Jerusalem*, see Joseph Viscomi, *Blake and the Idea of the Book* (Princeton, New Jersey: Princeton University Press, 1993), 339.

6 Quoted in Vincent Geoghegan, *Utopianism and Marxism* (London and New York: Methuen, 1987), 13.

7 Jon Mee, *Dangerous Enthusiasm: William Blake and the Culture of Radicalism in the 1790s* (Oxford: Clarendon Press, 1992), 214.

8 Morton D. Paley, *The Continuing City: William Blake's "Jerusalem"* (Oxford: Clarendon Press, 1970).

9 William Hazlitt, "On People with One Idea" in *The Complete Works of William Hazlitt*, vol. VIII, ed. P. P. Howe (London and Toronto: J. M. Dent, 1931), 66.

10 Robert Owen, "A New View of Society, or, Essays on the Principle of the Formation of the Human Character, and the Application of the Principle to Practice" in *A New View of Society and Other Writings*, ed. Gregory Claeys (Harmondsworth: Penguin, 1991), 43.

11 J. F. C. Harrison, *Quest for the New Moral World: Robert Owen and the Owenites in Britain and America* (New York: Scribner's, 1969), 80.

12 Owen, *The Life of Robert Owen*, xxxv–xxxvi.

13 Harrison, *Quest for the New Moral World*, 154.

14 A fuller consideration of the ideological inversion which Owen attempts would have to take into account other elements of the ideological implications of the experimental communities. Gregory Claeys provides some of this necessary background in analyzing the complex interplay of political and antipolitical thought in the Owenite movement, that is, those elements which would encourage pluralistic interaction in the communities' governance and those which see such participation as a "bourgeois" trifle, in *Citizens and Saints: Politics and Anti-Politics in Early British Socialism* (Cambridge: Cambridge University Press, 1989), especially chapter 3. Barbara Taylor usefully supplements this account in her consideration of the place of women in utopian communities in *Eve and the New Jerusalem* (London: Virago Press, 1983).

15 Northrop Frye, *Fearful Symmetry: A Study of William Blake* (Princeton, New Jersey: Princeton University Press, 1947), 391–403.

16 The idea that Blake's texts were produced by mirror-writing – a backward writing on the plate which then appears "normal" on the printed page – is not universally accepted. The leading opponent to this view, Ruthven Todd, proposes instead a "transfer" method which

would not require Blake to write backwards in order to produce the texts. For the most detailed and extensive commentary on this technical issue, and for a convincing defence of the mirror-writing thesis, see Viscomi's *Blake and the Idea of the Book*, especially the first chapter, "Fair Copies, Models, and Transfers: Printmaking as Paradigm" (3–15). For other discussions of *Jerusalem*'s inversive structures, see E. B. Murray, "*Jerusalem* Reversed," *Blake Studies* 7 (1974), 11–25; Edward J. Rose, "The Structure of Blake's *Jerusalem*," *Bucknell Review* 11 (1963), 35–54; and, for the "antithetical" structure of the illustrations, Henry G. Lesnick, "Narrative Structure and the Antithetical Vision of *Jerusalem*" in *Blake's Visionary Forms Dramatic* ed. David Erdman and John E. Grant (Princeton, New Jersey: Princeton University Press, 1970).

17 For a discussion of Blake's imagery in *Jerusalem* and its relationship to the new industrialism, see Eileen Sanzo's "Blake and the Symbolism of the New Iron Age" in *The Evidence of the Imagination*, ed. Donald H. Reiman, Michael C. Jaye, and Betty T. Bennett (New York: New York University Press, 1978). Of especial interest for our project is Sanzo's observation that "iron-making is a symbol with two faces: it can represent for Blake the oppression of the industrial age or it can represent the labors of man the maker guided by true utopian vision" (4).

18 See Kenneth R. Johnston's article on the subject, "Blake's Cities: Romantic Forms of Urban Renewal" in *Blake's Visionary Forms Dramatic*.

19 One might additionally note that these lines from the frontispiece are literally "obscured" by Blake's attempts to cover them with ink and incisions (see Erdman's textual note to *The Complete Poetry and Prose of William Blake*, E809). They thus replicate a pattern which we shall see at work in the poem as a whole, in that they are discernible to some readers (experts like Erdman and those who have bought his edition) and invisible to others, simultaneously within and without the text.

20 David V. Erdman, *Blake: Prophet Against Empire*, revised edition (Princeton, New Jersey: Princeton University Press, 1970), 410–1.

21 See *J*18:2–4, E162, for Los's version of Urizenic "outsideness": "There is an Outside spread Without, & an Outside spread Within / Beyond the Outline of Identity both ways, which meet in One: / An orbed Void of doubt, despair, hunger, & thirst & sorrow." Blake's purpose in *Jerusalem* is to deny this nonhuman "outside" projected by the fallen man, and to substitute for it a notion of the dialectical interdependence of the "without" and the "within."

22 Most helpful and interesting in this context is V. A. De Luca's consideration of Blake's "textual sublime" and his description of *Jerusalem* as "a hundred-panelled wall" in *Words of Eternity: Blake and the Poetics of the Sublime* (Princeton, New Jersey: Princeton University Press, 1991), 90. I hope to have supplemented De Luca's fine thesis by focusing not so much on a psychological theory of the sublime as on an historical

model of citybuilding, its reasons for exclusion and separatism, and their relation to Blake's poem.

23 For the possibly ironic significance of Blake's reference to these traditional English characters, see Susan Matthew's "*Jerusalem* and Nationalism" in *Beyond Romanticism: New Approaches to Texts and Contexts, 1780–1832*, ed. Stephen Copley and John Whale (London and New York: Routledge, 1992), 86–94.

24 See also, for another assessment of Blake's rhetoric in *Jerusalem* Roger R. Easson's article "William Blake and His Reader in *Jerusalem*" in Stuart Curran and Joseph A. Wittreich, eds., *Blake's Sublime Allergy: Essays on* The Four Zoas, Milton, *and* Jerusalem (Madison, Wisconsin: University of Wisconsin Press, 1973). For an example of a structural assessment of the poem, see Stuart Curran's article in the same volume, "The Structures of *Jerusalem*."

25 See Paley, *The Continuing City*, chapter 6, "The Form of *Jerusalem*." Paley, despite his dialectical thesis, implies a somewhat naive form/content dichotomy (antithetical to Blake) in his distinction between *Jerusalem*'s "organizational container" and "the work itself" (303).

26 Harold Bloom, commentary to *The Complete Poetry and Prose of William Blake*, 930–1.

27 For a fine assessment of Blake's notion of the public, in the context of his theory of painting, see the chapter "A Blake Dictionary" in John Barrell's *The Political Theory of Painting from Reynolds to Hazlitt: "The Body of the Public"* (New Haven and London: Yale University Press, 1986), 222–57. In the course of refuting an expressivist interpretation of Blake's theory of art, Barrell rightly identifies Blake's terms "character" and "individual" as corporate in nature. He underestimates, however, the degree of perspectival variety possible within Blake's corporate forms, proposing, for instance, that the distanced vision of the "One Man" is somehow inferior to the microscopic vision of "Multitudes of Nations" (250).

28 The distinction between different historical models of the public sphere and the description of the feudal "representative" public is the substance of chapter 1 of *The Structural Transformation of the Public Sphere*, trans. Thomas Burger (Cambridge, Massachusetts: MIT Press, 1991), 1–26.

29 See ibid., chapter 2 (27–56), for a description of the workings and institutions of the bourgeois public sphere.

30 Nancy Fraser, "Rethinking the Public Sphere: A Contribution to the Critique of Actually Existing Democracy" in *Habermas and the Public Sphere*, ed. Craig Calhoun (Cambridge, Massachusetts, and London: MIT Press, 1992), 129; Fraser's emphasis.

31 For a formulation which stresses even more clearly the direct dialectical link between the General and the Particular, see chapter 2, plate 38, which, in the course of a description of the Divine Humanity, "the Only

General and Universal Form" (20), states that "All broad & general principles belong to benevolence / Who protects minute particulars, every one in their own identity" (22–3, E185). This formulation nicely balances the passage from chapter 3 quoted in the text: where the other passage seems incapable of imagining a plea for the "General Good" which is not hypocrisy, this passage seems conversely to claim that "*all* broad & general principles" respect their origins in particulars. The distinction between these two passages, seemingly contradictory, is the distinction between the ideological and the utopian themselves, between a world in which general benevolence is always a cover for oppression and one in which the benevolent have always established their bona fides in attention to particulars. In the terms of my earlier discussion of *Jerusalem*, these two formulations reflect the utopian mirroring of Blake's strategy in this poem.

32 The phrase is Karl Popper's, *The Open Society and Its Enemies*, vol. I, *The Spell of Plato* (London: Routledge and Kegan Paul, 1945).

33 See Bourdieu's analysis in *Distinction: A Social Critique of the Judgment of Taste*, trans. Richard Nice (Cambridge, Massachusetts: Harvard University Press, 1984).

34 Jane Mansbridge, "Feminism and Democracy, *The American Prospect* 1 (spring 1990): 127.

35 For this hasty sketch of Habermas's complex ideas I draw particularly on section 6 of *The Theory of Communicative Action*, "Intermediate Reflections: System and Lifeworld," 2 vols., trans. Thomas McCarthy (Boston: Beacon Press, 1984) vol. II, 113–97.

36 See Susan Matthews, "*Jerusalem* and Nationalism," for a fine discussion of Blake's ambiguous use of the discourses of nationalism. I hope to extend her thesis regarding the complexity of Blake's nationalistic tendencies by suggesting a model of communalism which is neither narrowly jingoistic nor exclusionary. On the issue of Blake's gender politics, I might make the related but minor point that the description of the "One Man," with its internal reference to the "Female" and its logical opposition to the "One Male," suggests that Blake intended the word "Man" as gender neutral. Further evidence for this position is provided in plate 88:3–15, referred to below, where Blake describes the Eternal Conversation of "Man . . . with Man," while simultaneously sexing the Emanations of each Man as "both Male & Female." The language of the "One Man" of course retains its origins in sexist distinctions, but seems to be critiquing those distinctions while pointing beyond them to a reformulated inclusive public sphere.

37 Paul Ricouer has made some of these same points in regard to the formation of the self in *Oneself as Another*, trans. Kathleen Blamey (Chicago and London: University of Chicago Press, 1992). See particularly his distinction between two notions of identity, associated respectively with the Latin *ipse* and *idem* (2–3 *et passim*).

38 See, for instance, Michael Warner, "The Mass Public and the Mass Subject," 382–4, and Michael Schudson, "Was There Ever a Public Sphere? If So, When? Reflections on the American Case," 143–63, both in Calhoun, ed., *Habermas and the Public Sphere.*

39 Jürgen Habermas, "*Vorbereitende Bemerkungen zu einer Theorie der kommunikativen Kompetenz,*" quoted in John B. Thompson, *Studies in the Theory of Ideology* (Berkeley: University of California Press, 1984), 264.

40 Jürgen Habermas, "Wahrheitstheorien," quoted in Thomas McCarthy, "A Theory of Communicative Competence," *Philosophy of the Social Sciences* 3 (1973), 135–56.

7. CONCLUSION: THE FUNCTION OF UTOPIANISM AT THE PRESENT TIME

1 Karl Mannheim, *Ideology and Utopia: An Introduction to the Sociology of Knowledge*, trans. Louis Wirth and Edward Shils (New York: Harcourt Brace and World, 1936) 263.

2 For a typology of anti-utopian positions, see George Kateb's *Utopia and Its Enemies* (London: Free Press of Glencoe, 1963), which echoes in title Karl Popper's prominent anti-utopian book, *The Open Society and its Enemies*. Kateb's book is somewhat dated in the present context and one of the things I hope to achieve in this short conclusion is at least to raise the issue of the peculiar challenge to utopianism raised by postmodernism as a political and aesthetic movement. Fredric Jameson, in several sections of his important *Postmodernism or, The Cultural Logic of Late Capitalism* (Durham, North Carolina: Duke University Press, 1991), raises this confluence of ideas in several provocative contexts.

3 Daniel Bell, *The End of Ideology; On the Exhaustion of Political Ideas in the Fifties*, revised edition (New York: Free Press, 1967).

4 Daniel Bell, *The Coming of the Post-Industrial Society: A Venture in Social Forecasting* (New York: Basic Books, 1973).

5 Ernst Bloch, in a dialogue with Theodor Adorno entitled "Something's Missing: A Discussion Between Ernst Bloch and Theodor W. Adorno on the Contradictions of Utopian Longing" in Ernst Bloch, *The Utopian Function of Art and Literature: Selected Essays*, trans. Jack Zipes and Frank Mecklenburg (Cambridge, Massachusetts, and London: MIT Press, 1988), 2.

6 Jean-François Lyotard, "Answering the Question: What is Postmodernism?" in *The Postmodern Condition*, trans. Geoff Bennington and Brian Massumi (Minneapolis, Minnesota: University of Minnesota Press, 1984), 81.

7 Lyotard's treatment of the postmodern by no means disqualifies such anachronistic experimentation, defining the term not in historical so much as formal (or antiformal) terms. Thus, he can claim that "the

essay (Montaigne) is postmodern, while the fragment (*The Athaeneum*) is modern," ibid., 81.

8 Ibid., 78–82.

9 Jameson, *Postmodernism*, 322.

10 Lyotard, *The Postmodern Condition*, 9–11, 27–37.

11 Jameson, *Postmodernism*, 347.

12 Readers of W. J. T. Mitchell's groundbreaking *Blake's Composite Art: A Study of the Illuminated Poetry* (Princeton, New Jersey: Princeton University Press, 1978), will recognize the extension of Mitchell's arguments about the variable relation between text and image to the realm of relations between motto and main text. Another area ripe for speculation is the relation between title and main text: e.g., does the title of Blake's "The Little Black Boy" express the framing perspective of an adult ("big") white speaker or should it be conceived of as an objective appraisal of the poem which follows ("This is the voice of the little black boy")? Blake's simple, quasi-objective titles in the *Songs of Innocence and of Experience*, a kind of titling "degree zero," encourage this kind of speculation.

13 Complicating this textual relationship still further is the fact that the motto is obscured by pigment in all but three of the existing complete copies of *The Marriage.*

14 Lyotard, "What is Postmodernism?," 78.

Index

CAMBRIDGE STUDIES IN ROMANTICISM

GENERAL EDITORS
MARILYN BUTLER, *University of Oxford*
JAMES CHANDLER, *University of Chicago*

27. *Romantic Imperialism*
Universal Empire and the Culture of Modernity
SAREE MAKDISI

28. *Ideology and Utopia in the Poetry of William Blake*
NICHOLAS M. WILLIAMS